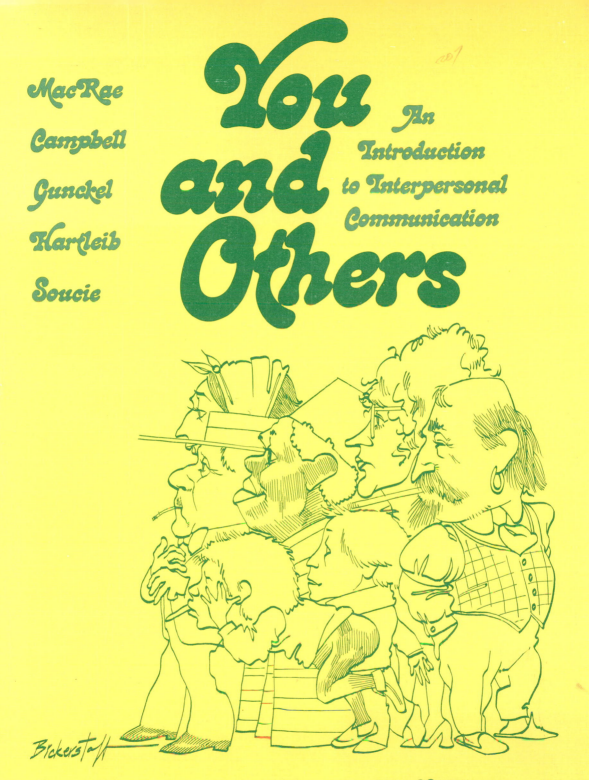

You and Others

An Introduction to Interpersonal Communication

MacRae
Campbell
Gunckel
Hartleib
Soucie

Bickerstaff

Introduction by Marshall McLuhan

YOU AND OTHERS

An Introduction to Interpersonal Communication

YOU AND OTHERS

An Introduction to Interpersonal Communication

Donald L. MacRae
Ronald F. G. Campbell
Vernon F. Gunckel
Carl J. Hartleib
Robert M. Soucie

Illustrated by Isaac Bickerstaff
Introduction by Marshall McLuhan

McGRAW-HILL RYERSON LIMITED

Toronto Montreal New York London Sydney
Johannesburg Mexico Panama Düsseldorf Singapore
São Paulo Kuala Lumpur New Delhi Auckland

YOU AND OTHERS
An Introduction to Interpersonal Communication

ISBN 0-07-082256-5
Printed and bound in Canada

1 2 3 4 5 6 7 8 9 0 JD 4 3 2 1 0 9 8 7 6 5

ACKNOWLEDGMENTS

Grateful acknowledgment is made to the following for permission to use copyrighted material: In Chapter 3, to Optometric Extension Program Foundation, Duncan, Oklahoma, for the photograph of a cow (Renshaw version); to Campbell-Ewald Company, Detroit, Michigan, for the advertisement "The Secret of Advertising"; and to John Hart and Field Enterprises Incorporated, Chicago, Illinois, for three cartoons from *B.C.* In Chapter 4, to Mayfield Publishing Company, Palo Alto, California, formerly National Press Books, for "The Johari Window" from Joseph Luft and Harry Ingham, *Group Processes: An Introduction to Group Dynamics,* copyright © by National Press Books; to Abingdon Press, Nashville, Tennessee, for the chart "Man the Manipulator and Actualizer" from *Man the Manipulator* by Everett Shostrom, copyright © 1967 by Abingdon Press; and to *Forum* Magazine for the table "Orientations That Help, Orientations That Hinder" by Jack R. Gibb from his article "Is Help Helpful?" in the February 1964 issue of *Forum* Magazine.

This book is dedicated to YOU,
the student of interpersonal communication

TABLE OF CONTENTS

FOREWORD

It is useful to approach the problem of developing communication abilities by focusing, not on content, but on process. The authors of this book explore human relationships by tracing their subliminal structures, which tend to determine communication dynamics. In *The Presentation of Self in Everyday Life, Interaction Ritual* and other works, Irving Goffman shows how social structure is reflected in the structure of face-to-face encounters, making them, in effect, microcosmic extensions of society itself. *You and Others* takes a look at communication as both a technological and a social process.

The rapidly extending concern with nonverbal communication needs to be put in the entire ecology context of environmental studies. Our time has discovered that there is a language of Forms and Gestures — a language which has its own grammar and syntax. *The Expression of the Emotions in Man and Animals* by Charles Darwin was a part of his own biological study in heredity and environment. Darwin's concern was with the nonverbal attitudes and postures, noting that: "...with mankind hardly any expression is more general than a widely open mouth under the sense of astonishment." Summing up, he stresses the close relationship between nonverbal and human communication:

> *Recapitulation.* — Men and women, and especially the young, have always valued, in a high degree, their personal appearance; and have likewise regarded the appearance of others. The face has been the chief object of attention, though, when man aboriginally went naked, the whole surface of his body would have been attended to. Our self-attention is excited almost exclusively by the opinion of others, for no person living in absolute solitude would care about his appearance. *(p. 345)*

If biology had enhanced the study of human communication in the nineteenth century, the twentieth century has turned to anthropology as a basis of observing human communication. Edward T. Hall's *The Silent Language* is only one such study of the deep expressiveness of the nonverbal positioning of people in daily life.

A quite different approach is represented by the work of Jacques Ellul in *Propaganda*, whose theme is that teaching and propaganda occur more by the subliminal shaping of perception and attitudes than by any direct expression. He considers all the institutions of language and society to constitute a total and irresistible propaganda. Ferdinand de Saussure, and others in linguistic studies, have taken a more specialized but similar approach to the problem of language and expression, directing attention to the great gap between *la langue* and *la parole*. Whereas *la langue* is total and subliminal, *la parole* is partial and verbal. Jacques Ellul is likewise saying that the main propaganda message of our institutions is embedded in the hidden *ground* of our institutions. However, the characteristic mark of twentieth century studies and awareness has been the increasing tendency of all subliminal *ground* to surface. Freud's *Interpretation of Dreams* was published in 1900, which provides a very convenient time mark by which to measure the steady rise of the subliminal to the surface of consciousness. Psychology and art and advertising alike provide wide testimonies to this pattern of change in awareness. It was Harold Innis who initiated communication studies into the observation of the hidden consequences of technical innovation in changing the environment.

In my own *Laws of the Media* I have tried to show that all technology, whether verbal or nonverbal, whether software or hardware, is linguistic in structure.

The work of Don MacRae, Ron Campbell, Vern Gunckel, Carl Hartleib and Bob Soucie is a definite step towards teaching and understanding interpersonal communication.

February 17, 1975   MARSHALL McLUHAN

PREFACE

"We seem to be experiencing some kind of communication breakdown." "What we have here, gentlemen, is a failure to communicate." "The problem is really a communications problem." "She can't communicate." "I just can't communicate with him."

Do all these frustrated voices sound familiar? They ought to: they are voices of our time. The world is shrinking, imploding in on us at a furious rate, forcing us as never before to plug into the lives of more and more people, here and around the globe. This increasing contact, as our mass media daily remind us, often spells not increasing harmony and cooperation, but increasing tension, misunderstanding, and war – failures at communication, breakdowns in communication. The unprecedented interest today in the *process* of communication, rather than, as traditionally, in the *content* of communication, perhaps derives in large measure from a slowly dawning realization that our very survival on this planet depends critically on this most difficult of human activities. In other words, we are beginning to feel it is time to take a good hard look at *how* we communicate, rather than just at *what* we communicate about.

And so all those frustrated voices. But though it is a first step, it is hardly enough merely to point to communication problems. You expect your mechanic to do more than point to your car and tell you, "What we have here is an automobile breakdown." What is he going to do about it? You have to be your own communication mechanic. You have to understand the process before you can make it better. And that is why this book has been written.

This book offers you, the beginning student, whether you are in school, in business and industry, or in the home, a clear, straightforward explanation of fundamental interpersonal communication theories and practices. It provides you with information you need to analyze communication problems and difficulties, as well as the opportunity to begin putting this knowledge to work in your own life.

There is now an urgent need for a Canadian book of this kind. Throughout this country courses are being offered, at all levels of education, in person-to-person communication, speech, writing, and discussion and conference techniques. We believe this book will help fill the growing demand for resources in these areas.

You and Others is written by five Seneca College teachers. Each deals with interpersonal communication from his own expertise, experience and point of view. No attempt was made to meld these diverse approaches into a single intellectual framework, or even into a common writing style. We feel this eclecticism, which mirrors that found in the field itself, constitutes a strength which the reader will appreciate.

The authors are indebted to a number of people whose efforts have made this book possible. We would like to recognize the editorial presence of Gordon Van Tighem and Herb Hilderley, whose advice and good humour have sustained us throughout. Don Evans (Isaac Bickerstaff), our illustrator, has contributed greatly to the book's appearance and readability, and we thank him for bending his creative imagination to that task, Lili Bartoletti, Mary Wilensky, Vivian Fitch and Lynn Greene have kindly helped us to prepare the manuscript. Finally, there are two groups of people to whom we are particularly indebted: our teachers, for their understanding and persistence; and our students, for their patience with us as we learned how to teach. We hope that our gratitude to them is expressed, in some small way, by the publication of *You and Others*.

THE AUTHORS

YOU AND OTHERS

An Introduction to Interpersonal Communication

1

COMMUNICATION
A Verbal and Nonverbal Process

Vernon F. Gunckel

INTRODUCTION

True being is self. In true experience every expression is creative, the creation of the person one is and is becoming.

Clarke E. Moustakas,
"True Experience and The Self"

What is *communication* to you?

In which of the following examples would you say communication is taking place?

You have brought your car to a stop at a red traffic signal.

While you are stopped at the signal, you admire the architecture of the museum across the street.

Because of a disagreement between you and your passenger friend, a bitter argument takes place.

Momentarily you have, in the heat of the argument, forgotten to observe the posted speed limit.

As a result, a police officer pulls you over and issues you a summons to appear in traffic court.

Your thinking about the incident is deflected by the smell of food.

Having reconciled your differences, you and your friend decide to stop for a hamburger.

In your conversation, your friend suggests that the two of you take in a movie.

Together you check the evening newspaper to see what is playing at the local theatres.

At the same time, the thought crosses your mind that you have a school assignment due the next day.

Despite every kind of excuse you can make for putting it off, it is decided that you had better pick another night for the movies.

Your dissatisfaction with the choice you have made is reflected by the frown on your face.

Saying good-bye to your friend, you set out for home.

How many of these situations would you say involve some form of communication? If you say *all* of them, you are right. Communication takes place in many situations, for a variety of reasons, and in several different ways.

We communicate by *visual symbols* and

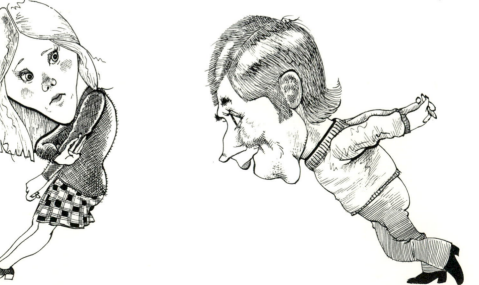

OUR INNERMOST THOUGHTS ARE COMMUNICATED TO OTHERS IN THE FORM OF NONVERBAL RESPONSES

signs as seen in the example of the traffic light. Our admiration of architecture demonstrates our appreciation of communication by *cultural values* as well as *artistic interpretations* gained through our experiences. Through *spoken language,* we can voice our opinions and thoughts. At times, we may find ourselves in the position of having talked ouselves into trouble as we can note in the disagreements between two friends. By the *actions of our society,* we have established laws which must be observed for the protection and safety of ourselves and others. When we break one of these laws, we must bear the consequences.

We receive communication through the *senses* of seeing, hearing, touching, smelling, and tasting. The *written,* as well as the spoken word, plays a major role in our communicative efforts.

While we spend a great amount of our time communicating with others, we can and often do *communicate with ourselves.* We accomplish this through the thought process and individual decision-making. Our innermost thoughts are sometimes communicated to others, consciously or unconsciously, when we show our reactions in the form of *nonverbal responses,* e.g. facial expressions and body gestures.

As you can see, our whole life is bound up in an interconnected series of continuous communication activities.

The purpose of this chapter is to examine the nature, scope and function of the process of communication. Because this chapter is introductory in content, our discussion will be limited to those basic concepts and definitions which should assist you in an understanding of the chapters that follow.

COMMUNICATION

What Is It?

Few words are used so much and understood so little as the word *communication*. It is a popular word in our day. It is a fashionable word to use. It is "in." It has become a cliché. Hardly a day passes when we do not come in contact with some form of the word. While it has been widely used by many, it is thoroughly misunderstood by most.

Why the popularity of this word? Is there something important about it? When it is fully understood, we discover just how very important communication is in our everyday lives. Our lives are based upon relationships with other people, and these relationships *depend* upon communication. However, we take communication so much for granted that it seldom occurs to us to examine its nature.

Isn't it strange that in a world with so much advanced communication technology we seem unable to communicate effectively with one another? In a world of the telephone, radio, television, newspaper, magazine, satellite, computer, and all the other evidence of man's so-called progress, we experience barriers and breakdowns in our efforts at communication. With all of our sophistication in communication hardware and technology, one can hear the cry, "Bring us together."

It is not that these "things"—products of man's inventiveness—cannot assist us as tools in our communication attempts; rather, we must first begin to understand ourselves as we seek, at the same time, to understand others. Herein lies the key to our efforts in communication, with self and others.

Basic Characteristics of Interpersonal Communication

A request for a definition of communication will result in an assortment of potentially valid interpretations of this commonly used word. Even authorities vary in their conception of the term. Technical definitions abound.

If we trace the etymology of the word, finding its origin, we discover that it comes from the Latin *communis,* "common." When we add the preface term "interpersonal," we direct our attention to a special type of human communication. It is a unique process of symbolic communication that involves interaction between persons.

When we communicate, we are trying to share information, an idea or an attitude. In this manner we may view communication as a process of sending and receiving messages. As far as we know, there are three main ways in which individuals can communicate with each other:

—by *actual physical contact,* such as a tap on the shoulder, a shake of the hand, or a loving caress;

—by our *gestures,* such as facial expressions and the visible movements of our bodies; and

—by the use of *symbols,* audible or visible.

Before we consider *how* communication works, let us take a look at some of the basic characteristics of interpersonal communication.

1. *Communication is Creative Meaning.*

The attempt to interchange meanings is intrinsic to human communication.

It is, however, in our search for meaning that we often encounter difficulties in our interpersonal communication. Meaning is not simply something that exists. It is something that *occurs.* Nothing in and of itself has meaning. *Meaning is created—it is invented, assigned, or given.*

A few years ago a little girl painted a picture for me with her water-colours. When one first looks at it, the painting appears only to be a child's wiggles and squiggles on paper. However, for *me* there is a deeper significance. The drawing often causes tears to well up in my eyes as I think of her. At seven years of age, this little girl was dying of leukemia, cancer of the blood. She had been told by her parents that she would not live. As much as a small child could understand that, she attempted to tell me that despite all that was happening to her—the painful blood transfusions and the weakness that had come over her body—life was still good. A few days before her death she painted the picture for me. It was her way of telling me about the times of joy she had with her parents, her brother and friends.

The picture for me had *creative meaning.* To anyone else, it was merely another child's drawing. To me, it was something very special.

On my desk is a small flat stone, a pebble. Those who enter my office wonder why I keep such an ordinary rock in such a prominent location. While the pebble has no particular significance for anyone else, it has meaning for me. During a holiday trip to England, I had picked up the stone from the seashore in the village of Tintagel, the site of the legendary King Arthur's castle.

Because of my interest in folklore, the day I visited that village was one of the high-lights of the trip. That pebble is a reminder of that journey. It has *creative meaning* for *me.* To anyone else, it is merely an ordinary stone. To me, it is something very special.

Objects have no meanings in themselves. Individuals give meanings and reality to them. These meanings reflect the individual's background. *Only people have meaning.* Creative meaning may be something personal or something shared in common with others.

Because of my friendship with the little girl, the picture she painted could only speak to *me* in the way that it did. This is *personal* creative meaning. Language experts have called this type of meaning *connotative.* Connotative meaning is most closely related to personal experience.

Our society has also invented *shared* creative meaning. This we may call *denotative.* Denotative meaning denotes or refers to something we basically share in common. We are trying to identify something in the physical world. To tell someone what a word means, we point to the object it represents. This becomes a word-object relationship. For example, I may point to a round object on the ground and say, "That is a ball." If you want to agree with me, we can say, together, "That is a ball."

In a similar manner, signs may also be denotative. Signs serve to inhibit or elicit specific action or response. Since I was a small boy, I have been told that when I see a red traffic light, I must stop. When it is green, I may go. Our society has created meaning for the object so that we may communicate with others on a common ground.

Symbols also are given expression through creative meaning. Symbols are different from signs in that they represent *things.* To Canadians, the maple leaf is more than just a leaf. It is a symbol for which we have assigned meaning. On our flag, it becomes part of our national identity.

An understanding of communication as creative meaning is important as we attempt to engage with one another in the sending and receiving of messages.

2. *Communication is Process.*

We began this section of the chapter with a question. Communication: What is it? This would seem to indicate that communication is a *thing.* We would be misinformed if we

FOR CANADIANS, THE MAPLE LEAF IS MORE THAN JUST A LEAF

were to consider communication in such a way. Communication is *not a thing* but a *process*; that is, it is not something which is static. It does not stand still like a photograph; it cannot be frozen in time and space. Unless we think in the terms of *process,* we will never fully comprehend the essence of communication.

A process signifies that something is in motion, ongoing, never static, and everchanging.

Like a circle, communication has no beginning and no end. Something has taken place before the communicative event and something will continue after the event.

Symbols and codes are subject to our concept of process for they are ever-changing. Symbols represent things. Each letter of the alphabet is a symbol. When a group of symbols are placed in a structure that is meaningful to some person, we say that we have created a code. However, meanings are never fixed. As experience changes, meanings change. People respond to what others say and do in the light of their own experience.

Not only do we create new words in our vocabulary but we also create new meanings for some old words. Even slang words are subject to change. When I was in high school, someone who was drunk was said to be "stoned." Today, to be "stoned" means that, among other things, one's mind is "blown," or one is "freaked out" on the use of drugs.

To illustrate how things change, list as many words as you can which have taken on meaning for *your* generation. Try to define them so that they are understood by most people. Now talk with your parents and see what words they have that might match your definitions. You might be surprised to find that you may both use the same word but have entirely different meanings for it.

A good example of new meanings created for old words can be seen in the word, "straight." Until recently, the term meant, for most people over thirty years of age, that someone was "square." However, because of the increasing impact of the Gay Liberation Movement, "straight" has now come to be used as an identification of one who is *not* gay.

Communication must be viewed as a process. When you see it in this manner, you will gain a fuller understanding of "self" and "others" as communicators.

3. *Communication is Unrepeatable.*

Because communication is a process, everchanging and ongoing, it cannot be repeated. We may do something in a *similar* way but we can never do a repeat of the *exact same thing* in the *exact same way.* Perfect repetition can be furnished by a computer, but people are not machines.

I recently visited the university from which I had received my undergraduate degree. In the thirteen years since I had been away, many changes had taken place. The campus was not the same place I had known when I studied there. But I wasn't the same person either. I was thirteen years older. The experiences I had as a student could not be repeated. Those experiences were now firmly rooted in my past. Class reunions sometimes try to recreate the feeling of those "good old days." But one can never go back.

Music is an important part of my life. I am especially fond of the works of J. S. Bach. No matter how many times I listen to the *Mass in B minor,* I will always hear and experience something new. Of course, I will still hear the same basic themes and will

CLASS REUNIONS TRY TO RECREATE THOSE "GOOD OLD DAYS." BUT YOU CAN NEVER GO BACK.

recognize those major sections of the composition. However, each time I listen I come to the event as a different person. My mood, attitude and impressions have changed. Perhaps I will hear something *this time* that I had not heard before. I may leave with entirely different feelings toward the work.

Some time ago I had the opportunity of hearing a great symphony orchestra and choir present this composition. My stereo records couldn't compare with the experience of seeing and hearing the *Mass* performed in person.

The evening was a thrill to me. If I were to hear the performance again, I could not repeat the same exact feeling I had that night. It is not that I wouldn't be excited at hearing it again, only this time it would be a new experience.

Have you seen the film, *2001: A Space Odyssey*?

If you have seen it a second time, can you say that the experience, the feelings and expectations of the first viewing, were repeated for you? On seeing the film again, you could anticipate certain segments and as a result experience new sensations and gain another perspective.

When I say that communication is unrepeatable, I don't mean that we don't do similar things in a similar manner. Life would be a little confusing if we didn't have some sense of consistency. We do perform acts which basically appear to be repeated. For example, except for holidays, I go to my office five days a week. I usually arrive about the same time each morning. The secretary even claims that she can set her watch by my arrival. We must keep in mind, however, that while we may appear to be creatures of repetition, we are at the same time influenced by changes taking place within and around us. Each day is a new day and we are a new person. We can sum up with the adage, "Today is the first day of the rest of your life."

4. *Communication is Irreversible.*

Have you ever, in anger, said something to a friend that you wish you had not said? The old rule to count to ten before saying something we might regret is really not such a bad idea. Given a few moments to think of what we are about to say could save embarrassment.

At one time or another, we have all said something, or may have done something, which we would like to say or do over again in a different way. Not only is communication unrepeatable but it is also irreversible. Once words have been spoken, they are on their way. We can't grab them back in mid air. For good or ill, they will be received and interpreted by the person with whom you are speaking. If we have verbally struck out in anger, we may find that we have unintentionally hurt a dear friend. Realizing what we have done, we may offer our apologies. But those original words of anger cannot be taken back. The two of you have entered into a new relationship. It may be a better one or it may have ended a friendship.

While watching a courtroom drama, you may have heard a witness testify to evidence which is not admissible in the proceedings of the trial. The judge directs the jury to disregard what was said. You and I know that it is not possible to disregard something which has been said; to pretend that it was never spoken at all. The statement, made by the witness, will have some influence upon the jury depending on the impact of the statement even if it is not officially on the court record.

When we talk about communication as being irreversible, we are not saying that *some* processes cannot be reversed. For example, we can freeze water to make ice. We can also reverse the process and melt the ice in order to have water. Unlike water or ice, people feel, interpret, affect others, and are affected by them. That is why we can say that communication is irreversible.

5. *Communication is Complex.*

What we have said up to this point should have convinced you that communication is complex. On the surface, communication may have seemed so simple. A person gets an idea and then verbalizes it to another person. That person hears what you have said and then interprets the idea. However, creative meaning takes place on many different levels. You must consider, among other things, the setting in which you will find yourself, certain personality traits in yourself as well as in others, and the reasons for communicating.

It has been said that whenever there is communication between two people there are at least six patterns of perceptions operative.

There is:

1. *Your* perception of how *you* see *yourself.*
2. Your *partner's* perception of how he sees *himself.*
3. *Your* perception of how you see your *partner.*
4. Your *partner's* perception of how he sees *you.*
5. *Your* perception of how *you think* your *partner* sees himself.
6. Your *partner's* perception of how *he thinks* you see yourself.

Does this sound complex? If you think this is confusing, just apply it to a *group* of people and you will begin to understand just how complicated the communication process can

YOUR PARTNER'S PERCEPTION OF YOUR PERCEPTION OF HIS PERCEPTION OF HOW YOU THINK YOUR PARTNER SEES HIMSELF

be. You may wonder how effective communication can ever take place. Perhaps you have come to a new appreciation of the dynamics of communication. It is not as simple as it would first appear. We must work at being good communicators.

6. *Communication is Persuasive Human Interaction.*

Why do people communicate?

What human need does it, or should it satisfy?

Interaction denotes reciprocal action. When we communicate we do so with a purpose. We can go so far as to say that *all* communication behaviour has as its purpose— its goal—the production of a response. As there are levels of communication, described earlier in this chapter, so are there degrees of purpose.

Very early in life we learn the basic techniques of persuasion. If you watch the development of a newborn baby as it progresses through the stages of infancy, you will see how quickly one discovers the process of persuasive communication. In a short period of time, the baby develops a highly sophisticated language system in the way it cries. A sensitive mother can determine, by the type of cry, whether the baby is hungry, wet, uncomfortable, or in need of loving.

The baby soon learns that not only does the world out there, beyond the crib, affect what happens to him but that *he* can also affect the world out there. Baby can therefore attempt to make his environment as comfortable as possible—*for himself.* Once this has been internalized, we proceed to adapt this principle throughout our lives. With each new experience, we increase our abilities to influence others so as to make our environment, that which is immediately around us, as comfortable as possible.

When we communicate verbally we are, in fact, doing so with the sole purpose of affecting the behaviour of others. It is done with intent. At times, our intentions may be so subtle, disguised, or even subconscious, that we may not be aware of what we are doing.

A simple "Hello" to our friend in the hall between classes has its purpose. In effect we are saying, "Look at me, notice me, I am *me*, I am important, I *am*." If our friend does not greet us back, we become very upset and be-

A SENSITIVE MOTHER CAN DETERMINE, BY THE TYPE OF CRY, WHETHER THE BABY IS HUNGRY, WET, UNCOMFORTABLE, OR IN NEED OF LOVING

gin to place all kinds of interpretations as to why he didn't acknowledge a gesture of friendship. It may never have occurred to you that maybe he didn't even see you. Has this not happened to you at some time? A person has become angry because you didn't say Hello to him. In actuality, you can't remember having seen him.

We are all affecting agents. Sometimes our persuasion is pretty direct. Let us say, for example, you want to go ice-skating tonight but you don't want to go alone. Your best friend says he can't go because he has to study for a chemistry test the next day. *But—you* want to go ice-skating. Depending on how badly you want to go, you will try to convince your friend that he should go with you. You may give such valid reasons as:

> It will relax your mind. Haven't you heard that you shouldn't study on the night before an exam?
>> *or*
> If you don't know it now, a few more hours won't make any difference.
>> *or*
> You are a brain, you'll have no trouble.

If these don't do the trick, I am sure you will try to find even stronger arguments in order to persuade your friend to come with you.

What about conversation at a party?

What about that report you are reading to the class?

In these situations, are we attempting to influence others with intent? Think about it.

Our interpersonal communication is the most important process in our lives. As human beings, we no longer live simply as a result of the products of our own hands, but through our dealings with others. Our basic purpose in communicating is to alter the original relationships between our own organism and the environment in which we find ourselves. More specifically, our basic purpose is to reduce the probability that we are solely a target of external forces, and increase the probability that we exert force ourselves.

Our basic purpose in communicating is to become an affecting agent, to affect others, our physical environment, and ourselves. We want to have a part in determining our destiny. We want to have a say in how things are. In short, *communication is persuasive human interaction*.

With an understanding of the basic characteristics of communication, we may now proceed in our discussion to a description of *how communication works*.

COMMUNICATION

How Does It Work?

Elements of the Communication Event

When people interact together, we call what happens a communication event. The communication process, as a total event, has been the subject of many studies.

If we view communication as a process, ongoing, continuous, and everchanging, we encounter difficulty when we try to describe it. We have said that communication cannot be frozen in time and space. It is not static. So, where do we begin when we seek to understand how communication works?

Every communication situation differs in some way or other from every other one, yet we can attempt to isolate certain elements that *all* communication situations have in common. It is these ingredients and their interrelationships we consider when we try to explain how communication works.

While we can draw a picture of how the communication event takes place, we must remember that it is only a picture of the event—much like a photograph. We can photograph a field-and-track meet or a hockey game but we cannot freeze time. Our photograph is only a fraction-of-a-second *representation* of the event and not the event itself. It is only an image on film. There is that which occurred before the picture was snapped and there is that which continued after the photograph was taken. We can never fully describe the event by simply looking at a photograph. We cannot recreate the emotions of excitement we had at the time of the event. Even those who were present will have different interpretations as to what had taken place.

When attempting to understand the nature and function of communication, we can only, at best, assimilate some reasonable facsimile of the event. We call this facsimile, a *communication model*. Like a photograph, a model represents a part of the communication process. Models in communication serve a very useful purpose. They can be designed for purposes of *description* or *prediction*.

When looking at an event which has occurred, a descriptive model can be used to identify the major details of what took place. Such models are helpful in analyzing and diagnosing communication failures.

A COMMUNICATION MODEL

If we have achieved successful communication in a particular situation, we may wish to attempt a similar approach at another time with a different event. When looked at in this manner, our model becomes predictive in purpose.

We will not concern ourselves with the many complex descriptive models researchers have used in explaining the communication process. Our attention will be directed toward an understanding of the *basic elements* found in the act of human communication.

There are three major elements in the communication process; the *sender*, the *receiver*, and the *message* which may be either verbal or nonverbal.

If we diagram these elements, it would look like this:

Sender
Field of
Experience

Receiver
Field of
Experience

A *sender* is the originator of the communication.
He is also sometimes called a *source*.
A source may be an individual speaking, writing, drawing, or a communication organization such as a newspaper, a printing house, radio or television station, etc.

A *message* is the information the sender, or source, sends to his receiver. The message may be verbal or nonverbal. A message is any signal capable of being interpreted meaningfully.

A *receiver* is the destination for the message.
A receiver is the one who receives the signal, the message, which has been sent by the sender or source. The receiver then, upon hearing or seeing the message, interprets its meaning in his own mind. All people are receivers of communication. Receivers may be an individual listening, watching, or reading. Receivers can also be a group of people such as observers at a football game.

But communication is not just one-way as seen in this diagram. Senders also become receivers and receivers can become senders.

We probably know if our message has been received by listening to the receiver's words or watching his gestures. The receiver tells you in some way how accurately he received your message. This is called *feedback*. It is the response the receiver sends back to the sender to tell him how he is doing. Feedback gives us the opportunity to correct our efforts if we do not succeed on the first attempt at communicating.

If we add feedback to our diagram, it would look like this:

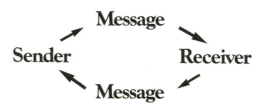

We can see, in this diagram, that communication is a two-way process. Notice that our model also shows us that communication can be thought of as a circle. This fits well into our description of communication as process, for it demonstrates the continuous nature of the communication event.

If our message is interpreted as we wanted it interpreted by the receiver, we say the communication had *high-fidelity*. We were pleased by the feedback we received.

If our message is not interpreted as we had wanted it to be interpreted, we say that the communication had *low-fidelity.*

Our goal in communication is to produce messages which will give us *high-fidelity.*

What causes us to have a *low-fidelity message?*

There are a variety of factors and reasons which we will discuss in more detail in the final section of this chapter. In general, we would say that anything which interferes with the reception of information could be classified as *noise.* Communication difficulties, or *noise,* can occur in one of five categories:

1. Difficulties that exist primarily within and about the sender.
2. Difficulties that exist within the receiver.
3. Difficulties which occur within both the sender and receiver, either jointly or separately.

4. Difficulties external to the sender and/or receiver.
5. Barriers and breakdowns related generally to the overall communication situation.

These difficulties are discussed in great detail in the chapter "Overcoming Communication Barriers."

Noise need not be considered a detriment unless it produces significant interference with the reception of the message.

There is one more element we must include in our diagram of the communication event. Before we can attempt to communicate, each person must share a commonness with one another. This common area of contact we call the *field of experience.*

The sender can send messages and the receiver can interpret the messages only in terms of the experiences each has had.

An obvious field of experience is a common understanding of a language code. If I speak German and you speak French, we will have great difficulty in communicating. However, if we both speak Spanish, we share a common field of experience, and communication then becomes possible.

In our diagram, this field of experience may be illustrated by two overlapping circles. The more they overlap the greater the possibilities for high-fidelity communication.

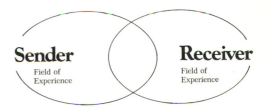

A RECEIVER

A field of experience includes not only an understanding of a language code but also an understanding of cultural values, attitudes, beliefs, level of knowledge, and one's social system. It is the sum total of each person's experiences. Communication takes place at those points where these experiences interact between the sender and the receiver.

Sender   Receiver
Field of   Field of
Experience Experience

With an understanding of *how communication works*, we may now proceed to a discussion of those factors which *determine communication effectiveness.*

COMMUNICATION

What Determines Its Effectiveness?

How do we determine whether or not our efforts at communication have been successful?

A SENDER OR SOURCE

We have said that when a message is received and interpreted in a manner which pleases us, we have *high-fidelity* communication. Therefore, through the process of feedback, we have ascertained that we were successful. But what factors must we consider in attempting to produce a *high-fidelity message*?

The purpose of this book is to make you aware of those factors which will help you improve your understanding of human communication. By studying the relationship between basic theories of human behaviour and communication events, you should be able to improve your facility for analyzing the determinants and the consequences of communication.

By way of introduction to the chapters that follow, let me briefly touch on some of these factors which determine communication effectiveness. These factors must be recognized and evaluated in terms of their impact on our own behaviour and that of others.

1. *We must recognize that one cannot* NOT *communicate.*

There are many ways in which we communicate, some intentional, some not. Some form of communication is always taking place. There is no such thing as noncommunication.

Every communication situation involves the production of a message by someone and the receipt of that message by someone. Our refusal to speak with a person, communicates a message in itself. You may be indicating to the other person that you are angry, anti-social, jealous, or you just don't want to be bothered. On the other hand, you may want the other person to make some response, such as an apology, recognition or gesture of friendship.

Let us say, for instance, that you are seated on a bus and a complete stranger comes on and sits down next to you. Not a word is spoken.

Is communication taking place?
Is a message being sent and received?

Although the two of you are not speaking verbally, communication *is* taking place on a nonverbal level. You are interpreting, in your own mind, definite impressions about the individual from what you see.

What do you see?
How do you look at this stranger?
Do you look at him critically, noticing that his shoes are unshined, the hair too long, drabby clothes, an unpleasing odour about him?
   or
Do you tend to look at him with friendly interest and to think that, despite some unfavourable external evidence, he seems to be a decent sort, perhaps even a potential friend?

What we see in a person is often not so much a revelation of the person as it is of ourselves.

Thomas Carlyle looked at his own nation and said, "England has a population of forty million people, mainly fools." That tells you something about Carlyle, doesn't it?

David Livingston, the great explorer-missionary, looked at Africa and said, "An unhappy people to whom I must dedicate my life." See the difference in the two men revealed in their outlook. What we see in others is often a greater revelation of ourselves than it is of the person looked at.

Communication takes place on many different levels.

One cannot *not* communicate.

2. *We must recognize that each person is unique.*

When we say that a person is unique, we mean that there is no other person like him; there never was nor will there ever be again.

You are unique. *You* are an event in history.

When you come to a communication situation, you bring with you everything that makes *you* who *you* are. Even though the receiver of your communication is of the same age, goes to the same school, and speaks the same language, each of you will interpret messages in different ways. This is because each person brings with him to the communication event all of the experiences which make him an individual.

Recently a group of students were working out-of-doors on an assignment project. The area that they had selected for their work was near a busy traffic intersection.

Shortly after they had arrived, a traffic accident happened right in front of them.

YOU ARE UNIQUE. YOU ARE AN EVENT IN HISTORY.

Each had seen the accident. However, each had a different interpretation of what had occurred.

Have you ever had someone tell you that they know how you feel when you relate some experience that has happened to you? I am sure you have had someone say to you, "I know how you feel, the same thing happened to me!" Perhaps you have wanted to respond by saying, "Oh no, it didn't. This is my very own experience. You are not me. How could *you* possibly know how I feel?"

While many situations may *appear* to be the same on the surface, such experiences are only *similar. No one ever has the same exact interpretations for anything.*

Because each person is unique, he brings to every communication situation his own attitudes, beliefs, opinions, personality traits, and all the things which make him who he is. You must approach every communication event with the knowledge that each person is unique.

3. *We must recognize the field of experience.*

In the previous section of this chapter in which we described how communication works, the *field of experience* was said to be those areas which the sender and the receiver share. The sender can send messages and the receiver can interpret the messages only in terms of the experiences each has had.

A person's field of experience includes:

1. Basic communication skills, *e.g.* reading, writing, speaking.
2. Level of knowledge, *e.g.* educational background, life experience.
3. Attitudes, *e.g.* personality, beliefs, opinions.
4. Social background, *e.g.* the nature of the society in which one has lived.
5. Cultural Heritage, *e.g.* those things which make groups of people distinct from one another.

If individuals do not recognize that fields of experience are different, then failure in effective communication is guaranteed.

4. *We must recognize the importance of feedback.*

Through feedback, we can correct our communication failures. We must be alert and receptive to verbal and nonverbal cues and clues. Listening, interpreting, and understanding what one says or does is a vital determinant in effective communication.

Not only do we receive feedback from

others but we can also experience feedback within ourselves. Have you ever been speaking with someone and suddenly realized you have made a mistake in what you have just said? Quickly you will correct yourself by changing a word or rephrasing a statement. You have experienced feedback with yourself.

Feedback serves as an excellent guide in being able to determine whether or not we are effectively communicating with others. However, unless we share some common field of experience with those with whom we wish to communicate, we may misinterpret what we see, read, or hear.

An incident that comes to mind occurred some time ago in a small town in the southwestern United States. A new teacher, who had just moved from a New England state, was disciplining a small Mexican-American boy. She kept insisting that the boy look at her while she spoke to him. She became very angry because he would look at the ground instead of at her. She thought him to be very rude and disrespectful. However, she didn't understand certain things about his sociocultural heritage. She didn't realize that, in Mexico, when a person was to show respect for an adult, it was customary to look at the ground when being disciplined.

For feedback to be useful, we must *accurately* interpret verbal and nonverbal cues and clues in the light of the experience each individual has had.

There are many factors in our communication attempts which determine our effectiveness. Among those is the recognition that one cannot *not* communicate, a realization that each person is unique, taking into account a person's field of experience, and being able accurately to interpret feedback. These principles are only a few basic examples of what each person must consider as they communicate with others. In no way is this list complete. As you proceed through the pages of this book, you will recognize other determinants which you will be able to add to the list.

SELECTED READINGS

Berlo, David K. *The Process of Communication.* New York: Holt, Rinehart and Winston, Inc., 1960.

Bormann, Ernest G. and Nancy C. *Speech Communication: An Interpersonal Approach.* New York: Harper and Row, Publishers, 1972.

Brown, Charles T. and Charles Van Riper. *Communication in Human Relationships.* Skokie, Illinois: National Textbook Corp., 1973.

DeVito, Joseph A. *Communication: Concepts and Processes.* Englewood Cliffs, New Jersey: Prentice-Hall, Inc., 1971.

Fabun, Don. *Communications: The Transfer of Meaning.* Beverly Hills, California: Glencoe Press, 1968.

Felber, Stanley B. and Arthur Koch. *What Did You Say?* Englewood Cliffs, New Jersey: Prentice-Hall, Inc., 1973.

Galvan, Kathleen and Cassandra Book. *Person-To-Person: An Introduction to Speech Communication.* Skokie, Illinois: National Textbook Corp., 1973.

Giffin, Kim and Bobby R. Patton. *Fundamentals of Interpersonal Communication.* New York: Harper and Row, Publishers, 1971.

————. *Basic Readings in Interpersonal Communication.* New York: Harper and Row, Publishers, 1971.

Keltner, John W. *Interpersonal Communication: Elements and Structure.* Belmont, California: Wadsworth Publishing Co., Inc., 1970.

McLuhan, Marshall. *Understanding Media: The Extensions of Man.* New York: McGraw-Hill Book Company, 1964.

Pace, Wayne and Robert R. Boren. *The Human Transaction.* Glenview, Illinois: Scott, Foresman and Company, 1973.

Sathre, Freda S., Roy W. Olson, and Clarissa I. Whitney. *Let's Talk.* Glenview, Illinois: Scott, Foresman and Company, 1973.

Schramm, Wilbur. *Men, Messages, and Media: A Look at Human Communication.* New York: Harper and Row, Publishers, 1973.

2

DYADIC COMMUNICATION

Carl J. Hartleib

THE BEGINNING

Who Will?

To be within myself and alone with shaking thoughts,
Who will enter my world and yet not trample my
*   trembling self?*
I wish to be with you,
Not to talk, not to analyze, nor to solve.

What is it?
Can you touch me and nourish my clenched heart?
And yet keep within my bounds of safety,
For my feeling is unknown and new to me.

From where did it come?
Who will recognize where I am?
Is it enough to be inside oneself and allow you in?

Perhaps!!

What was the writer of this poem attempting to convey to others?

Could you read this poem and "tune in" (be with him in his emotions and his thoughts) to this person, or are you in a personal space that will not allow you to reach beyond your own internal anxiety and your own concerns to recognize and experience others?

Is it important for you as a person to increase your ability to encounter with another in meaningful dyadic communication?

Read This Chapter
If This Human Process
Is of Value to You

Our Concern

The poem, "Who Will" was written by me to symbolize a message that I have heard repeatedly in my work with groups and individual counselling. People need to develop the human skills of communicating with each other to enable themselves to share their inner concerns more freely and honestly with significant others who are important to them. It was this concern of helping people to communicate their inner needs and thoughts with each other that prompted us to write this book. I was especially concerned with face to face inter-relating with two people who were emotionally and socially close to each other.

I will present a model of communication that emphasizes components and skills that I have found helpful in facilitating close communication with caring people, in hopes that you the reader may improve and be more aware of yourself and others in moments of meaningful encounter. We will return to the poem after we have examined our dyadic model of interpersonal communication and really hear what people are saying in the poem.

WHAT IS MEANINGFUL HUMAN DYADIC COMMUNICATION?

How does one know that he has experienced "meaningful" dyadic communication with another human being? This is a difficult question to answer in print, and is similar to answering the question of a young person who asks, "What's it like to be in love?" For a person in love, there is no doubt in his mind about the experience, but this love experience takes on dimensions which are individualized and different for each person. So it is with someone who has the human skill to communicate at meaningful levels with others. He knows it's happening, but often it is difficult to analyze and describe to others.

For our purposes we will describe dyadic conversation as what occurs when two people who are important to each other engage in an intimate, special communication, face to

and by focusing on these criteria the reader will become aware of the human dimensions of his own conversations. It is not within the scope of this chapter to present a manual of dyadic conversation, but to bring to the reader's awareness human communication skills that are identifiable and learnable.

A Model of Core Elements
That Increase
Meaningful Interpersonal Communication

How Do You KNOW IF YOU HAVE EXPERIENCED "MEANINGFUL" COMMUNICATION WITH ANOTHER HUMAN BEING ?

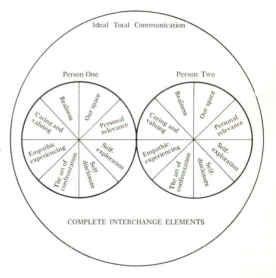

face. They really hear each other and reach out to each other with both their verbal and nonverbal language. The two people involved sense an atmosphere of closeness, of exciting learning and human acceptance of each other that makes this contact between them special and unique. The importance of this kind of relating to each other cannot be overstressed, for through it you will learn to experience yourself and others more fully and add that richness to your communicating life that we as humans need to develop.

Many social scientists who are concerned with this human dimension of communication have approached the subject in many ways; but when one studies each approach there seem to be common key elements that continually come to the fore. These I will identify and describe.

I will attempt to describe my relationship with communication. This is analogous to a painter attempting to describe his painting without the listener being able to see it. How does one take the art of communicating with another, which is a whole, and break it down into its parts for descriptive purposes, and yet maintain the authenticity of this communication? I will attempt to identify criteria that facilitate interpersonal communication,

THE MODEL OF CORE ELEMENTS

The preceding diagram helps illustrate what I mean about transposing a process into its components. For our purposes, the model is an ideal situation in which two people possess the following eight human communication skills:

a) Realness
b) Caring and Valuing
c) Empathic Experiencing
d) The Art of Confrontation
e) Self-disclosure
f) Self-exploration
g) Personal Relevance
h) Our Space

The more of these components that are present in any interaction between two humans, the more opportunity for meaningful communication and learning. The two people bring the necessary elements of good conversation with them to the encounter. However, not all individuals possess these eight characteristics in their fullest potential, and one person could bring any combination of the core elements to the conversation while another person may bring a different combination of the elements to the conversation. If both people, however, bring together all eight elements then eventually a total conversation will develop. This occurs because humans can learn from each other and each acts as a model for the other in those criteria that he possesses. Let us diagram an example of that.

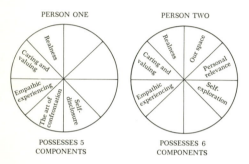

PERSON ONE   PERSON TWO

POSSESSES 5 COMPONENTS   POSSESSES 6 COMPONENTS

Listed below are the component skills that person one possesses and that person two possesses:

Person One	Person Two
Realness	Realness
Self-disclosure	. . . . .
. . . . .	Personal relevance
. . . . .	Our space
. . . . .	Self-exploration
Empathic experiencing	Empathic experiencing
Art of confrontation	. . . . .
Caring and valuing	Caring and valuing

So, for our purposes, person one will be modelling self-disclosure and the art of confrontation for person two, while person two will model personal relevance, our space, and self-exploration for person one. In other words, people model skills that are missing in the person with whom they are conversing. You will also note in our example that between both people, all eight components were present in the conversation, and eventually both persons would have experienced all eight components.

In some conversations all eight components are not present because both people are deficient in the same components; for example, if both people are lacking the skills of self-disclosure and realness, neither could experience from the other such skills, and the richness of the dyadic experience would be limited to only six of the eight components, and because of these missing components the possibility for misunderstanding would be increased.

If you as a person have experienced communication with another where all eight components eventually were exercised in the experience, you will remember it and value it for the human experience that it is, and wonder why it does not occur more often. The beauty of this interaction is that it can happen between any and all persons in any and all settings, in any and all periods of time, if the two people will take the time and the caring for each other that is necessary. It may seem simplistic, but I have discovered if people will actually commit themselves to spending time with each other for the purpose of actively caring and listening to each other, that these components will come into operation. Now let us examine the components.

Empathic Experiencing

It has been my experience, after working with people for a number of years, that each individual brings with him to a communication relationship a certain amount of empathic experiencing. By this I mean that one can respond verbally and nonverbally to a person in such ways as to add deeper feeling and meaning to the expression of the second person, so that the latter can begin to explore those deeper themes. He is able to move into the feeling space of the other and be tuned in to him in such a way that he is responding with a full awareness of who the other person is, and what his deepest feelings are, by being fully with him in his deepest moments. The listener is so free to sense what the other person is experiencing that it is as if they were two vibrating tuning forks humming at the same frequency. The degree of quickness with which one can zero in on another's feelings can be an expanding experience for the other, or a scary experience that inhibits him from really sensing his own feelings. It is as if you have met someone who appears to

CHILDREN ARE FREER AND MORE SPONTANEOUS
IN EXPRESSING THEIR UNDERSTANDING
OF ANOTHER'S FEELINGS

or another. The need to nurture others and be nurtured by others has been displayed by mankind and animals since time began. All one has to do is observe a loving mother caring and nurturing her child to grasp the sense of this human dimension. This need does not disappear in adulthood; and at critical, vulnerable times, human beings need to be nurtured and loved for their own sakes alone, without conditions or expectations. When someone realizes that another really cares about his feelings, experiences and potentials, it allows him to feel free to be himself and experience being valued as an individual. If you can communicate your commitment of valuing another person as a human being, that other person will be able to begin experiencing a deep respect and a caring for himself. What you are communicating is, "With me, you are free to be who you are." This expression of respect for each other will help in disclosing one's attitudes and behaviours, both negative and positive, about oneself and others. This acceptance by one person of another is very crucial.

know you as well or better than you know yourself, even though you have never met him before. This gives him an awesome power with which you may, or may not, trust him, because you are afraid of what you don't know about yourself that he might tell you. The choice to continue exploring these deeper feelings and thoughts will depend upon how gently the other person responds to your newly emerging discoveries. The key to this process is the listener's sensitivity to the other person's emotional space; and it is often unwise to move in too quickly and chance going beyond the surface feelings being expressed. It may be wiser to simply reflect verbally what the other person is saying, and not to either add to or subtract from what the other is expressing. If one can really be with another in his feelings, and express it to the other in a way that is acceptable to him, a bond of trust will begin to grow and greatly enhance the communicative relationship. Children often display this empathic sensing of another's feelings but, unlike adults, they are freer and more spontaneous in expressing this understanding to the other person.

TENDER LOVING CARE

Caring and Valuing

All of us need acceptance and tender loving care (TLC) from others at one time

Realness

How many times have you heard the expression, "What a phony that guy is!" Probably what this means is that this person's verbalizations to the listener were clearly unrelated to what he was actually feeling and thinking at the moment, and this kind of response has a destructive effect upon others. The person's thoughts and feelings are not being expressed in harmony, and this disharmony is detected by the listener. He is actually saying one thing when it appears he means something else or is feeling something else related to the topic. In other words, there is a discrepancy between the inner experiencing by the person and what he is outwardly expressing. If that "phony" could respond with many of his own feelings in a sincere way, he would appear more genuine to the second person and the relationship could grow. Both could then be freely and deeply themselves in a nonexploitive relationship and be open to experiences of all types with each other.

Self-disclosure

Closely connected to being genuine there is a dimension where one may choose either to disclose nothing about one's own feelings or personality, or, where one volunteers very intimate material about oneself. In the first instance one person actively attempts to remain detached, and by doing so remains an unknown quantity to the second person, who then loses faith in the first person. In the second instance, where the first person is free and spontaneous in volunteering personal information about himself, he gives the impression of holding nothing back in disclosing his feelings and ideas fully and completely, and this acts as a basis for encouraging open-ended inquiry. So, one has the choice to remain ambiguous and private or one can freely volunteer information about one's personal ideas, attitudes, and experiences in accordance with the conversation.

Often when one senses a person having difficulty discussing some personal intimate material, one can ease the situation by voluntarily revealing private concerns and by so doing free the other person to share also those matters which, to this point, he has not been able to express, thus facilitating more self-exploration.

Personal Relevance

Have you ever heard the expression, after listening to someone talk, "What the hell was that all about?" Probably the person dealt only with vague and anonymous generalities, and avoided personally relevant, specific situations and feelings. This person probably uses the term "they" to refer to the general

A SESQUIPEDALIAN BROMIDE

PEOPLE WHO CONTINUALLY EXPRESS THEMSELVES IN ABSTRACT AND HIGHLY INTELLECTUAL WAYS LEAVE OTHERS INDIFFERENT

group of people that do things to you. For instance, "They always pick days like this to complain and tell me about things that are wrong," which does not make much sense to anyone; if he had been personally more specific and indicated what person had done what act to him, then there would have been no ambiguity to deal with. People who continually express themselves in abstract and highly intellectual ways leave others feeling that the discussion is irrelevant. Conversely, if one can discuss specific feelings, situations, and events, then one is left with a sense of direct expression of personally relevant feelings and experiences. In other words, the conversation is about concrete and specific terms that are seen as personally relevant to what was being discussed. To discuss fluently, directly and completely, specific feelings and experiences, leaves both parties knowing exactly what was discussed, and no one has to fill in blank general areas with information that may or may not be correct.

The Art of Confrontation

"Only a friend could have told you that," is a statement referring to the gentle art of confrontation. When a person becomes aware of discrepancies in another person's behaviour, he may choose to accept them passively and remain silent concerning them, or relate directly and specifically to them. Perhaps you have a friend who doesn't seem to be aware of what he does to some people, and it would take a great deal of courage and diplomacy on your part to confront him with this behaviour. The discrepancy is that he feels he acts a certain way, but in reality his behaviour is not in harmony with what he thinks, so it would be up to the person seeing this difference to point it out to him. Usually it has been my experience that when one attends directly and specifically to discrepancies in others' behaviour and communication, in a sensitive and perceptive manner, potentially fruitful inquiry and communication results. In other words, the person can begin to become aware of discrepancies and choose to explore them and perhaps change these inconsistencies.

Our Space

Have you ever been in a tense conversation where you could feel your anger growing and

YOU SHOULD POINT OUT THE DISCREPANCIES IN SOMEONE ELSE'S BEHAVIOUR TO HIM

yet the content of the conversation with the other person was not directed to you or to him? What was happening in the immediate conversation was that each of you was sending messages to the other that you weren't appreciating because both of you chose to disregard the dynamic of anger that was occurring between you. You can't quite put your finger on the process, but something immediate has happened to your relationship with the other during the conversation. Probably what has happened is that either of you has simply disregarded all those messages to each other that concern your relationship, and you choose to remain silent or just not relate the content of your discussion to yourself. You choose not to interpret what is going on between you and the other person in the immediate moment. It's easier to avoid confronting the other person with what is happening between you at the moment, so you let it ride only to find later that you wish you could have interpreted, more quickly and accurately, the dynamic that was occurring in the relationship: Was he putting me down? Was he making fun of me? Was he trying to be sincere, but I couldn't recognize it? What was he actually trying to communicate to me, even though he really didn't say it to me directly? Many important messages that are sent in a camouflaged way are only vaguely understood and leave the person with an uneasy, unresolved feeling. I have found that if I cautiously relate the reflections and expressions that are occurring in our relationship at the moment, it helps in interpreting our relationship generally. In other words, what is happening between you and me at this particular time is an important avenue for increasing our communication and awareness of each other.

Self-exploration

Some people have the art of dealing openly with themselves in full view of others. A person spontaneously will probe inwardly to discover new feelings and experiences which have been triggered by another person introducing personally relevant material. He will actively focus upon himself and explore himself in his world even though he may be doing so fearfully and tentatively. This kind of personal modelling encourages others to begin to explore themselves more freely. This has been brought to my attention many times in group situations where an open and honest individual has become aware of some personal inner focus and has shared this inward searching with others; this in turn has encouraged others to relate to themselves and share things within themselves that they never could before. This is a beautiful process to observe and actively practise.

TOWARDS AUTHENTIC COMMUNICATION

Our model has been presented and described in hopes of making you more aware of the process of dyadic communication. Each of these eight components adds human dimensions to your conversations that increase the opportunity for fuller understanding and authenic relating between people. Many people can increase their ability to express themselves more autonomously, spontaneously and authentically, and by doing so increase their opportunity for a more productive, communicative life. It is towards this end that you read this chapter and we hope increased your dyadic relating potential. Therefore, in summary, would you consider the following:

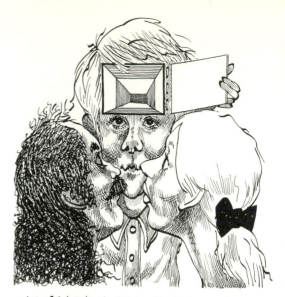

AN OPEN AND HONEST INDIVIDUAL SHARES HIS INWARD SEARCHING WITH OTHERS

Now that you have read this chapter, do you have a greater appreciation and awareness of the factors affecting meaningful dyadic communication?

Do you recognize more fully, human communication characteristics that each person brings to any communication relationship?

Do you recognize in yourself those factors that you possess and those that you don't demonstrate within this model?

Can you begin to consider how to express better those human communication qualities that increase and facilitate communication between two people in a developing relationship?

We hope so.

AS IN THE BEGINNING—*Who Will?*

Let us now consider our total model of interpersonal communication and re-read the poem, "Who Will"; then reconsider our responses to this person. Empathically, can you experience this person's aloneness, and hope that someone will care and value his or her inner state of feeling and be with him with no sense of exploitation, but gentle acceptance? Can you respond to the plea for recognition and help, but move within his delicate space of this new experiencing of opening himself?

Do you recognize his puzzlement about what is happening within him? Can you understand him at the level he is feeling? Do you think perhaps just being with him totally and allowing him to experience you there will be the beginning of a communication process for him that will lead to further personal growth?

SELECTED READINGS

Carkhuff, R. R. and G. B. Bernard. *Beyond Counselling and Therapy.* Toronto: Holt, Rinehart and Winston, Inc., 1967.

Combs, A., D. Avila, and W. Purkey. *Helping Relationships.* Boston: Allyn and Bacon, Inc., 1971.

Johnson, David W. *Reaching Out,* Englewood Cliffs, New Jersey: Prentice-Hall, Inc., 1972.

Jourard, Sidney M. *The Transparent Self.* Toronto: Van Nostrand Reinhold, Ltd., 1971.

Rogers, Carl R. *On Becoming A Person.* Boston: Houghton Mifflin Company, 1970.

3

COMMUNICATION BARRIERS

Donald L. MacRae

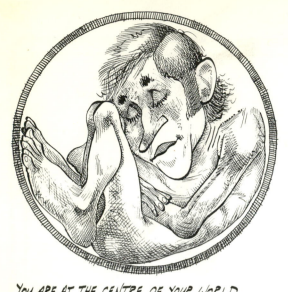

YOU ARE AT THE CENTRE OF YOUR WORLD...

The quality of the lives we lead is shaped in large measure by our ability to relate to our fellow human beings. Those relationships are developed primarily through interpersonal communication.

It would be nice if this process that we call interpersonal communication was a very simple one—one that each of us could master quickly and easily; however, it isn't. It is a very complex process of human interaction that is more complex than human nature itself. It is a process that challenges each of us to understand its complexities, its problems, and to develop solutions to those problems so that we might use the process of interpersonal communication to further develop the quality of our lives.

Each chapter in this book has been written to help you understand the complex nature of interpersonal communication. The objective of this chapter, in particular, is to identify and explore some of the most common problems—more frequently referred to as communication barriers—that develop as we try to communicate. The next chapter will explore some of the solutions for overcoming these communication barriers.

Each of us has, on many occasions during our lives, experienced communication breakdown. Those times when we have attempted to establish a relationship with another person and share our ideas and feelings, and something was just not right. There seemed to be a tension in the air or we did not under-

stand each other or did not seem to be listening to each other. On many of those occasions we felt really frustrated because we knew we were failing to communicate with the other person, but we just couldn't put our finger on the reason why.

In a very general sense, the reason for most communication breakdowns is the fact that there is no common world—you are at the centre of your world and I am at the centre of mine. The closeness of our worlds depends on the closeness of our language, experience, culture, beliefs, attitudes, philosophies and so on. The effectiveness that we can achieve in interpersonal communication depends on the extent to which our worlds overlap each other. In effect, we are able to communicate because we see similarities in each other's world. Communication breaks down when we are not able to see the similarities in each other's world.

There are a number of barriers that frequently develop as we try to communicate with each other that prevent us from seeing the similarities in each other's world and thus lead to communication breakdown. I have chosen what I consider to be seven of the most prominent barriers to communication. They will be discussed in this chapter in the following sequence:

1. Perception
2. The self and the self-concept
3. Living a role vs. playing a role
4. The masks we wear

AND I AM AT THE CENTRE OF MINE

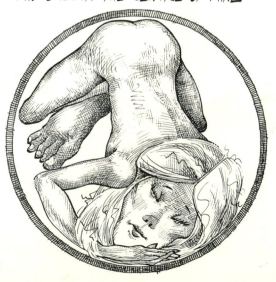

WHY ERECT BARRIERS?

5. Motivation—what makes us say the things we do?
6. Words and meanings, and people and meanings
7. Listening vs. hearing

Before beginning our discussion of communication barriers let me offer you a definition of interpersonal communication in the hope that it will indicate to you the complexity of the process that we engage in hundreds of times each day, yet so frequently take for granted.

Interpersonal communication is a complex process of human interaction in which information is conveyed from person to person verbally and nonverbally through shared language, experience and perception in such a way as to achieve the transfer of a close approximation of intended meaning.

If you accept this definition of interpersonal communication you will agree that if we, as communicators, do everything we should do in order to communicate effectively, the best we can hope for is "to achieve the transfer of a *close approximation* of the intended meaning." If that is correct, if we are barely able to communicate with any degree of accuracy when everything in the system is working effectively, what kinds of results can we expect if we place barriers in the paths of our communication attempts?

If we are to overcome the negative effects of barriers on interpersonal communication, we must first identify the barriers and understand their causes and effects—the objectives of this chapter.

PERCEPTION

Perception is the name we give to the process of selecting, organizing and interpreting the information we receive from our five senses (vision, touch, taste, smell, hearing). It is one of the most important factors affecting our ability to communicate with each other.

"Do you see what I mean?" is a question that we are frequently asked after we have received a verbal message from another person. What the question means is, "Do you see in your mind's eye what I see in my mind's eye at this particular moment?" which in turn means, "Did you select the information that I wanted you to select, organize it the way I intended you to and interpret it exactly the way I do?"

The answer to each of the preceding questions is *No*. However, most of us would probably answer yes to the question, "Do you see what I mean?" because we do see what the other person means but in terms of *our own experience*. In order to understand a little more clearly why the answer to the question in the previous paragraph would be no, let's take a closer look at the three phases of the perception process: (1) *The world around us* or what J. Samuel Bois, in his book *The Art of Awareness*, referred to as the WIGO, (2) *selecting information* which we will refer to as the WIS, and (3) *organizing and interpreting* that information which we will refer to as the WIMTU.

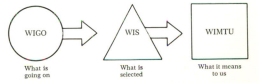

I will define the WIGO, for our purposes, as what is going on around each of us at a particular moment in time that we are capable of sensing (through one of the five senses) and therefore capable of selecting for interpretation either consciously or unconsciously. Let me give you an example. As you walk down the street, everything that you are able to see, hear, touch, taste or smell at that particular time is part of your WIGO. Things that are happening inside the buildings you are walking by; things that are happening two blocks, two miles or two oceans away from you are *not* part of your WIGO unless you are able to receive information from them through one of your senses. If you were walking past a television store in Vancouver and a television set in the window was showing events that were happening live in Montreal, then of course, the events that were happening in Montreal would be part of the WIGO for you at that particular moment in time.

What we must understand when we talk about the role of the WIGO in perception is that no two WIGOs are exactly the same. I can never receive information through your senses and you can never receive information through my senses. What is going on for *you* is never *exactly* the same as what is going on for *me*. You experience your WIGO from the centre of your world and I experience my WIGO from the centre of my world. It is when I think *what is going on for me* is the same as *what is going on for you* that we tend to confuse each other in communication.

The WIS represents what we select from the WIGO for interpretation. The WIS represents the sounds, sights, smells, tastes and touching experiences that we concentrate on or pay attention to at a particular moment in time. As we walk down that street in Vancouver there are many sensory stimuli available to us; however, we choose to ignore most of them and select those that have special interest for us. We normally select from the information available to us according to our particular interests, needs or desires *at that moment* and we are more likely to select information that we are familiar with or can anticipate. In other words, we tend to see what we want to see and see it according to how we have seen it in the past.

Let's use a visual example. Read the information in the triangles below quickly and out loud.

Did you select *ALL* of the words in each of the triangles? If you didn't can you explain why you didn't? If you did, can you explain why you did? Did you "see" what you wanted to see?

We each select information from our environment differently. You select what is important to you and I select what is important to me. What is important to you is not *necessarily* important to me. If you think it is, we are going to find each other's communication misleading. You select information from a world that is different than mine and you select information from your world according to *your* needs, which are also different than mine.

So far we have found your WIGO to be different than mine at any moment in time and what you select to be different than what I select at any moment in time. Let us suppose for a moment that part of your WIGO was also part of my WIGO and that both of us selected that shared piece of information. Could both of us perceive that information in exactly the same way? No, we couldn't because of the third part of our model the WIMTU.

WIMTU stands for *what it means to us*— the "it" being the WIS. Now that we have selected information we have to organize it and interpret what it means to us at the particular moment we selected it. We normally organize and interpret this information according to: (1) our purposes for choosing the information in the first place, (2) our assumptions about the information in the present circumstances, and (3) perhaps most important, our past experience.

Let's go back to some visual examples to illustrate how these three factors affect our interpretations of information we select from the world around us.

When you look at the following shapes, how do you organize the information you see?

Do you see nine lines or three sets of three lines each? Do you see a bunch of X's and O's or do you see vertical columns of X's and vertical columns of O's? Do you see a number of dots or do you see a circle and a box?

We normally try to organize information into familiar patterns that we can interpret in terms of our previous experience. However, if we have had limited experience or perhaps no experience with certain pieces of information that have been selected for interpretation, then chances of interpreting the information *incorrectly* or not being able to interpret it at all increase dramatically.

When you look at the information below, how do you interpret it? What do you see?

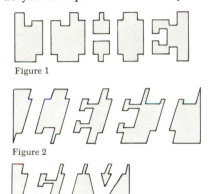

Figure 1

Figure 2

Figure 3

In Figure 1 you should see the word THE. Do you see it? Did you see it immediately? Probably not! When you first look at Figure 1 your past experience tells you to look at the black shapes because they seem to stand out. They are in the foreground. At the same time, we are not used to seeing white letters on a partial black field. We normally see black letters on a white background.

Now that you have interpreted the information in Figure 1 correctly, when you look at Figures 2 and 3 your purpose for choosing the information, your assumptions about the information and your past experience have all changed and you very quickly interpret the information as the words LEFT and FLY.

Have you seen the cow yet in Figure 4?

Well, even if you haven't seen the cow yet I am sure you can see that you and I will never interpret information from the world around us in *exactly* the same way. You interpret the information you select according to your past experience, purposes and assumptions and I according to mine. In other words, we interpret the "reality" of the world around us differently—you from your internal frame of reference and I from mine. It is when we think we see the world around

Figure 4.

us *in the same way* that we begin to misinterpret our communications to each other.

Now that we have discussed the three phases of the perception process, I hope you understand why the answer to the question, "Did you select the information I wanted you to select, organize it the way I intended you to and interpret it exactly the way I do?" is *No* and must always be *No!* We perceive things *differently* and as a result you and I frequently *understand* different messages from the same communication.

Summary

1. I experience things from the centre of *my* world and you experience things from the centre of *your* world. We perceive things differently! *What is going on* for you is not necessarily *what is going on* for me. It is when we think we do see things in the same way that we tend to confuse each other in communication.

2. We select information from our environment differently. What is important to you is not necessarily important to me. If we think it is we might find our communication misleading.

3. We interpret the "reality" of the world around us differently—you from your experience and I from mine. If you think we see the world around us in the same way, you will misinterpret my communication to you.

4. I tend to perceive what I expect or want to perceive and you do the same. We are influenced by our interests, emotions, attitudes, motives and drives. As a result we can easily *understand* different messages from the same communication.

THE SELF AND THE SELF-CONCEPT

To know men is to be wise;
to know one's self is to be illumined;
to conquer men is to have strength;
to conquer one's self is to be stronger still;
and to know when you have enough is to be rich.

For vigorous action may bring a man what he is
determined to have; but to keep one's place, that is,
in the order of the universe, is to endure;
and to die and not be lost, this is the real blessing
of long life.

Lao-tzu,
Chinese philosopher

Now that we have talked about the perception of things or events, let's have a look at how your perception of *yourself* can contribute to the creation of barriers in interpersonal communication.

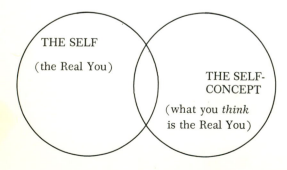

THE SELF
(the Real You)

THE SELF-CONCEPT
(what you *think*
is the Real You)

The *self* is the *real you*. It is the sum total of your experiences with yourself and with others. If it was ever possible to paint a completely objective picture of *you*—your personality, character, feelings, beliefs and attitudes—then you would have what is symbolized in the illustration as the *self*. It is constantly changing as we add new experiences, change our attitudes, reshape our beliefs and perhaps even our personalities.

The *self-concept*, on the other hand, is the way you *see* yourself. It is the sum total of the beliefs you have about the kind of person you are. You develop your self-concept in two ways: (1) based on your observations of your own behaviour and (2) based on your observations and interpretations of other

THE SELF-CONCEPT IS THE WAY YOU SEE YOURSELF

people's behaviour towards you in a wide variety of situations and circumstances. In other words, your self-concept represents your perception of who and what you really are and that self-concept is one of your most important possessions. It is just as important to you as an arm or a leg and just as real. The question we must answer here is, "How *real* is your self-concept in terms of its accuracy and how does the self-concept affect interpersonal communication?"

Remember the WIGO, WIS and WIMTU? Perception is a highly selective process. Much of the time we see and hear what we want or expect to see and hear. Well, our self-concept is a product of this same process of perception. We frequently see in our own behaviour what we want to see and we frequently interpret feedback from others as reinforcement for what we have already seen or already think we know about ourselves. We build our self-concepts by interpreting selected experiences with ourselves and with others in a positive manner, i.e. I am a good guy, a leader, trustworthy, dependable, and so on, and thereby shaping a very positive image of yourself; *or* in a negative manner, i.e. I am not nice, not liked, dependent on others, insecure, untrustworthy, and so on, and thereby shaping a very negative self-image. Chances are your self-concept is

based on a combination of positive and negative interpretations. Whatever the case may be, however, you perceive yourself, that self-concept is *very real* to you. In fact, it becomes in your own mind the *real you,* for who should know who and what you are better than you?

We put a lot of faith in our self-concept and we soon find that it controls, to a large degree, how we behave. If you think of yourself as a leader (and haven't you proven it to yourself through previous experiences?) then you should act like a leader and you probably do. But what if you have interpreted *incorrectly* those experiences that led you to believe you were a leader? As the illustration of the self and the self-concept indicates, we can be quite inaccurate with our self perceptions. The self-concept in the illustration is composed of two parts. The part of the self-concept within the wall of the self, represents an *accurate* perception *on your part* of the way you really are, i.e. you believe yourself to be good in sports, and you are; you believe yourself to be honest, dependable and kind, and you are. The other part of the self-concept is outside the wall of the self.

This part of your self-concept represents images that you have of yourself that *do not* reflect the way you really are. This is not the way other people see you. In other words, you have interpreted some of your previous experiences *incorrectly* and have come up with a partly false image of *who* and *what* you are.

Let's go back to the leadership example and suggest that your image of yourself as a leader came from that part of the self-concept that is outside the wall of the self. You think of yourself as a leader. You believe it and your self-image is reflected in your behaviour. However, the people you relate to have interpreted their experiences with you differently. They *do not* see you as a leader but *see you as you really* are and the feedback they give you indicates that they do *not* see you as a leader. Well they are *wrong!* They don't *really* know you! Who *knows* you better than you!

It is *threatening,* isn't it, when someone indicates to you that you are *not* what you *think* you are! Just as you become defensive when someone threatens your physical well-being, similarly, you become defensive when someone threatens your psychological well-being by attacking your self-concept. You erect barriers for defence and any further attempt at communication must penetrate those barriers in an atmosphere filled with a certain degree of tension.

There are a number of ways that our self-concepts contribute to the development of barriers in interpersonal communication. We have just talked about what happens when someone *threatens* your self-concept.

You erect barriers for defence. Well the same thing happens when you threaten someone else's self-concept. They will respond in the same way even if you threaten their self-concept unknowingly. For example, if your opinion of yourself is too high, you tend to take an attitude of superiority into the communication situation. You don't mean to threaten the other person's self-concept; however, this superior attitude is saying to the other person that they are inferior to you. This threatens their self-concept and barriers are erected. In the same way, if your opinion of yourself is too low you take a feeling of inferiority into the communication situation. This attitude leads you to feel threatened by the other person, and barriers are erected.

In order for you to become better acquainted with your self-concept and its effect on your communication patterns you might want to try the following exercises.

Exercise 1
1. Make a list of the first ten words that come to your mind that describe the way you see yourself.
2. Ask a friend to list the first ten words that come to his/her mind that describes the way he/she sees you.
3. Ask a person who doesn't seem to like you to list the first ten words that come to his/her mind that describes the way he/she sees you.
4. Ask a person whom you do not seem to like to list the first ten words that come to his/her mind that describes the way he/she sees you.

After you have compared and analyzed the lists, you might want to discuss the discrepancies you find with your class or with a group of friends.

Exercise 2
Divide yourselves into groups of four to six people. Each person in the group decides on a colour that he thinks best represents his image of himself. Each person in the group then decides on a colour for every other person in the group that reflects the way he sees each of the other people. Start with one member of the group. Each of the other members of the group in turn explain the colour they chose that reflected their image of that person and explain the reasons for their choice. That person then indicates the colour he chose for himself and explains the reasons for his choice. This exercise is repeated with each member of the group.

Summary
1. How we behave and how we communicate is consistent with our self-concepts. We act like the person we think we are. However, if we are not the person that we think we are, our communication behaviour can be quite confusing to those who see us in a different light.

2. Our self-concept is one of our most important possessions. It is as much a part of us as an arm or a leg. Just as you become defensive when someone threatens your physical well-being; similarly, you become defensive when someone threatens your psychological well-being by attacking your self-concept. You erect barriers for defense and any further attempt at communication must penetrate those barriers.

3. Similarly, if you do not understand the importance the other party in the communication situation attaches to the protection of his self-concept, you might knowingly or unknowingly threaten his self-image. A tension is created and barriers to communication are erected.

4. If my opinion of myself is too high, I tend to take an attitude of superiority into the communication situation. This attitude is normally interpreted in a threatening manner by the other person and tends to create a tension between us.

5. If my opinion of myself is too low, I tend to take a feeling of inferiority into the communication situation. This attitude leads me to feel threatened by the other person or what the other person communicates and, as a result, tension is created between us.

THE ROLES WE PLAY

All the world's a stage
And all the men and women merely players;
They have their exits and their entrances,
And one man in his time plays many parts.

Shakespeare was right! We do play many parts or roles in the course of a lifetime or in the course of a day for that matter. *We have to!* It is society's way of telling us how to cooperate in order to meet the work and social pressures and responsibilities of each day. The roles that we play have certain duties that must be performed and certain expectations as to how they must be performed. When we accept the role of student, or teacher, or father or mother, or butcher or baker or candlestick maker, we accept the script that goes with that role.

Since each of us plays many roles in any one day, it is important for us to be able to adjust quickly to each different role. Most of us will be able to adjust freely and easily to the many roles we play if we do not take our role-playing *too seriously*; in other words, if we constantly realize that we are *playing* a role. On occasion, we might find ourselves *playing* the role *less* and *living* the role *more*. When this happens communication barriers are not far behind!

What is the difference between *playing* a role and *living* a role? When you are playing a role you realize that the foundation for that role is the Real You. You realize that you are playing a part. You allow your personality to be highly visible in the role. As you change roles, you keep the Real You as the *foundation* for the new role and allow people to relate to the Real You *playing* a role, rather than having them relate only to the role itself.

Let's look at an illustration of the Real You as the *foundation* of the roles you play.

In the illustration the Real You has changed its configuration in order to meet the challenges of the different roles, but it is still quite visible. As a result, people, when relating to you playing a role can also relate to you as a person, on a person-to-person basis. They are still mindful of the role and the requirements of the role, but they are usually much more confident of establishing genuine communication when you make the Real You visible in the role you are playing.

When you are *living* the role, you have lost sight of the fact that role-playing is just the Real You playing a part. The role and the expectations of the role as you see them consume the Real You and take the place of the Real You as you communicate with other people. This is sometimes referred to as "really playing the role". When this happens communication begins to break down. People quickly see that they are not communicating to the Real You, but rather are communicating to a Role. Communication then takes on a staged or artificial quality and ceases to be a process of human interaction. It became a game called *role-to-role communication!*

This game of role-to-role communication that is played by people who are *living* a role is not at all easy and is certainly not very rewarding. First, you must be an exceptional actor in order to play your part at all times and you must have extensive knowledge of the rules of the game. When you are living a role you must expend your energy and concentration on something you are not. Instead of concentrating on the requirements of the communication situation—sensitivity to the needs of the other person and the feedback from the other person—you must spend most of your time concentrating on your role. Are you saying the "right" things? Do you look the way you should? Are you relating to that other person's role the way you should? Are you communicating effectively? No!

If you are not careful you *become* the role you are living. The more you live a role, the more it becomes part of your existence. As a

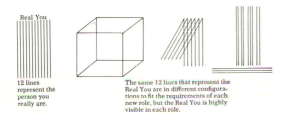

Real You

12 lines represent the person you really are.

The same 12 lines that represent the Real You are in different configurations to fit the requirements of each new role, but the Real You is highly visible in each role.

IF YOU ARE NOT CAREFUL YOU BECOME THE
ROLE YOU ARE LIVING

result, you start sending two sets of messages that might be both contradictory and confusing. One set of messages would come verbally from the role you are living and another set of messages nonverbally from the Real You. The people you are trying to communicate with don't know which set of messages to relate to and are probably beginning not to care.

Perhaps the most important barrier that you erect when you are living a role is the one that denies the communication process its most important ingredient—You. The one thing that most of us want and need for effective interpersonal communication is cooperative, open and honest sharing of each other, and when you are living a role you just can't share what ain't there!

Some Questions for Discussion:
1. How many roles can you identify that you play in a day?
2. Which is easier—to *live* a role or to *play* a role? Why?
3. Can you ever stop role-playing and just be yourself? When? With whom?
4. Can you identify people who "really play the role"?
5. Can you identify the reasons they won't let the Real Self show through?

Summary
1. Playing roles is a necessary and important part of our everyday lives—*living roles is not*. When you *live* the role you tend to communicate more and more of the role and less and less of yourself. This type of role behaviour is normally perceived as artificial or phony behaviour and tends to create a lack of trust in the communication situation.

2. When you *live* a role, you normally play the game called "role-to-role communication". In order to "play the game" you must be an exceptional actor and have extensive knowledge of the rules. Even with these "qualities" the communication situation takes on a very "staged" atmosphere and frequently leaves both participants with an empty and somewhat depressed feeling.

3. When you are *living* a role, it takes a lot of energy and concentration trying to be something that you are not. Instead of concentrating on the requirements of the communication situation—the needs of the other person and the feedback from the other person—you must spend most of your time concentrating on the role. Your communication effectiveness is severely diminished.

4. The more you *live* a role, the more it becomes a part of your existence. As a result you might be sending two sets of messages that might be contradictory—the role you are living *verbally* and the Real You *nonverbally*.

5. Most important, when you are *living* a role you are denying the communication process its most important ingredient—You! The one thing that most of us want and need for effective communication is cooperative, honest sharing of each other and *you just can't share what ain't there!*

THE MASKS WE WEAR

What is this mask we wear? Well, it's like a screen. It could be a screen of words, a screen of actions or a screen of silence. It is there to protect us from the unknown, and that *unknown* is the way people might react to the Real Self behind the mask. The advertisement on the next page illustrates visually and verbally the masks that we wear in communication.

The mask is one of the most difficult barriers to overcome in interpersonal communication and in the development and growth of

other person is, "Well, in that case, I don't trust you with my feelings either, so here, have a word with *my* mask!"

We use the mask as a protective barrier to keep people away from our Real Selves. We reason that if people don't get *too close* then we are not going to get *too hurt*. The mask seems like the simple and logical answer; yet, most of us look at the mask with ambivalence. We face a dilemma similar to the one faced by the two cold porcupines who wanted to get close enough to share each others' warmth yet not so close so as to risk being pricked by the other's quills. *They couldn't do it and neither can we!*

Some Questions for Discussion:
1. Do you agree that we wear masks?
2. Do you think we *have* to? Do you think we should?
3. Do you wear the same mask or do you change it frequently?
4. Do you attempt to hide different parts of the Real Self from different people? Why?
5. Will you ever get to the point that you will not have to wear a mask at all? If yes, then when?
6. Below is the poem "The Desiderata." Read the poem over carefully. Can you relate the recommendations in the poem to your own experience?

The Desiderata
Go placidly amid the noise and haste and remember what peace there may be in silence. As far as possible without surrender be on good terms with all persons. Speak your truth quietly and clearly; and listen to others, even the dull and ignorant; they too have their story. Avoid loud and aggressive persons, they are vexations to the spirit. If you compare yourself with others, you may become vain and bitter, for always there will be greater and lesser persons than yourself.

Enjoy your achievements as well as your plans. Keep interested in your own career, however humble; it is a real possession in the changing fortunes of time. Exercise caution in your business affairs; for the world is full of trickery. But let this not blind you to what virtue there is; many persons strive for high ideals; and

everywhere life is full of heroism. Be yourself. Especially, do not feign affection. Neither be cynical about love, for in the face of all aridity and disenchantment it is perennial as the grass. Take kindly the counsel of the years, gracefully surrendering the things of youth. Nurture strength of spirit to shield you in sudden misfortune. But do not distress yourself with imaginings. Many fears are born of fatigue and loneliness. Beyond a wholesome discipline, be gentle with yourself. You are a child of the universe, no less than the trees and the stars; you have a right to be here. And whether or not it is clear to you, no doubt the universe is unfolding as it should. Therefore be at peace with God, whatever you conceive Him to be; and whatever your labours and aspirations, in the noisy confusion of life keep peace with your soul. With all its sham, drudgery and broken dreams, it is still a beautiful world. Be careful. Strive to be happy.
MAX EHRMANN

7. Can you discuss the poem in relation to the self and the self-concept theory and the role-playing theory?
8. Do you agree with the statements expressed in the poem?
9. Are there any contradictions in the poem?
10. Do people have personality traits that make it difficult to follow the advice in the poem?

Summary
1. Communication is made up of two major components: (1) content and (2) emotion. If I deprive my communication of the emotion component, I greatly reduce my effectiveness. If I am *not prepared* to *share* myself with you will you be prepared to share yourself with me? No!

2. When I try to mask my feelings while communicating, I frequently experience a tension that affects my ability to establish a rapport with the other person. This tension is transmitted nonverbally, and ... ...ed by the other person can cause additio... riers to communication.

3. When I mask my real thoughts, opinions and feelings in order to protect my self-concept (in other words not give people a

chance to give me negative feedback), then all I am doing is contributing to the establishment of a completely inaccurate and immature self-concept.

4. When you wear the mask, you are saying to yourself and to others, "I cannot *face* what I am and what I feel". If you can't accept yourself as you are, can you accept others as they are?

5. When you wear the mask you are saying to the other person, "I do not trust you with my feelings." If you can't trust others with your feelings, should you expect others to trust you with their feelings?

MOTIVATION

Why do we do the things we do? Why do we want some things and not others? Why do we react to people and situations the way we do? Why do we communicate in one way to one person and in quite another way to another person? Part of the answer to these questions is *motivation*.

In order to understand the role motivation plays in interpersonal communication, let's first explore a brief summary of a theory of motivation outlined by Dr. Abraham Maslow in his book, *Motivation and Personality*.

1. Motivation is born of five distinct needs that are part of our nature from the moment we are born. They appear successively in the life of the individual in the following order:

a) *Physiological needs*—are concerned with the survival of the individual. They are the strongest needs. If they are not satisfied, they dominate the behaviour of the individual. These needs include food, water, rest, exercise, air and sex.

b) *Security needs*—emerge when the physiological needs have received minimal satisfaction. They refer to our desires for safety and security. These needs are disturbed by anything that is unexpected or threatening, i.e. new situations, new faces, unfamiliar environment. The security needs are concerned primarily with *psychological* safety as opposed to *physical* safety.

c) *Belongingness or love needs*—This set of needs reflects our desire to be loved for our own sake and to be able to love others. We want to be accepted, to belong, to be loved by our close friends and the groups we choose to belong to.

d) *Recognition or esteem needs*—As we become more and more a part of various groups, we become aware of the need to preserve our own identity and uniqueness. The result is a desire for recognition—attention, appreciation, status, prestige and dominance.

e) *Self-actualization or self-development needs*—the mature person. At this stage the individual has a high degree of self-acceptance and self-confidence and a very low degree of self-defensiveness. He accepts what happens easily. He is open minded, but not easily led. A person striving to satisfy this set of needs is striving to reach his full potential.

2. The first set of needs (Physiological) must be satisfied *to some degree* before the second set (Security) appears. The Security needs then have to be satisfied *to some degree* before the third set appears and so on. It is as if we were trying to reach the top of a five-step ladder.

Just as the most important step on a long journey is the first one, similarly, the most important step on the ladder is the first one (Physiological needs). The second most important step on the ladder is the second one (Security needs) and so on up the ladder. After we have adequately satisfied the physiological needs on the first step of the ladder,

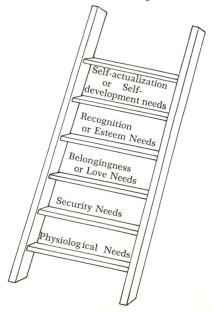

we move to the second step. Our behaviour is now motivated by a desire to satisfy our security needs and so it goes. If, at any point in time, a set of needs on a lower step of the ladder than the one we are on are threatened and require satisfaction, then we must go back down the ladder and satisfy them before we begin our climb upward again. For example, if you are working on satisfying your belongingness or love needs and suddenly your survival is threatened, then your physiological needs immediately become the primary motivating factors in your behaviour. You have to go back and re-climb that step on the ladder.

3. Most members of society have *partially* satisfied all of their basic needs. Maslow suggested in his writings that the "average" person would have satisfied his needs in something approaching the following relationship:

OUR GOAL BECOMES *MANIPULATION OF* RATHER THAN *COMMUNICATION WITH*

(1) Physiological needs   85%
(2) Safety needs   70%
(3) Belongingness or Love needs 50%
(4) Recognition or Esteem needs 40%
(5) Self-actualization or
    Self-development needs   10%

These figures are meant to indicate where the "average" person *might* be in terms of need satisfaction. They are *not* meant to indicate where you, as an average person, *should* be in terms of your need satisfaction.

4. Only unsatisfied needs act as motivators for behaviour. If you use the "average" person figures cited in the previous point as an example, you will see that the love, esteem and self-actualization needs would be stronger motivators than the physiological and safety needs that seem pretty well satisfied.

5. When our needs are *denied* satisfaction, they can cause a number of negative conditions in the individual, such as anxiety, tension, fear and resentment.

If we accept Maslow's theory of motivation then we may apply it in some interesting ways to the process of interpersonal communication. Each of us has five sets of human needs that we want to satisfy and our communication patterns are closely tied to our desires to satisfy those basic needs. The barriers to interpersonal communication develop when our desires to satisfy *our own needs* overcome our sensitivity to the needs of others. We become *manipulators* rather

than partners in a relationship and our goal becomes *manipulation of* rather than *communication with*. When this happens, we use communication in order to satisfy our own needs without regard for the need satisfaction of others.

Communication barriers develop primarily in two ways when a manipulator is involved in the relationship. First the manipulator erects barriers around himself by refusing to share himself openly and honestly in the interaction. He creates a shield around himself in order to conceal what he really thinks and feels. He communicates what people want to hear or what he thinks they want to hear in order to get positive need-satisfying feedback. Honesty, in the mind of the manipulator, is *not* the best policy!

The manipulator also creates a barrier for *open* communication by avoiding the expression of negative thoughts or feelings for fear of receiving negative feedback that would deny *him* need satisfaction. In other words, the manipulator's concern is not for the other person. He is not withholding negative thoughts or feelings because he is sensitive to the other person's needs. He just doesn't want to create a situation that might result in his receiving negative feedback, thereby denying him need satisfaction.

The second way that communication barriers develop happens when the person involved in the interaction with the manipulator perceives that he is being used. People quickly perceive the difference between open, honest, trusting, sharing communication and that which is manipulative. As soon as they recognize their communication partner as a manipulator—competing for need satisfaction—they quickly put up defensive barriers and any meaningful communication relationship is doomed. The game now is "Manipulate the manipulator!"

Some Questions for Discussion:
1. In terms of percentages, how well do you think you have satisfied each of your sets of needs?
2. Which group of needs is motivating you right now?
3. Which group of needs might predominate in a discussion with your teacher? A fellow student? A friend?
4. Could a person be working at satisfying his self-actualizing needs one minute and his physiological needs the next? Under what circumstances?
5. Do you recognize any characteristics of the manipulator in your communication behaviour? What are they? When do you notice them?
6. Have you ever been in a communication situation in which you thought you were being manipulated? How did you feel? How did you respond?

Summary
1. Our communication patterns are closely tied to our desires to satisfy our basic needs system. If we are not careful, our desire to satisfy our needs overcomes our sensitivity to the needs of others and we become *manipulators* rather than *partners* in interpersonal communication. Our goal becomes *manipulation of* rather than *communication with*.

2. When we become manipulators we tend to:
a) communicate thoughts and feelings in such a way as to get positive need-satisfying feedback even if our communication and/or the other person's feedback is dishonest.
b) avoid expressing negative thoughts and feelings for fear of receiving negative feedback that would deny us need satisfaction.

3. People quickly perceive the difference between open, honest, trusting, sharing communication and that which is manipulative. As soon as they recognize their communication partner as a manipulator—*competing with them for need satisfaction*—they quickly put up defensive barriers and any meaningful communication relationship has ceased to exist.

WORDS AND MEANINGS AND PEOPLE AND MEANINGS

"When I use a word," Humpty Dumpty said, in a rather scornful tone, "it means just what I choose it to mean, neither more nor less."

"The question is," said Alice, "whether you can make words mean so many different things."

"The question is," said Humpty Dumpty, "which is to be master—that's all."

Lewis Carroll,
Through the Looking Glass

If you listen to Humpty Dumpty, words *do not* have meaning. They are simply symbols devoid of any meaning, other than that which he attaches to them. This is an argument that has appeared in a number of communication and language textbooks and it goes something like this:
(1) Words do *not* contain meaning. Meaning is in people.
(2) *People, not* dictionaries, give meaning to words. Dictionaries simply *describe* word usage.
(3) We use words to *elicit* meaning in people.

(4) The meaning(s) a word might elicit in a person changes as the person's experiences change.

I am not sure what the four previous points *mean* to you, but to me they mean that old Humpty was right—that a word can mean "what I choose it to mean, neither more nor less." They mean that I can make a promise to you without crossing my fingers and have no intention of keeping that promise. They mean that I have a new defence in court when I break a law written in meaningless words. They mean that since they are only words written on a page, they have no meaning and might mean whatever I choose them to mean.

Well, we could go around and around on this one for some time. Perhaps the real problem facing us in understanding the relationship between words and meanings and people and meanings is how we define the word *meaning*.

If you choose Humpty's use of "meaning", then we define meaning as *our own experiences, nothing more and nothing less*. For our purposes, I will be a little more generous and define the meaning of a word as *the symbolizing or signifying or representing all experiences, both private and public, that could attach themselves to the word*. Now our problem is not one of a word having no meaning but rather a problem of the word having *too many meanings!*

The problem facing the communicator becomes one of choosing enough of the correct words in order to accurately present his message. This is not an easy task! It takes an uncommon understanding of the ways in which public meanings and private meanings are combined to give an accurate meaning to a particular word in a particular situation.

A word has many, many meanings. It has *public* meanings, referred to commonly as the *denotative* or *dictionary* meanings and *private* meanings of the people using the language, commonly referred to as the *connotative* meaning.

The *denotative* meanings of a word are brief, *objective* dictionary explanations of how the word is normally used in a number of situations. Synonyms and pictures are frequently used to indicate more precisely the denotative meaning.

The *connotative* meaning, on the other

Word Symbol

Denotative Meaning   **Connotative Meaning**

hand, is a much more *subjective*, much more private and personal meaning(s) for a word. It represents all of our personal thoughts, feelings and experiences about the thing, event or concept that the word refers to. Obviously, since no two people experience things in *exactly* the same way, the connotative meanings that I have for a word are going to be somewhat (and perhaps a lot) different than the connotative meanings that you have for the same word.

Let's look at an example of the difference between denotative and connotative. If you looked the word "hockey" up in the dictionary, you might find the following kind of denotative meaning—a game played on an ice surface, in which two opposing teams of skaters, using curved sticks, try to drive a rubber disk, or puck, into the opponents' goal. If you could only use the *denotative* meaning as representing your understanding of the word hockey, you might come up with the picture on page 42.

The word hockey might *mean* a lot more when you add the connotative meaning. If the person using the word hockey and the person hearing the word hockey have both had a lot of experiences with the game, then they are able to understand more of the meaning of the word. The combination of the denotative meaning and the connotative meaning allows the two participants, in this case, to share *more of the meaning* of the word. If, on the other hand, one of the two participants in this discussion did not have any experiences with the game, either as a spectator or as a participant, then that person would not be able to add connotative meaning to the denotative meaning, and would therefore understand much less of the *meaning* of the word hockey.

When we find ourselves in a situation in which we do not know either the denotative meaning or the connotative meaning of a word then it is going to be very difficult for us to understand the intended meaning of the message. It has been estimated that no one person knows more than one hundred

HOCKEY: A GAME PLAYED ON AN ICE SURFACE IN WHICH TWO OPPOSING TEAMS OF SKATERS, USING CURVED STICKS, TRY TO DRIVE A RUBBER DISK OR PUCK INTO THE OPPONENT'S GOAL

thousand of the one million or so words in the English language. If that is the case, then we will run into words that we don't "know" quite frequently. When we find ourselves in that situation, we can do one of two things: (1) ask what the word means (2) don't ask what the word means for fear of appearing "stupid." B.C. gives us a few examples of what happens if you choose the latter. (See page 43.)

I have suggested in this section that:

1. Words do have meaning, in fact, many, many meanings.
2. Word meaning should be defined as *symbolizing or signifying or representing all experiences, both public (denotative) and private (connotative) that could attach themselves to a word.*
3. The degree to which we understand the meaning of a word, depends on our knowledge of the word's denotative and connotative meanings in a given situation.

Some Questions for Discussion:

1. Do you see what I *mean*? (Sorry about that.)
2. Do you agree that words *do* have meaning or do you believe that meaning is *only* in people?
3. Can you think of any words whose denota-

tive and connotative meanings are quite different?

4. What does the word context mean? How does context affect the meaning of a word?
5. How might word meaning affect communication?
6. Do you think each of us should be held responsible for knowing the meaning (according to the definition above) of the words we use? Is this possible? Is it probable?
7. The Roman rhetorician Quintillian set a standard for the clarity of language when he said: "One should not aim at being possible to understand, but at being impossible to misunderstand." Can we ever meet that standard if words do not have meaning? Can we ever meet that standard if words do have meaning?

Summary

1. It has been estimated that there are more than one million words in the English language and that no person knows more than one hundred thousand. We know less than one out of ten words in our own language. When we hear one of those other nine hundred thousand words that we don't know used in conversation, we frequently fail to

ask the meaning of it for fear we will appear "stupid." Communication begins to break down.

2. The problem is *not* that words do not have meaning but rather that they have so many meanings, that the receiver of the message frequently chooses a different set of meanings (denotative and connotative) than the sender intended.

3. Language is a tool of communication but it is not and cannot be an absolutely precise tool. The precision with which you and I use words to communicate depends on: (1) the closeness of our vocabulary levels (2) the closeness of our understanding of the denotative and connotative meanings of a word when used in a particular context. We run into communication barriers when we assume that the other person understands *exactly* what we mean when we use the English language to communicate. It never happens!

ARE YOU LISTENING OR ARE YOU HEARING?

The difference between listening and hearing is an important one and a factor that we should constantly be aware of in interpersonal communication. In order to explore the difference between the two terms, let's go back to our perception diagram of the WIGO, WIS and WIMTU and talk about information received through the auditory sense.

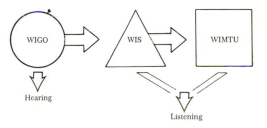

Let's suppose that you are sitting in a cafeteria and someone is talking to you from across the table. There are people sitting all around the cafeteria talking in large and small groups. There are all sorts of sounds around you—tables being cleaned, dishes dropping, the crunch of an apple being consumed nearby. All of these sounds are part of the WIGO. If they are loud enough for you to hear, then you will *hear* them and the auditory sense will send the information to your brain. It is *at this point* that the process of hearing continues or the process of listening begins. If our attention is drawn to one of the sounds in the WIGO (i.e. the person talking to us from across the table) and we begin to *select* that sound over the others and proceed to *organize* and *interpret* the meaning of that sound, then we are listening. If our attention is *not* selective, and therefore we do *not* try to organize and interpret the meaning of one or a group of sounds in the WIGO, then we are only *hearing*.

The main purpose of listening is to *understand* what the *speaker means* by what he is saying. Therefore, the most important part of the listening process becomes *interpretation*. It takes a conscious effort on the part of the listener to try to interpret what he hears in terms of the *speaker's experience* rather than in terms of his own. In other words, when we are listening we must make a *conscious effort* to get inside the speaker's world and try to see things the way he does. Most of us find this to be a very difficult task. Frequently we *think* we are listening but in fact we are only *hearing*. For example, when we listen only to be better able to refute or contradict what the speaker is saying; when we try to interpret information received from the speaker *only* in terms of our own experience; when we are busy preparing our reply when the speaker is still talking; when we become impatient because the speaker does not seem to be speaking as fast as we are thinking—all are examples of hearing. They leave us little hope of understanding the speaker's message and add greatly to the probability of communication breakdown.

What do *you* do? The person who is talking to you is probably speaking at between 125 and 175 words per minute. Yet you are capable of hearing and interpreting 300 to 400 words per minute, perhaps more! What do you do with all that spare time? Do you concentrate on *listening*—trying to understand the content and emotion components of the speaker's message in terms of his experience? Or are you evaluating, relating to your own experience, preparing a reply, or just off on a little side trip back to a pleasurable experience that happened last week? If you are doing the latter then you are erecting barriers to communication.

Firstly, you will not be "interpreting" the complete message and as a result, will have an incomplete understanding of the intended meaning. Secondly, if you are not *concentrating* on listening, you will probably fail to interpret the emotion component in the message, i.e. the feelings the other person is transmitting or, perhaps more important, not transmitting. Thirdly, even though we try to give the impression we are listening when we are not, the message that we are *not* listening and therefore not interested, is usually transmitted to the other person nonverbally. This nonverbal message is picked up consciously or unconsciously and the resulting tension that develops in the person who feels "not important enough to be listened to" creates a barrier to further communication that is going to be very difficult to remove.

The real barrier for most of us is the fact that we don't know how to listen or we are just not willing to commit the necessary time, energy and concentration. As a result, we just don't know *how much* we are missing. Let me give you a visual example.

If you look at the picture on page 45 quickly, without paying much attention (the way we *hear*), you will get a general picture of *what is going on*. If you look at the picture carefully, selecting, organizing and interpreting its various parts (as you would when actively listening) you will find a number of hidden messages.

Some Questions for Discussion:
1. Why do we find it difficult to listen actively and objectively?
2. Why do we find it difficult to suspend judgment when listening?
3. Have you ever been interrupted in midsentence? How did you feel? What was the person who interrupted you saying to you in addition to his verbal message? What did the interruption do to your desire to continue the dialogue?

Summary
1. The first problem with listening is that it is just plain hard work. It takes a constant effort on our part to concentrate on the tasks of listening. It is much easier for us to spend much of our time *hearing* and only a small portion actively *listening*. As a result, our chances of interpreting the sender's message

with any degree of accuracy are greatly de-creased.

2. Most of us have *not* been trained to be effective listeners. Consequently, we spend much of the time that we should be actively listening in preparing what we are going to say next. We try to *evaluate* what is being said and prepare counter arguments rather than trying to understand what the message means to the sender. Listening is 50 per cent of the interpersonal communication process.

If you miss that much, can you expect to be an effective communicator?

3. Communication has two components that we must be prepared to listen for: (1) the information component and (2) the feel-ings component. Frequently we listen to the words but ignore the feelings or emotions that are being transmitted with them. Often the most important part of the message is exposed in the feelings that are transmitted, or *are not transmitted.*

SELECTED READINGS

Allport, F.   *Theories of Perception.* New York: John Wiley & Sons, Inc., 1955.

Bois, J. Samuel.   *Explorations in Awareness.* New York: Harper & Row, Pub-lishers, 1957.

————.   *The Art of Awareness.* Dubuque, Iowa: William C. Brown Company, Publishers, 1966.

Brown, Roger.   *Words and Things: An Introduction to Language.* New York: The Free Press, 1958.

Campbell, James R., and Hall W. Hepler, eds.   *Dimensions in Communication.* Belmont, California: Wadsworth Publishing Co. Inc., 1965.

Clark, Tony, Doug Brock and Mike Cornett.   *Is That You Out There?* Columbus, Ohio: Charles E. Merrill Books, Inc., 1973.

Giffin, Kim and Bobby R. Patton, eds.   *Basic Readings in Interpersonal Communication*. New York: Harper and Row, 1971.

Hayakawa, S. I.   *Language in Thought and Action,* 3rd ed. New York: Harcourt Brace Jovanovich Inc., 1972.

Johnson, Kenneth G.; John J. Senatore; Mark C. Liebig and Gene Minor.   *Nothing Never Happens*. Beverly Hills, California: Glencoe Press, 1974.

Johnson, W.   *People in Quandaries*. New York: Harper & Row, Publishers, 1946.

Maslow, Abraham H.   *Motivation and Personality*. New York: Harper & Row, Publishers, 1970.

Myers, Gail E. and Michele Tolela Myers.   *The Dynamics of Human Communication*. New York: McGraw-Hill Book Company, 1973.

Nichols, R. G. and L. A. Stevens.   *Are You Listening?* New York: McGraw-Hill Book Company, 1957.

Powell, John S. J.   *Why I Am Afraid To Tell You Who I Am*. Chicago: Argus Communications, 1969.

Vernon, Magdalen D.   *The Psychology of Perception*. Baltimore: Penguin Books, Inc., 1962.

4

OVERCOMING COMMUNICATION BARRIERS

Donald L. MacRae

In the last chapter, we explored seven factors that frequently have an adverse effect on our ability to communicate effectively with another person. Since these seven factors can lead to complete communication breakdown, and often do, we identified them as *barriers* to communication and studied their causes and effects in relation to the negative roles they play in the process of communication.

Our objective in this chapter will be to explore some of the ways in which we can overcome these seven barriers and in the process of overcoming them as communication *barriers*, turn them into *vehicles* for successful interpersonal communication.

OVERCOMING PERCEPTION BARRIERS

Baby, what you see isn't necessarily what you get. So, have another look!

You wouldn't have seen the "cow" so quickly this time if you hadn't had another look the last time—and another look—and another look—until you finally broke away from the narrowness of your previous experience and perceived more accurately what was in the picture. This is the first key to overcoming communication barriers caused by differences in perception—be willing to have another look before you decide What Is Going On. Try to break away from the grip of your previous experience and see the WIGO and the people around you in a different light. Then are you ready to say with certainty "My perception is completely accurate"? No, you are not, but your perception would probably be more accurate this time than the first time.

The main reason that our perception would not be "completely" accurate after revising it a number of times seems to be the way we select information. For example:

1. We select information that seems to have relevance for *our* personal goals.
2. We select information that helps us satisfy *our* basic needs.
3. We select information that reinforces *our* beliefs and expectations.
4. We select information that *we* do not expect, i.e. that which is out of the ordinary.
5. We pay attention to *our* friends and *our* things.

Everything we select as information from the world around us seems to have *some meaning* for us *already* and seems to relate closely to *our* internal frame of reference, *our* subjective world. This is perhaps the biggest hurdle in overcoming perception barriers in communication. We must learn to overcome our own narrow internal frame of reference when selecting information from the WIGO. That is easy to say but—

There seem to be two ways that we can at least begin to overcome our internal frame of reference; the first way relates to how we perceive information, things and events from the world around us and the second relates to the way we perceive people.

In the first case, when we are looking at the inanimate objects of the world, we should try to be more objective than subjective in our perceptions. We should not be satisfied to look at things from only one perspective. We should look for things that might normally escape us, for detail that we would normally not bother with. We should be much more flexible and open in our selection of information, selecting information not only because it has relevance for our goals, or satisfies our needs or reinforces our beliefs, but because it helps us to expand our fields of experience and see things in a different light. That would be a start!

In the second case, to increase the accuracy of our perceptions of people, we must obviously try to understand the behaviour of that other person from the centre of *his* world, from *his* internal frame of reference, through *his* eyes. If I am able to understand how he sees the world around him, then I will have a much better chance of perceiving him a little more accurately as a person.

There is one other perception barrier that we must overcome in order to be effective communicators and that is our tendency to draw inferences from our perceptions—inferences that we seem to put a good deal of faith in. We seem to do this most frequently (and most incorrectly) when we are dealing with people perceptions. You have all had the experience of meeting someone for the first time and in a matter of minutes you *know* that you don't like that person. From a few spoken sentences and a few gestures we draw conclusions about the person's beliefs, attitudes, feelings—about his whole personality! We infer so much from so little and so frequently *we are wrong!* We should learn to be a little less hasty in drawing inferences about people and things based on such limited, highly selective and narrowly interpreted pieces of information. Withhold judgment and have another look!

IN A MATTER OF MINUTES, YOU KNOW THAT YOU DON'T LIKE THAT PERSON

Summary

1. We should recognize the problems associated with perception and learn not to put so much faith in the accuracy of our perceptions of the world around us. Be willing to have another look—and another—

2. We must recognize that the best vantage point for understanding What Is Going On for another person is from that other person's internal frame of reference.

3. We should recognize that the biggest problem in accurately perceiving the world around us is *our* internal frame of reference. Everything we select from the WIGO seems to have some meaning for us already and relates closely to our subjective world, our needs. We should be more open and flexible when selecting information from the world around us.

4. We should be much more careful about the inferences we make about people, things and events. Our inferences are based on limited, highly selective, subjectively interpreted bits of information and are frequently quite incorrect.

OVERCOMING SELF AND SELF-CONCEPT BARRIERS

We know that the self-concept is extremely important in shaping our communication behaviour. We know that we develop the self-concept (1) based on our observations and interpretations of our own behaviour and (2) based on our observations and interpretations of other people's behaviour towards us in a wide variety of situations and circumstances. We know that our self-concept is one of our most valuable possessions. We know that we try to protect our self-concept when communicating with others. What we frequently *don't* know is how distorted our self-concept really is!

If the self-concept is as important to the communication process and our own psychological well-being as has been suggested, then it is obvious that we must have as accurate a perception of our real selves as is possible. However, as you know, perceiving things completely objectively is very difficult and when the object of your perception is *you*, then it becomes even more difficult.

How about you? Do you think that you

WHAT WE DON'T KNOW IS HOW DISTORTED OUR SELF-CONCEPT REALLY IS

have an accurate self-concept? Give some thought to the following questions before answering:

1. Do you have a *balanced* self-concept? Do you objectively recognize the positive and negative factors of the real you?
2. On the whole, do you view your self-concept more positively than negatively?
3. Are you open to feedback from others concerning the accuracy of your self-concept?
4. Are you sensitive to the verbal and non-verbal feedback from others that relates to your self-concept?
5. Are you always prepared to accept negative feedback about your self-concept and act on it in a positive way?

If you answered *yes* to all of the above questions you have probably been giving these kinds of questions a good deal of thought for some time and are well on your way to developing an accurate self-concept. If you answered *no* to any of the questions, *welcome to the club!* It is very difficult for most of us to be as objective about the way we see ourselves and the way we think other people see us as we would have to be in order to answer yes to the questions above. However, in order to develop a more accurate self-concept, that is what we must do!

First, let's have a look at whether our communication behaviour is being shaped by a *balanced* self-concept or is being shaped primarily by the positive or negative factors we see as part of our self-image. Try making a list for yourself (you may or may not decide to discuss this list later in class). On the *positive* side list all of your accomplishments, qualities you like in yourself, positive feelings, goals that you have reached—anything that you are proud of, anything that you like about yourself. On the *negative* side list those characteristics, attitudes, shortcomings, failures—anything that you do not like about yourself or your past or present behaviour. Now ask yourself, "Which side of the list is governing my behaviour? Which side of the list predominates in my self-concept?"

Many of our self-concepts are controlled primarily by the positive side. We tend to forget the fact that we are human and subject to the same human frailties as others. We approach everything and everyone with an air of superiority. We so easily forget our own shortcomings, yet are so quick to point out the shortcomings of others.

Others of us are controlled primarily by the negative side and approach everything and everybody with a feeling of inferiority. We are frequently the ones who are so considerate of others, yet so critical of ourselves.

In order to overcome this problem of having our self-concepts controlled by our positive factors or by our negative factors, we must come to understand that our personality is not made up *primarily* of positive *or primarily* of negative factors but rather a *combination* of the two. If we look at ourselves realistically, we will normally see enough negative factors to keep our self-concepts from being *controlled* by our positive factors and enough positive factors to keep our self-concepts from being *controlled* by the negative factors.

Although our self-concepts should be shaped by a balanced, realistic, objective appraisal of who and what we really are, *on the whole* we should view ourselves with a sense of optimism. Although we all carry the burden of our human frailties, we all have the most important positive factor on our sides and that is the potential each of us has for personal growth and development. In other words we should learn to accept ourselves for *what we are* and *where we are right now* and view our potential for future growth as the most positive element of our self-concepts. We must also learn to accept other people for what they are and where they are right now and view their potential for personal growth as the most important factor in your perception of them. In short, we must be able to like and accept ourselves before we will be able to like and accept others and we will have to be able to like and accept others before they will be able to like and accept us.

Assuming that all of us will be moving optimistically towards more realistic, objective, balanced self-concepts that will allow us to be more accepting of ourselves and others, the question is how to keep it that way, while at the same time providing a climate for growth. Our biggest problem is that we try to protect the self-concept that we arrive at. We select information that agrees with and reinforces our self-concept and filter or block completely information that threatens it. We think we are "protecting" *ourselves* by protecting our self-concepts. What we are really doing is completely inhibiting our own growth and maturity. Once we begin to realize that *personal growth* rather than personal security should be the by-product of human interaction then we can begin to treat communication that relates to our self-concept quite differently. We might begin to be more open and accepting of feedback from other people concerning how *they* see us. We might become more sensitive to the way we *really* see ourselves and we might be more willing to accept negative feedback from ourselves and from others and act on that feedback in a positive way.

Summary

1. We should learn to balance our self-concepts—objectively recognizing the positive and negative factors.

2. We should learn to view our self-concepts, *on the whole*, more positively than negatively. Our potential for growth gives the positive side the advantage.

3. We should learn to accept ourselves and others for what we are and where we are in terms of personal development as of this moment.

4. We should become more open to and

sensitive to feedback from others as to the accuracy of our self-concepts.

5. We should be prepared to accept negative feedback about our self-concepts and act on that feedback in a positive way.

OVERCOMING ROLE BARRIERS

To be nobody-but-yourself in a world which is doing its best, night and day, to make you everybody else—means to fight the hardest battle which any human being can fight; and never stop fighting.

e. e. cummings

Many of us make the mistake of confusing the difference between *playing* a role and *living* a role. We fall into the trap because we become more concerned with what we *think* other people expect of us rather than what we expect of ourselves. We become more concerned with how people *think* we are performing in the role than how we *are* performing as a person. We soon become afraid to let the real person surface for fear of destroying the artificial image we have learned to project. This is *living* the role!

In order to overcome the communication problems associated with living a role, we must learn to become more effective at role-playing.

When we are playing a role, we are concerned with two components of the role— (1) the task orientation and (2) the person orientation. The *task orientation* is a rather objective set of expectations of how we should act when playing a particular role.

For example, how we should interact with our children when we are playing the role of father (or of mother), what kind of language we should use, how we would expect to be addressed and so on. We could use similar lists for the task orientation of students and teachers, or presidents of businesses. The task orientation is an indication of how society expects us to act when performing the tasks associated with the role.

The *person orientation*, on the other hand, recognizes the people needs of interpersonal communication. It recognizes that the key ingredient in any human interaction, especially communication, is a willingness to share yourself openly and honestly with that other person. The person orientation makes "the real you" a visible part of the role. It allows people to relate to *you* while you are *playing* a role rather than forcing them to engage in the game of "role to role communication".

If you are going to be an effective role player you must learn how to combine the task orientation and the person orientation in the most effective combinations for you as you play your various roles. In some cases the task orientation might have to be much more prominent and in other cases the person orientation might have to predominate but in *each* role you play both components should be *visible*.

The natural question we come to now is, "How do I make my person orientation more visible and to what extent should I be willing to share the real me with the other person?"

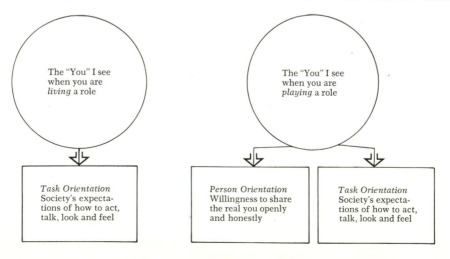

The "You" I see when you are *living* a role

Task Orientation Society's expectations of how to act, talk, look and feel

The "You" I see when you are *playing* a role

Person Orientation Willingness to share the real you openly and honestly

Task Orientation Society's expectations of how to act, talk, look and feel

PEOPLE ARE NOT USED TO ENCOUNTERING SELF-DISCLOSURE

The answer to the first part of the question is *self-disclosure* and the answer to the second part of the question depends on (1) the level of trust or the closeness of the relationship with that other person and (2) how much you want to learn about yourself and your ability to relate to other people.

Self-disclosure means to reveal information about yourself that would normally not be available to the other person through the task orientation component of the role. In other words this information would not be considered "public" information. It is the kind of information that could only come from you. Some of the kinds of things you might be willing to share with another person through self-disclosure are as follows:

> beliefs
> prejudices
> loves
> hates
> needs
> hopes
> fears
> feelings
> self-perceptions
> attitudes
> perceptions of others
> past experiences
> future expectations

As you can see from the list, this kind of information is *not easily* shared with others. In fact, you have probably thought of a number of hazards involved in self-disclosure already. The *extent* to which you reveal your real self as part of the role would of course depend on the level of trust and closeness that exists between you and the other person. With a person that you did not know well, or with someone that you have just recently met, you would make your person orientation visible in your role—that is you would show your willingness to share the real you, openly and honestly in the relationship—but the extent to which you disclosed information from your "private world" would be severely limited until mutual trust and mutual self-disclosure became a part of the interaction.

Let's look at some of the negative and some of the positive factors to be considered when deciding whether or not self-disclosure should become a part of our person orientation in role-playing.

Negative Factors

1. Tends to arouse suspicions—people are not used to hearing this sort of information.

2. Can never be sure how disclosure will be received. Other person might be offended.

3. You might learn things about yourself that will take a good deal of courage to deal with (things that you suspected but preferred to ignore or reject).

4. Self-disclosure requires intimacy, which strikes fear in the hearts of many. Some people feel very threatened if they think you are getting too close to them or they are getting too close to you.

5. Might provide information that could prove embarrassing at some future date.

6. We might lose the acceptance or respect of the other person.

7. Other person might try to use the disclosed information to manipulate us.

Positive Factors

1. You experience communicating on a person-to-person rather than on a role-to-role basis. This experience will help you share your needs, thoughts and feelings with others.

2. You experience becoming more personally involved in interpersonal communication.

3. You experience the development of a unique, open, honest, trusting relationship with another person.

4. The self knowledge you gain would not otherwise be available to you. This knowledge will help you change the real you if desirable.

5. You have taken a major step towards developing your full potential as a human being.

Well, those negative factors sure look pretty imposing, don't they! It is not easy sharing yourself openly and honestly as a visible part of the roles that you play each day and it is even more difficult to experiment with self-disclosure in order to develop a closer relationship with another person. On the other hand, the reward potential is great! The ability to relate to people on a person-to-person rather than on a role-to-role basis is certainly worth making your person orientation a visible part of the roles you play and in terms of your personal growth, the experience of developing a close, open, honest, trusting relationship with another person might well be worth the risks involved in self-disclosure.

Summary

1. We should recognize that we must all *play* many roles. It is important for us to be flexible enough to change roles quickly and easily. At the same time, we should be careful that our communication behaviour does not become a slave to the role expectations. The *person orientation* should always be *visible* if we are to *play* roles rather than *live* them.

2. Although the "real" you (person orientation) should be visible in each of your roles, the degrees of visibility will depend on the situation. Some situations require the task orientation to predominate, others require more visibility on the part of the person orientation.

3. Self-disclosure is an important method of developing a closer relationship with another person, while at the same time learning more about your own ability to relate to other people. Self-disclosure is not without its risks; however, the potential rewards, in terms of personal growth, seem to make the risks worth taking.

OVERCOMING MASK BARRIERS

Most of us wear masks when we communicate! We think we *have* to in order to protect ourselves from that other person. We ask ourselves, "What would happen if I let the mask down and let that person in to see the real me through my hopes and fears and prides and prejudices and my needs and feelings and emotions?" and we answer, "He wouldn't understand me. I would feel rejected. I would lose a friend. I would be looked at with strangeness. I would feel naked and alone. I would feel terrible." With that kind of answer what would you do? Right! You would get the mask in place and keep it in place. Who needs the problems? Who needs the frustrations? Well, the answer to those questions is, "We all do if we hope to develop our full potential as human beings and as effective communicators."

In the chapter on communication barriers we discussed the two major components of communication—content and emotion. If we are to become successful communicators we must first develop a good communication climate—a sharing climate—in which we indicate to each other that we are prepared to share *both* information and open, honest feelings. When we wear our masks, we are denying the communication process the emotional component—our feelings and our needs. For some reason, we think we must isolate the emotional component, suppress it, hide it behind the mask. We must be rational and objective when communicating with another person and the only way we can do that is to keep our feelings out of sight. Right? Wrong! Our feelings, our needs, our hopes and fears are a very important part of us. They must be expressed and even when we try to mask them they still find expression in our nonverbal behaviour. I am sure you have had the experience of talking with someone who had negative feelings about you. They were trying to mask their feelings but you could tell. You could feel the tension. You could see the negative feelings in their eyes and hear it in their speech. They probably wanted to express their emotional stress verbally but they couldn't. You probably wished they had so that the causes for the negative feelings could be discussed openly and honestly.

You will find that many interpersonal conflicts and barriers to communication result from emotional stresses (negative feelings) that are hidden behind the mask and never given a chance to surface. The only way that the relationship can develop is if the emotional stresses can be replaced by emotional bonds (positive feelings) and the only way that change will come about is if both parties *express* their feelings verbally. In other words, if we can't *talk about the problem* there is not much chance of solving it.

In order to overcome the barriers that the mask represents in communication, why not try putting the emotion component back into your communication behaviour. If you are feeling up to the challenge, then let's talk about two of the ways that you can help yourself make the transition: (1) by establishing a climate of interpersonal trust and (2) by learning to be more open and honest in expressing your feelings.

The first task facing us is to reduce our own defensiveness (thickness of the mask) and the defensiveness of others by trying to establish a *climate of interpersonal trust* for each other. If we wear these masks to protect ourselves from a potential threat and if it becomes clear to us that the potential threat does not exist, then it becomes much easier for us to drop the mask and work towards developing a good communication climate. There are a number of ways for you to indicate to the other person that you do not wish

YOU MUST BE INVOLVED

to pose a threat. You might try some of the following:

1. Do not criticize unnecessarily—speak in terms that are positive in flavour rather than negative.

2. Regard the other person as an equal in the interaction. Consider yourself neither superior nor inferior. There should not be a feeling that one person is trying to manipulate or control the other.

3. Do not try to hide your motivations, or develop complex communication strategies. As much as possible, be open, honest and spontaneous.

4. Do not give the impression of neutrality or a lack of interest in the interaction. You must be *involved* and conveying a sensitivity to the feelings and needs of the other person.

5. Do not be dogmatic. If you give the impression of arrogance and mirror the "I am always right" attitude, it will be perceived as trying to exercize control. You must communicate the idea that your viewpoints are not carved in stone and that you are willing to change your ideas, attitudes and behaviour.

The second task facing us, once we have begun to develop a climate of interpersonal trust, is to learn to be more open and honest in expressing our feelings. We must learn how to verbalize our feelings instead of masking them. If we can learn to do this we will benefit greatly, both in terms of personal growth and in terms of communication effectiveness. I would like to use the Johari Window, more properly referred to as the Johari Awareness Model, which was developed by Joseph Luft and Harry Ingham (*Group Processes: An Introduction to Group Dynamics*, National Press) to help visualize the benefits that can be derived from a more open, honest expression of our feelings.

Quadrant 1—The Open Area—represents information, feelings, motivations and behaviour that are known to others and known to ourselves. This is the completely "public" area.

Quadrant 2—The Blind Area—represents information, feelings, motivations and behaviour that are known to other people that we are not aware of.

Quadrant 3—The Hidden Area—represents information, feelings, motivations and behaviour that we know about ourselves but do not want other people to know. This is our completely "private" area.

Quadrant 4—The Unknown Area—represents information, feelings, motivations and behaviour unknown to ourselves and unknown to others.

Let's assume for a moment that the Johari Window represents you. Let's also assume for a moment that you want to be an effective communicator. You want to develop a sharing climate for communication. How much of yourself are you willing or able to share? If we use the diagram as an illustration of *you* in a communication situation, the answer appears to be only 25 per cent. You are willing to share 25 per cent in the Open Area, unwilling to share the 25 per cent in the Hidden Area and unable to share the 50 per cent of yourself in the Blind and Unknown Areas because they represent information and feelings that you are unaware of or that are unknown to you. Well, being willing to share 25 per cent of yourself is really not going a long way towards developing a sharing climate for communication; however, under the circumstances, that is all you *can* share.

Now let's look at what would happen if you decided to be more open and honest in expressing information about yourself, your feelings, motivation and behaviour. In order to do this, you would have to drop the mask a bit and extend the Open Area into the Hidden Area through self-disclosure. You would reveal information about your "private" self from the Hidden Area—for example, your feelings.

When you increase your Open Area, into the Hidden Area, something happens to the Blind and Unknown Areas as well. When you express your previously hidden feelings

The Johari Window

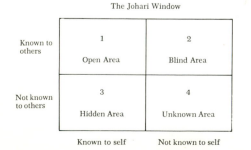

	Known to self	Not known to self
Known to others	1 Open Area	2 Blind Area
Not known to others	3 Hidden Area	4 Unknown Area

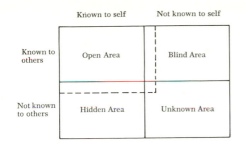

	Known to self	Not known to self
Known to others	Open Area	Blind Area
Not known to others	Hidden Area	Unknown Area

openly and honestly, this allows others to express their feelings towards you more openly and honestly. As a result, information about yourself, to which you were previously blind, becomes known to you. In a similar way, the Unknown Area decreases in size. Neither you nor others knew how you would react to the feedback you received after revealing a little more of yourself. Now you know!

As a result of being more open and honest in expressing your feelings, motivations etc., that 25 per cent of yourself that you were able to contribute to the establishment of a sharing, trusting communication climate has grown considerably and so have you.

Learning to express our feelings, learning to strip away the mask, bit by bit, learning to commit more and more of ourselves to the communication process does not happen overnight. For most of us it will take a lifetime, for others the process might never begin.

If you decide to accept the challenge, here are two exercises that you might find interesting:

1. Form into groups of three. The students in each group should not know each other. Student one takes about two to three minutes to tell the other two students as much about himself as he feels comfortable in doing. Students two and three then take four to five minutes to tell student number one what they heard him say and also what they inferred from what he said or left unsaid. This process is then followed with student two and student three.

2. Select a partner in class, preferably a person that you don't know well. Sit facing each other. Describe your perceptions of your partner and your reactions to him/her at that particular time. Be as specific as possible in identifying how you perceive your partner

DESCRIBE YOUR PERCEPTIONS OF YOUR PARTNER

and in explaining your feelings. Your partner should then repeat the exercise.

Summary

1. We should recognize that the masks we wear are barriers, not only to effective communication, but also to our growth as unique human beings.

2. In order to develop our full potential in personal growth and communication, we should learn to be more open and honest in our communication with ourselves and others.

3 We should stop suppressing our feelings! We are denying the communication process a major component. We should learn to express our feelings verbally while at the same time recognizing the sensitivities of others—their needs, feelings and human frailties.

4. We should become less defensive about the fact that we sometimes experience negative feelings and emotional stresses in interpersonal communication. If the relationship is to develop, the negative feelings or emotional stresses must be recognized and dealt with by both parties before they can be replaced with positive feelings and emotional bonds.

5. We should try to reduce the defensive-

ness of others by trying to establish a climate of interpersonal trust.

OVERCOMING MOTIVATIONAL BARRIERS

Are you a Manipulator or an Actualizor? What's the difference? Well, a manipulator is a person who tries to satisfy his basic needs by manipulating people. He doesn't care about the needs of others. He doesn't care about the relationship between himself and others. He lacks sensitivity. All he cares about is satisfying his own needs. He is constantly competing with others for need satisfaction. The term actualizor is derived from what Abraham Maslow called the "self-actualizing person"—a person who has reached a high degree of self-fulfillment. Actualizors operate from a position of self worth rather than deficiency. They appreciate their own uniqueness and the uniqueness of others. They understand and respect their own desires for need satisfaction and personal growth while at the same time recognizing the need satisfaction and personal

growth need of others. Actualizors do not compete with others for need satisfaction; instead, they try to establish a relationship with others within which mutual need satisfaction is possible.

Everett Shostrom, in his book *Man, the Manipulator* (Abingdon Press) listed what he saw as the fundamental characteristics of manipulators and actualizors in order to show the contrast between the two. As you read the characteristics of each, ask yourself this question, "Which is of primary importance to manipulators and actualizors—need satisfaction or the establishment of a sharing relationship?"

You will probably come to the conclusion that manipulators are concerned with need satisfaction and the actualizors are concerned primarily with the establishment of a sharing relationship and it would seem that you are right. What most of us quickly forget when we begin to adopt some of the characteristics of the manipulator is the importance of the *relationship* for need satisfaction. Most of our needs, with the exception of some of

---

FUNDAMENTAL CHARACTERISTICS OF MANIPULATORS AND ACTUALIZORS CONTRASTED

Manipulators

1. Deception (phoniness, knavery)
The manipulator uses tricks, techniques and maneuvers. He put on an act, plays roles to create an impression. His expressed feelings are deliberately chosen to fit the occasion.

2. Unawareness (deadness, boredom)
The manipulator is unaware of the really important concerns of living. He has "tunnel vision." He sees only what he wishes to see and hears only what he wishes to hear.

3. Control (closed, deliberate)
The manipulator plays life like a game of chess. He appears relaxed, yet is very controlled and controlling, concealing his motives from his "opponent."

4. Cynicism (distrust)
The manipulator is basically distrusting of himself and others. Down deep he doesn't trust human nature. He sees relationships with humans as having two alternatives: to control or to be controlled.

Actualizors

1. Honesty (transparency, genuineness, authenticity)
The actualizor is able honestly to be his feelings, whatever they may be. He is characterized by candidness, expression, and genuinely being himself.

2. Awareness (responsiveness, aliveness, interest)
The actualizor fully looks and listens to himself and others. He is fully aware of nature, art, music, and the other real dimensions of living.

3. Freedom (spontaneity, openness)
The actualizor is spontaneous. He has the freedom to be and express his potentials. He is master of his life, a subject and not a puppet or object.

4. Trust (faith, belief)
The actualizor has a deep trust in himself and others to relate to and cope with life in the here and now.

BOTH THE MANIPULATOR AND THE ACTUALIZOR ARE EASY TO DETECT

our physiological needs, cannot be satisfied alone. We need other people. The relationship must be developed first! Needs are satisfied through a sharing relationship. The manipulators think that they can speed the need satisfaction process up by trying to develop a quick artificial relationship. Lie! Tell them what you think they want to hear! Pretend you like them! Pretend you are sensitive to their needs! Anything! Just get the kind of feedback you need to satisfy your needs. Manipulate!

Fortunately for us, and perhaps unfortunately for the manipulator, he is fairly easy to detect through both his verbal and his nonverbal behaviour. When we recognize a manipulator we usually feel somewhat tense and threatened by the artificiality of the situation. We want to protect ourselves from being manipulated. Communication barriers go up very quickly and as a result, there is now no chance of developing the kind of relationship that would allow mutual need satisfaction. The manipulator might *think* that he is satisfying his needs but that is because he has not wanted to or not been able to develop the kind of relationship with another person that would allow that other person to be open

and honest enough to give him evidence to the contrary.

The actualizor is also easy to detect. He recognizes the importance of establishing a sharing relationship. He is not in competition with us. We feel comfortable with him. We do not feel we are being used or manipulated. He is concerned about us and expects us to be concerned about him. It is easy to communicate with him and to feel that we are sharing a relationship. There seems to be a climate for mutual need satisfaction. Why do we feel this way? Why do we feel so positive towards the actualizor? The first reason is that we are not threatened. We see that the actualizor puts us and our relationship ahead of his own need satisfaction. Secondly, he knows how to develop a relationship that will help us move towards mutual growth and need satisfaction. Jack R. Gibb, in an article entitled "Is Help Helpful?" (*Forum* Magazine, February 1964) listed the following orientations that would lead to the development of a helping relationship. The helping orientations seem to characterize the actualizor and the hindering orientations seem characteristic of the manipulator.

Orientations that Help	*Orientations that Hinder*
1. Reciprocal trust (confidence, warmth, acceptance)	1. Distrust (fear, punitiveness, defensiveness)
2. Cooperative learning (inquiry, exploration, quest)	2. Teaching (training, advice giving, indoctrinating)
3. Mutual growth (becoming, actualizing, fulfilling)	3. Evaluating (fixing, correcting, providing a remedy)
4. Reciprocal openness (spontaneity, candour, honesty)	4. Strategy (planning for, maneuvering, gamesmanship)
5. Shared problem solving (defining, producing alternatives, testing)	5. Modeling (demonstrating, information giving, guiding)
6. Autonomy (freedom, interdependence, equality)	6. Coaching (molding, steering, controlling)
7. Experimentation (play, innovation, provisional try)	7. Patterning (standard, static, fixed)

If we are to become effective communicators, if we hope to overcome the communication barriers caused by our desires for need satisfaction, then *we must learn to become actualizors!*

Summary
1. First, we should have a look at how we try to satisfy our basic needs through interpersonal communication. Are we manipulators or actualizors?

2. Most of us will find that we have some of the characteristics of the manipulator in our communication behaviour. We should then recognize the effect that competitive, manipulative need satisfaction has on interpersonal communication. This kind of behaviour is normally perceived as threatening, and the result is a quick deterioration of the communication relationship.

3. We should try to adopt more and more of the characteristics of the actualizor in our communication with others—honesty, awareness, freedom and trust.

4. We should work towards building helping relationships that allow mutual growth and need satisfaction rather than competitive, manipulative relationships that allow for the satisfaction of one person's needs only at the expense of the needs of the other.

OVERCOMING WORD MEANING BARRIERS

One should not aim at being possible to understand, but at being impossible to misunderstand.

　　　　Quintillian (Roman rhetorician)

We have often heard the saying, "A picture is worth a thousand words" used to indicate the tremendous number of words that would be necessary to describe accurately the visual impression one receives when looking at a picture. Now that we understand how many meanings (denotative and connotative) that a single word may have, it is probably accurate to say that, "A word is worth a thousand pictures." If we are to overcome effectively the communication barriers caused by word meanings, then we must help each other choose the one picture in a thousand that accurately reflects the meaning we intend in any particular communication situation. In other words, one of our primary goals in communication must be to strive for an independence of word meaning—to remove any doubt as to the intended meaning of the words we are using in our message. In order to meet that goal we should discuss the following suggestions:

1. Understand the barriers that different word meanings can create in communication and constantly be on guard against the development of those barriers.
2. Accept the responsibility for clarifying the intended meaning of the words we use.
3. Improve our ability to interpret more accurately the denotative and connotative meanings of words.

By now, we all realize that it is impossible to be *absolutely precise* when using the English language to communicate a message. I can never communicate *exactly* what I have on my mind because you and I have *somewhat* different understandings of the denotative meanings of the words being used and, quite likely, *very* different understandings of the connotative meanings of the words being used. However, although we can never be *absolutely* precise, our purpose in using language to communicate must be to strive for the highest level of precision that we are capable of attaining. Once we are aware of the many barriers that can develop when people associate incorrect meanings with the words being used in a message, we can constantly be on guard against the development of those barriers by compensating for the potential problems while we are communicating.

One of the ways to do this is to accept the responsibility for *clarifying the intended meaning* of the words we are using in situations where we think there might be room for doubt or misunderstanding. We might clarify the intended meaning of a word by explaining the denotative and connotative meaning in terms that the listener would understand or we might want to narrow the intended meaning of a word by qualifying its meaning—explaining the limitations you are placing on the meaning in a particular context.

Although the primary responsibility for clarifying the intended meaning of a message rests with the sender, the receiver is not without responsibility. If the sender expresses an idea that you do not understand or uses language that you do not understand and fails to clarify the meaning for you, it is your responsibility to ask for clarification. We might say, "What do you mean by . . .?" or "What do you mean when you say . . .?" or "How are you using the word . . .?" or "I don't understand the meaning of the word . . . could you give me some examples?" If both the sender and the receiver accept responsibility for the clarity and level of understanding of the message then we will be moving closer to the level of precision we are capable of attaining in communication.

There is one other way to help ourselves overcome word meaning barriers to communication and that is by improving our ability to interpret more accurately the denotative meanings of words. Since the various denotative meanings of words are found in the dictionary, we should become better acquainted with our dictionaries and use them frequently. We must also develop our vocabu-

AT TIMES LIKE THIS, IT IS A BIT AWKWARD FLIPPING THROUGH THE PAGES OF A DICTIONARY TRYING TO FIND THE RIGHT WORD

laries in order to be more effective in getting our message across and in understanding the messages of others. It is a bit awkward flipping through pages of a dictionary trying to find the right word when we are in the middle of a conversation with someone. We have to depend on the words we have in our vocabulary at that moment. The more words we have at our disposal, the better will be our chances for constructing a clear message. Here are a few suggestions for vocabulary improvement:

1. Purchase a vocabulary improvement book and read it at your leisure.
2. When you hear or see a word that you do not understand, look it up in a dictionary at your earliest convenience.
3. Keep a list of new words you have learned and refer to it frequently.
4. Practice using new words in your vocabulary in conversation.

Improving our ability to interpret more accurately the connotative meaning of words is not quite so straightforward. We recognize that connotative meanings are based on our *personal* experiences with whatever is signified, symbolized or represented by the word. It is important for us as listeners, if we are to understand the *intended* meaning of a word, to try to interpret the connotative meaning in terms of the speaker's experience as well as our own. Since the speaker doesn't have time to stop and explain the connotative meaning he is intending, he normally tries to indicate this meaning through metacommunication (i.e. vocal inflection, loudness, pitch, rate and nonverbal indicators such as facial expressions and gestures). Metacommunication messages send instructions to the receiver indicating how the receiver is to interpret the verbal symbols with the emphasis on connotative meaning. If we are to improve our ability to interpret more accurately the connotative meaning that is *intended* by the sender we must be acutely aware of metacommunication messages and accept them as an integral part of the verbal message.

Summary

1. We should constantly be aware of how easy it is for a person to misunderstand the intended meaning of a word.

2. We should strive to attain the highest level of precision that we are capable of when using language as a tool of communication.

3. The communicator (sender) should be responsible for clarifying the intended meaning of the words he is using if there is any room for doubt or misunderstanding. If he does not receive feedback from the listener that would indicate understanding, then he should ask for it.

4. The listener is not without responsibility for clarifying meaning. If the sender does not clarify his intended meaning to the listener's satisfaction, then the listener should seek clarification.

5. The receiver should be acutely aware of the metacommunication messages that indicate how a message should be interpreted.

OVERCOMING LISTENING BARRIERS

Communication is a process of close co-operation, of sharing information and feelings with another person. The sender tries to construct a message that will relate to the experience of the listener, that can be understood by the listener, that is clear, that is sensitive to the needs of the listener, that is not manipulative and that is sent openly and honestly. The listener actively participates in the communication process by giving his undivided attention to the task of *understanding the intended message* of the sender. Well,

that is the way it is supposed to be! We have spent a good deal of this chapter discussing how to become more effective message originators, so now let's look at how to become more effective listeners.

When most of us *think* we are listening we are really only partially listening for the intended meaning while the other part of our concentration is engaged in a seemingly natural tendency to evaluate and judge or to approve or disapprove of the information and feelings that are being transmitted. Perhaps just as important is the fact that we evaluate and judge what is being communicated in terms of our own experience, our own point of view rather than the speaker's. In effect, we are partially listening to the speaker and partially listening to ourselves. Our primary goal when listening seems to be evaluation rather than understanding.

If we are to become effective listeners, then we must make the goal of listening—*understanding*. If we are to reach this goal we must concentrate on what the speaker is saying and *what it means to him*. We must get inside the speaker's mind, his feelings, beliefs, experience and needs and try to understand his frame of reference, his view of the world *as if it were our own*. We must listen *empathically!*

Empathic listening involves listening *with* another person not listening *to*; seeing the other person *not* as *you* see him but as he sees himself; moving away from the centre of your world and experiencing the centre of the other person's world. Empathic listening involves listening in order to understand rather than to evaluate, for it is only when we understand what the message means to the speaker that we will be able to judge with any accuracy what the message means to us.

Here is an exercise that you may want to try that will help you understand more fully the meaning of empathic listening. The purpose of the exercise is to get you to understand the meaning of the message from the sender's point of view.

Two students who firmly believe in opposite sides of a controversial issue are to discuss their views in front of the class. After the first person has given his side of the issue the second person must restate the ideas and especially the feelings of the first person

WE MUST GET INSIDE THE SPEAKER'S MIND, HIS FEELINGS, BELIEFS, EXPERIENCE AND NEEDS

to his satisfaction. When the second person has done that, he may present his side of the issue. Before the first person speaks again, he must restate the ideas and feelings expressed by the second person to that person's satisfaction before he continues explaining his side of the issue—and so it continues.

Listening is just plain hard work and it requires a deliberate effort if it is to be successful. It is an investment in both the communicative process and the development of a closer human relationship. The reward will depend on the size and quality of the investment.

Summary
1. We should recognize that the communication process is cooperative—a sharing experience. Part of the necessary cooperation is being prepared to commit the necessary energy and concentration that listening requires.

2. We should recognize that the goal of listening is *understanding* and *not* evaluation. We should learn to reserve judgment when listening.

3. We should listen EMPATHICALLY—listening *with* another person not *to* another person. Our energy and concentration should be aimed at understanding *what the message means to the speaker.*

4. We should constantly try to improve our ability to listen empathically when we find ourselves interrupting the speaker, or evaluating what he is saying in terms of our own experience; then we should remind ourselves that we are not listening—we are only hearing.

5. We should recognize that listening is an important investment in the communicative process and in the development of a closer human relationship. The reward will depend on the size and quality of the investment.

SELECTED READINGS

Culbert, Samuel A.   *The Interpersonal Process of Self-Disclosure: It Takes Two to See One*. New York: Renaissance Editions, Inc., 1967.
Goffman, E.   *The Presentation of Self in Everyday Life*. New York: Doubleday-Anchor, 1959.

Keltner, John W.   *Interpersonal Speech-Communication*. Belmont, California: Wadsworth Publishing Company, Inc., 1970.

Jouard, Sidney M.   *Disclosing Man to Himself*. New York: Van Nostrand Rinehold, 1968.

————.   *The Transparent Self*. New York: Van Nostrand Rinehold, 1964.

Lee, I. and Lee, L. L.   *Handling Barriers in Communication*. New York: Harper & Brothers, 1956.

Rogers, Carl R.   *On Becoming A Person*. Boston: Houghton Mifflin Co., 1970.

Smith, Henry Clay.   *Sensitivity To People*. New York: McGraw-Hill Book Company, 1966.

Stewart, John, ed.   *Bridges Not Walls*. Reading, Mass.: Addison-Wesley Publishing Co., 1973.

Strauss, Anselm.   *Mirrors and Masks: The Search for Identity*. Glencoe: Free Press, 1959.

5

NONVERBAL COMMUNICATION
An Introduction

Robert M. Soucie

Consciously and unconsciously, we send and receive many thousands of messages every day; occasionally these messages involve words.

INTRODUCTION: GETTING THE FEEL OF IT

In a small town in southern Italy, every bus on the line has a sign that reads: "Please don't talk to the driver; he must keep his hands on the steering wheel."

You were probably talking about nonverbal communication the last time you said:
   "There was just something about her that . . . ."
   "It wasn't anything he said."
   "Somehow I sensed that he . . . ."

Attention, Marshall McLuhan
   The sender is the receiver is the medium is the message is you. In face-to-face interaction, you send and receive messages simultaneously (the sender is the receiver). Your body is the medium—face, eyes, trunk, limbs, skin and the second skin—clothes (the sender is the receiver is the medium). Of all the messages generated by the body medium, the most numerous and crucial are messages about *you*—your personality, attitudes, temperament, mood, status, role, sex, and so on (the sender is the receiver is the medium is the message is you). One of the prime functions of nonverbal behaviour is therefore to reveal

YOU

continuously, efficiently, and in depth. In nonverbal communication, you are the message, you are the content of your body medium. Once you get a feel for this concept, you will be getting a feel for this entire chapter.

For Openers: Clichés
   A good way to get the feel of nonverbal communication is to start with some of our nonverbal clichés—our old nonverbal chestnuts, as it were. Crack a cliché today! Open one up! You'll find that, like nuts, clams and politicians (and quite unlike streakers), they conceal more than they reveal. Inside many of them are stored generations of fascinating collective insight into face, body, and other nonverbal communication forms. Take, for example, some of the things we've all been

saying for years about the face and the role it plays in human interaction:

Fill in the blanks with clichés from the list below.

   Sometimes, you can read people ___1___ _____ because it is ___2___ _____. But at other times (___3___ _____), they may ___4___ _____, and with a ___5___ _____, tell you a bunch of ___6___. ___7___ _____ persons, however, aren't the only ones you can't always take ___8___. In everyday, ordinary ___9___ interaction, even people you are ___10___ with will often control and manipulate their faces to avoid ___11___, or to ___12___ —either yours or theirs. ___13___ then, there's sometimes ___14___ _____.

ONE OF THE PRIME FUNCTIONS OF NONVERBAL BEHAVIOUR IS TO REVEAL YOU

   11 *seeing eye to eye*
   7 *two-faced*
   8 *at face value*
   2 *written all over their face*
   3 *let's face it*
   6 *bare-faced lies*

9 face-to-face
12 save face
1 like an open book
11 losing face
5 straight face
4 look you right in the eye
14 more than meets the eye
18 on the face of it

The face is certainly a marvellous communication medium. It's fast, highly complex, and very visible, and so we all pay a great deal of attention to it, as both senders and receivers.* So much attention, in fact, that we know we can use it effectively to play all kinds of subtle games with people when we meet them face-to-face. Erving Goffman called these games "facework," which is something like "fancy footwork." The net result is that you can't always believe what you see on others' faces, and they can't always believe what they see on yours. It's a good thing there is more to nonverbal communication than the face—a lot more.

Another consequence of the fact that the

face has great communication potential is that we tend, both as senders and receivers, to neglect body communication. In this chapter we will have to pay close attention to body communication.

First we will frame a definition of nonverbal communication, then examine the range of behaviours that play a part in this process. We will seek to discover why they are important ingredients in face-to-face interaction, and how they function with language when *you* and *others* get together.

In the second nonverbal chapter, "Improving Nonverbal Communication Skills," you will learn about some of the most common difficulties people experience in communicating nonverbally (perhaps even without knowing they are experiencing them!). You will receive some practical advice on how to improve both your knowledge and your skills in nonverbal communication.

Now that you have some sort of feel for what nonverbal communication is all about, let's go on and try to define the process as sharply as possible.

SECTION ONE: DEFINING NONVERBAL COMMUNICATION

Non = "non"
Verbal = "word"
Nonverbal = "nonword"

Communication
one
uni-
union
communion
communicate
The essential idea is "one."

You are walking slowly through a vast golden blanket of rolling prairie wheat. The sky is bright and large and incredibly blue, and a sweet wave of pleasure spreads through your body. You feel one *with nature. You are communicating with nature.* One.

What is communication? Well, let's start with the wheat field example. You are *one* with nature. You and nature have formed a

union. You are in *communion* with nature. You are *communicating* with nature. ONEness. That's the essential element of communication. Two or more things becoming *one*. Sounds great, doesn't it? The only problem is that it never happens, except metaphorically, because it's impossible.

When we say people communicate, we are really using the word loosely. We label as "communication" *any movement towards unity.* The closer this ideal is reached, the better is the communication. But we simply cannot get there—ever.

*Man's reach should exceed his grasp/Or what's communication for?***

What counts then, as communication? What constitutes a movement in the direction of unity? The processing of information about someone or something is the minimum requirement for communication. Communication is information processing.

*See Paul Ekman's writings in the Selected Readings section of this chapter.

**Apologies to the poet Robert Browning, who wrote: "Man's reach should exceed his grasp,/ Or what's a heaven for?"

Why? Because the processing of information about someone or something puts you into a relationship with that thing or person. This relationship ties you together, binds you, links you, however temporarily and however superficially. When you process information, you enter into a relationship with what is perceived. This is called an information relationship, or a communication relationship, or simply communication.

Communication is the process of establishing an information relationship.

Can you see that it's impossible *not* to become related to what you perceive? Again, it is not a matter of how deep or lasting the relationship is. You don't have to, and in fact *can't* have an *actual* union with what you perceive; as soon as you perceive someone or something, you have communication because you have established an information relationship: an approach to a union. When you perceive, you communicate.

Can you think of other kinds of relationships? Ones that don't involve information processing? How about the relationship between the items on your desk, or in your room? The relationships of night to day, summer to winter, cold to hot?

Here are some examples of communication situations. Note that some of the relationships are deeper, stronger and more lasting than others, but that they all involve information processing. Note also that communication does not have to be a mutual or two-way affair; one-way communication is still communication.

1. Encounters on the street, in elevators or in restaurants.
2. Reading a book.
3. Watching a film; watching television.
4. Having a long "heart-to-heart" with your friend, spouse, parent or boss.
5. Feeling a lush piece of velvet.
6. Thinking.
7. Smelling and eating food.
8. Engaging in small talk with casual acquaintances.

Look up the meanings of the following terms in the Appendix at the back of this book: sender, receiver, channel, medium, message, information.

Now discuss each of the communication situations above in terms of each of these items. For example, in reading a book, who is the sender? Who is the receiver? What are the channel and medium?

As you can see, communication is hardly restricted to the processing of verbal, or "word" information. Also, you will notice examples above where messages are not deliberately or consciously sent or received; but communication still takes place. Finally, note that communication may involve different senses, or channels, and that the media may range from human voice mechanisms to television, to the body itself.

WHAT IS NONVERBAL COMMUNICATION?

Now that you have some understanding of what communication in general is, let's go on and define *nonverbal* communication as precisely as we can.

Nonverbal communication is the process of establishing relationships based on information mediated by body and body-related variables, and by paralinguistic and extralinguistic variables.

A variable is some factor that takes on different values in different circumstances. Thus, the nonverbal variables mentioned here are factors which mediate information by changing their values. They are sources of information, in short, because they vary.

This definition seems formidable, but actually it's a rather simple statement. What it says is that nonverbal communication involves information processing, and thus the establishment of relationships. That you already know. It also says that this information is mediated by the body, and body-related variables, and by paralinguistic and extralinguistic variables. You need to know what these variables are to understand the definition, so here they are:

1. *Body appearance and behaviour.* Body size and shape, body colour, body hair, etc. Facial expressions, eye behaviour, body motions, limb behaviour, etc.

2. *Body-related natural and artificial objects.* Flowers, food, clothes, chairs, cigar-

BODY APPEARANCE...

PARALANGUAGE & EXTRALANGUAGE

BODY-RELATED NATURAL AND ARTIFICIAL OBJECTS

BODY-RELATED SPATIAL BEHAVIOURS

...AND BEHAVIOUR

VARIABLES

ettes, and anything that one touches or manipulates during interaction.

3. *Body-related spatial behaviours.* Conversational distance (how close we stand when conversing); personal space (the space around our bodies, the penetration of which is treated as a penetration of our skins); and territory (some area we claim as our private preserve).

4. *Paralanguage and extralanguage.* Such variables as tone, pitch, rhythm, volume, etc. are paralanguage variables. Extralanguage variables include gasps, snores, whistling, laughing, etc.

> "*I understand a fury in your words,
> But not the words.*"
> Shakespeare's Othello

A good example of paralanguage in operation. You don't have to understand a language to decipher the fury behind it.

Nonverbal communication, as you can see, encompasses an extraordinarily wide range of variables. Here are a few more, all of which fit into one of the four categories listed above, but which have not been mentioned yet:

Make-up
Facial configuration

Body smell
Distinguishing marks
Eye sparkle
Pupil dilation and contraction
Posture
Gait
Body lean (forward, backward,
   left or right)
Body twisting
Tension in face and body
Head movements

You will learn a great deal about these and other variables from the books listed in the Suggested Readings section of this chapter. You are encouraged to take a close look at as many of them as you can.

So far, we have examined the definition of communication and nonverbal communication. But definitions are poor things. To *understand* nonverbal communication, you have to know something of its importance, and the roles it plays in face-to-face interaction. You also have to appreciate the similarities and differences between nonverbal and verbal communication, and the ways in which these two systems operate together. These are issues that will be discussed in the second, third and fourth sections of this chapter.

SECTION TWO: THE IMPORTANCE OF NONVERBAL COMMUNICATION

Think how poor our lives would be if we stopped relating to each other every time we stopped talking.

One of the things that separates us from the rest of the animal kingdom is our greater ability to manipulate and control the external world by using symbols which "stand for" objects, events and characteristics of that world. While animals certainly have communication abilities—very sophisticated ones in many cases—they seem to lack the kind of symbol we call language. Without it, they will remain bound by their own situations, unable to communicate, except crudely, about the past, about the present (unless they are directly involved in it), and about the future. Without the distancing from the environment that language provides through its complex symbol system, they are more like prisoners of their world than masters of it. Language delivers us from the time/space bind other animals are caught in. Language makes possible history, dreams, philosophy, and radical, abrupt changes in our patterns of living, and our orientations to others. Animal patterns evolve. Language opens the door to revolution.

But when the word arrived on the scene we did not, and could not discard our nonverbal communication systems. While they are prior to language in time, they were never, and are not now primitive systems, in the sense of "crude," "ineffective" or "clumsy." On the contrary, they play, as they always have, absolutely crucial roles in the daily lives of each one of us, and play them well. In this section, you will explore several reasons why such a statement can be made. The conclusion to be drawn is not that nonverbal communication is more important than verbal communication, or vice versa, but that each, in its own way, contributes something special to the process we have been calling human interaction.

Here are some clichés to think about:

"One picture is worth a thousand words."
"Two-cents worth."
"Words are cheap."
"Seeing is believing."
"Actions speak louder than words."
"Lip service."
"Speak with forked tongue."
"Do you get the picture?"
"Do you see what I mean?"
"See right through him."
"Put up or shut up."

SIX REASONS WHY NONVERBAL COMMUNICATION IS IMPORTANT WHEN YOU AND OTHERS GET TOGETHER

1. The great amount of time we spend communicating nonverbally.
2. The great amount of information generated by nonverbal variables.
3. The crucial nature of nonverbal information.
4. The trustworthiness of nonverbal information.
5. The efficiency of nonverbal communication systems.
6. What nonverbal does for language.

In this section we will examine each of these six reasons in turn.

Reason One: The Great Amount of Time We Spend Communicating Nonverbally

As long as you are in the presence of others, you can't stop communicating nonverbally. You can stop verbal communication, but not nonverbal communication. You cannot not communicate nonverbally. Even if you died, you'd still be sending information: "dead!"

Compare language. Ray Birdwhistell, a nonverbal authority, estimates that the average person spends a mere ten to eleven minutes a day actually speaking words! Don't include schoolteachers, politicians, salesmen or Muhammed Ali in there! And the average English sentence lasts only two and a half seconds.

How much talking did you do before breakfast this morning? During breakfast? On your way to work or school? While working? During lunch? On your way home? At supper? While watching TV?

So nonverbal is an "always-on" communication system, whereas language is a "some-

YOU KEEP RELATING TO PEOPLE
EVEN WHEN YOU'VE SHUT UP VERBALLY

times-on," and "mostly-off" one. You keep relating to people, keep processing information about them, even when you've shut up verbally. And they do the same. That's the first reason why nonverbal communication is important.

Can you think of a reason this "always-on" nonverbal system makes for more accurate communication?

Try to inhibit sending any nonverbal signals. Then take a look in the mirror and see all the signals you're sending!

Reason Two: The Great Amount of Information Generated by Nonverbal Variables

Most of our interactions during the day don't involve words. Think of all the people you meet, yet don't speak to, in the course of an average day: people in corridors, in restaurants and shopping plazas, on the streets and in classrooms. But as we've seen earlier, these interactions are hardly communication-free; nonverbal information sending and receiving goes on constantly during these silent encounters.

In those interactions that *do* involve words, the proportion of nonverbal messages is amazingly high, according to Ray Birdwhis-

tell, who suggested the following figures as rough estimates:

35 per cent of all messages are traceable to language

35 per cent of all messages are traceable to paralanguage

30 per cent of all messages are traceable to face, body, clothes and all other nonverbal variables

So 65 per cent of the messages in verbal interactions are traceable to nonverbal sources! Remember that this is merely an estimate for the "average" encounter, whatever that may mean. Still, if you consider the three points below, you will probably be willing to grant that, whatever the percentages, nonverbal *does* account for a very large proportion of the total message content of our daily interactions with others.

1. We spend far more *time* per day communicating nonverbally than we do verbally, as we've just seen above.

2. Our bodies are multi-media systems—which include the face, eyes, limbs, body, clothes, paralanguage, etc. There is only a *single* medium in the case of language.

3. Some nonverbal variables like clothes, body shape and skin colour mediate only a limited amount of information, especially when we are dealing with someone we already know. But other variables are ones which change rapidly, and are very complex: the eyes, facial expressions, and paralinguistic elements like speech rate, intonation, volume, etc. These latter variables can and do reflect a whole host of rapidly changing things about a person: changes in emotions and their intensity, changes in attitudes, mood, etc.

So it is clear that a great amount of information is generated by nonverbal variables. That's the second reason why nonverbal communication is important.

Reason Three: The Crucial Nature of Nonverbal Information

We have just seen that we spend a lot of time communicating nonverbally, and that, proportionately, nonverbal messages are probably more numerous than verbal ones. The question is, however: how salient are nonverbal messages? How much weight should we assign to them? Despite their numbers, could we get along without them?

Suppose you decide that. Which of the items below would you prefer to code nonverbally, and which ones verbally? Which ones *could* you code verbally as *efficiently* and *accurately* as you could nonverbally? Remember that efficiency and accuracy are very important factors in human relationships.

1. Your mood, and *all* the changes in it throughout the interaction, *as* they occur.
2. Your age, sex, occupation, status, health, role.
3. Your personality and your emotions.
4. All your attitudes—towards yourself and your own words, towards the other person and his behaviour, including his language behaviour, towards the relationship itself, towards the environment around you. All these, on a moment-to-moment basis, as they are experienced by you.
5. Your physical attractiveness.
6. The weather.
7. Your temperament.
8. Your thoughts on the Leaf hockey game last night.
9. What you ate on your trip to Vancouver.
10. The fact that you wish to speak, at each point in the interaction.
11. The fact that you don't understand what is being said, or that you don't want to be interrupted—each time this occurs.
12. The fact that you've finished a point, and wish to move on to another one.
13. Your philosophy of life.
14. Your opinions of community colleges.

As you went through this list, did you feel that you wouldn't want to, or couldn't communicate verbally about certain items? Which ones and why? How many things on the list do you feel you could refrain from communicating, if you wanted to? How many when you're tired, or angry, or depressed or nervous?

By this point you ought to be convinced that we prefer to let our nonverbal behaviours handle a good many very important messages—because they are difficult or impossible to code verbally, or because the nonverbal behaviours are simply more eloquent than their verbal counterparts. Try to imagine what interaction would be like if we

could not express our emotions and attitudes nonverbally! Nonverbal behaviours also serve to keep the verbal stream moving along, by acting like stage directions—indicating the "correct" tone of a conversation, the proper content, the alternation of speaking roles, and so on.

The simple truth is that nonverbal information is responsible for a great deal of the richness and fluidity of the face-to-face communication process. Without it, interaction would come close to resembling a rapid exchange of written notes. That's the third reason why nonverbal communication is important.

"Language is a poor thing. You fill your lungs with wind and shake a little slit in your throat, and make mouths, and that shakes the air; and the air shakes a pair of little drums in my head—a very complicated arrangement, with lots of bones behind—and my brain seizes your meaning in the rough. What a roundabout way, and what a waste of time."

Du Maurier

Reason Four: The Trustworthiness of Nonverbal Information

By and large, nonverbal information is considerably more trustworthy than verbal information. That's a pretty broad statement. But consider these facts, and see if you don't arrive at precisely the same conclusion.

1. A large amount of the nonverbal information available to others during interaction is unintentionally produced, in the sense that we don't *mean* to produce it.
2. A large amount of the information is also unconsciously produced, in the sense that we are not *aware* that we are producing it.
3. It is relatively more difficult to deliberately control our nonverbal behaviours than our verbal ones, particularly when we are under emotional pressure. This is true not only for our attempts to inhibit information, hide it from others, but also for our attempts to act out something we do not genuinely feel. One of the reasons for this is that our nonverbal behaviours are directed more by our autonomic nervous systems than are our

verbal behaviours. The autonomic nervous system is the one over which we exercise relatively little control, compared to the central nervous system. Another reason is that there are simply more nonverbal channels to control than there are verbal ones.

Thus, if we observe a contradiction between what a person says and what he does, most of the time we quite rightly give less weight to the verbal information. We trust the nonverbal more. That's the fourth reason why nonverbal communication is important.

How would the concepts of innuendo, slips of the lip, hidden meanings and sarcasm fit into this discussion?

Do you think paralanguage is a better source of information in a contradictory-message situation than eye behaviours or facial expressions? Why?

"For him who has eyes to see and ears to hear no mortal can hide his secret; he whose lips are silent chatters with his fingertips and betrays himself through all his pores."

Sigmund Freud

Reason Five: The Efficiency of Nonverbal Communication Systems

The efficiency of nonverbal communication systems derives from the following characteristics:

1. *Nonverbal communication is multimedia communication.* While the face is sending messages, a person can use his body or voice to generate messages simultaneously. No need to wait until some channel is clear and open to inject a message. Note that language doesn't work this way. Language is most efficient when speakers and listeners alternate roles. This forces delays in responding to a verbal message verbally. The whole back-and-forth character of verbal interaction, compared to the simultaneity of nonverbal multimedia information generation, is slow and inflexible.

2. *Nonverbal communication patterns are deeply rooted in emotion and physiology.* Many of our nonverbal behaviours code information efficiently because they are directly linked to physiological and emotional changes occurring within us. Facial expressions, eye movements and many trunk and limb movements are spontaneous manifestations of internal processes, and thus are

FACIAL EXPRESSIONS, EYE MOVEMENTS AND MANY TRUNK AND LIMB MOVEMENTS ARE SPONTANEOUS MANIFESTATIONS OF INTERNAL PROCESSES

authentic and effective sources of information. Language, by comparison, is often generated in a more contrived, controlled fashion, routed as it is through the conscious mind via the central nervous system. This is not to say nonverbal behaviours are not themselves under conscious control at times; they are. Only that a greater proportion of our nonverbal behaviours are reflexive and habitual in nature, and that for this reason they are less likely to be distorted sources of information. Given its artificiality, the door is open, in language, for a certain degree of inefficiency in reflecting internal events.

3. *Nonverbal communication codes are well-suited to deal with certain kinds of meaning.* Nonverbal behaviours are exceedingly poor substitutes for language when it comes to the communication of ideas and concepts. We have great difficulty in using nonverbal behaviours to refer to realities that are not immediately in our environment. There is no substitute—no efficient substitute—for language for communicating linear, logical thought processes.

But nonverbal behaviours are extremely efficient—and eloquent—when it comes to communicating *presently felt* emotions, attitudes and moods, and *our own* personality, role, status, age, health, etc. And as we saw above, the nonverbal mode fits in well with the dynamics of the interpersonal situation. Our expressive actions are often rapid and don't interfere with each other or language; they are often coded pictorially, and that can make for clarity and precision and subtlety; and finally, they tend to be complete, integrated events that need no further elaboration or explanation: a smiling face *is* the message, the slow, shuffling gait *is* the message. That is to say, these behaviours are not reports of events—they are the events themselves.

Reason Six: What Nonverbal Does for Language

The relationships between nonverbal and verbal communication will be spelled out in detail in Section Four of this chapter, and you should peruse that section for a fuller account of the importance of nonverbal from the point of view of its contribution to language.

Briefly, nonverbal behaviours serve the function of providing continuous, multichannel feedback on the verbal stream. Reactions to language can be seen on the face and in the body, even while a sender continues to speak. This feedback guides the speaker in his choice of words and tone, the selection of topics, his volume and countless other decisions.

Nonverbal behaviours also serve to clarify, underline, qualify and elaborate on the verbal messages. It is the nonverbal information stream that keeps the interactants in contact with each other, keeps them relating, even though only one of them is speaking, or neither of them. Nonverbal fills in and around language. It is the information that provides encounters with their "here and now" quality, their life and vitality. Without nonverbal communication, persons could not truly meet each other.

We have explored six reasons why nonverbal behaviours are such an important part of interpersonal communication. In the following section let's attempt to deepen our understanding of nonverbal communication by investigating several functions nonverbal behaviours serve when *you and others* meet face-to-face.

SECTION THREE: THE FUNCTIONS OF NONVERBAL INFORMATION

The sender is the receiver is the medium is the message is you. Remember? The *prime* function of nonverbal information is to reveal *you* continuously, efficiently, and in depth. In nonverbal communication, you are the message, you are the content of your body medium.

A second function of nonverbal information is to serve as a substitute for language itself when verbal behaviour is impossible, difficult, or undesirable for some reason. This is a minor function of nonverbal behaviour.

The third function of nonverbal information is to regulate interactions by aiding in their initiation, maintenance and termination. Let's take a close look at each of these three functions in turn.

Function One: Revealing the Interactants

You are a psychological, social, cultural and physiological being. Other people get to know you partly from what you say, and partly from your appearance and behaviour. Unlike language, however, the main and specialized role of nonverbal behaviours is to reveal the self. The content of language may be you, but it may also be motorcycles, philosophy, Aunt Sarah, or pizza. It is most difficult to use nonverbal behaviours to refer to anything but you as you are at the moment, and your reactions to the people, events and things in the immediate vicinity. Your nonverbal behaviours certainly have this limited scope, but make up for it with their ability to reveal you continuously, efficiently and in depth. Take, for example, you as a psychological being . . .

Who are you? I see part of you in the way you dress, move your eyes, your hands, your legs. You reveal yourself to me by the way you make up your face, by the way you walk, by the way you sit. Your needs and your attitudes are communicated to me by the way you purse your lips, toss your head, and grin. How close are you standing to me? Are your arms folded? Through these actions you reveal yourself. Do you move quickly, jerkily, or smoothly and deliberately? Is your voice pitched high? Do you speak slowly or do you spray out your words without stopping for breath? Are you hesitant? Do you mispronounce or stumble over words? Who are you? I see part of you. I hear part of you. I touch and smell part of you. You reveal yourself in countless ways to me.

You are also a social being. I observe your clothes, your accent, your choice of words. I notice the places you frequent, where you work. I visit your home and meet your family. Through these things I see and hear about your role in society. I judge your status. You are part of society, and through you, I see that society.

You are a cultural being. You act differently from your friend from Sweden. You look somewhat different too—in your features, your clothes, your style of gesturing. Your speech is different, and your eating

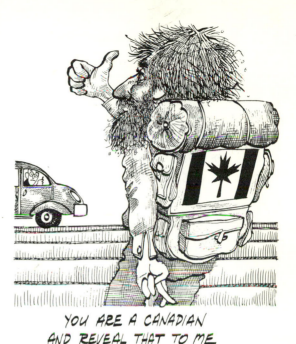

YOU ARE A CANADIAN
AND REVEAL THAT TO ME

habits. You live in a different kind of home, and hold your cigarette in a subtly different way. You are a Canadian, and reveal that to me.

Physically, you are unique. I can often tell if you are feeling ill or depressed or tired or in shock. I can guess your age. I know your sex and I have opinions about your attractiveness. I recognize you instantly. You reveal your physical self to me.

And your reactions. What do you think of my ideas? That look on her face? This restaurant? Do you like my clothes? Are you in favour of the three-day week? Are you disappointed because I have to go now? You seem to approve of that last comment by Lil. You can answer all these questions verbally, but you can—and do—often show me by your actions what you are thinking.

And Not a Word Was Spoken

"*I worked for several years as a crossing guard, shepherding people across a busy street. Over the years I came to make a lot of friends just by doing my job. Some of them were drivers and passengers in cars that passed by. But you know, I never said a single word to many of them all that time, and they never spoke to me. Yet I feel I knew them well."*

A Mature Student

You never stop—and you cannot stop—revealing yourself nonverbally. Physically, culturally, socially and psychologically, you let me know who you are. This information is detailed and it is often the kind of information you don't or cannot give me verbally. I need it to relate to you, to carry on a conversation with you, however simple or brief.

Function Two: Substituting for Language

Do you know the nonverbal equivalents for these messages?

> OK.
> Peace!
> I want to hitch a ride.
> Come here.
> Over there.
> There, there now; it'll be OK.
> What a square!
> What a beautiful figure!
> Hooray!
> It's a deal.
> She's a little crazy.
> Hurry, hurry!
> Two minutes for cross-checking.
> Set it down right here.
> Lift it up.
> I'm a gorilla.
> The scene is Japan.
> Don't go through the screen door, Granny, you'll strain yourself.
> Ben Hur.
> Now is the time for all good men to come to the aid of the party.

Those last five were considerably more difficult than the others, weren't they? That's because we're asking nonverbal behaviours to communicate things that they are really ill-equipped to do. We have worked out signs for a number of words and phrases, but the stock of these language substitutes is pretty meagre. And when we try to communicate about things that aren't part of that small supply, we find nonverbal breaking down. It's simply not the kind of system we use to communicate "Now is the time for all good men to come to the aid of the party."

Deaf mutes though, would have little trouble with that sentence, because they have devised a very complex nonverbal sign system out of necessity. It's so complex, in fact, that it *is* a form of language.

So, you can see that while we *can,* by elaborate pantomiming and charades, communicate about people and events beyond our immediate situation, or about ideas and concepts strung together into sentences, it's a pretty exhausting task most of the time. Why bother? We have language to do that for us.

Yet we do have a need for simple nonverbal signs like the peace sign, and "come here," and "lift it up." When verbal communication is impossible, difficult or undesirable, these language substitutes may come into play.

If another person is too far away, or there is too much noise in the environment—at football games, for example, or on the deck of an aircraft carrier—we may use these nonverbal signs which Paul Ekman calls "emblems" (see Selected Readings). If you don't want to disturb someone or something by speaking you may decide to "gesture" your message. Sometimes we simply opt for an emblem because it seems to have more force and point than the spoken word (obscene gestures, ritual gestures).

When faced with the necessity to communicate with someone who doesn't speak our language we realize just how poor a substitute an emblem is for the "real thing." The fact is that these language substitutes weren't meant to do language's job.

Function Three: Regulating Interactions

A most important function of nonverbal behaviour is to regulate the very process of interaction—to start it off "on the right foot," to keep it running smoothly, and to end it satisfactorily. If you don't think this is too important a function, you may be the kind of person who can't appreciate the work of people who organize and supervise a rock concert, or some sporting event. Rock concerts and sporting events don't just happen; an awful lot of decisions and hard work are involved. We need the regulation provided by laws, signs, traffic lights, and common courtesy to keep our traffic from becoming hopelessly fouled up. Schools and governments need rules and procedures to operate efficiently.

So does the process of interaction. How do you know who to interact with, and when?

IF YOU DON'T WANT TO DISTURB SOMEONE BY SPEAKING, YOU CAN "GESTURE" YOUR MESSAGE

How do you begin an interaction? What tone do you take? What do you say first? When do you speak and when do you listen? How do you react to the other person? What if there's a disagreement? When do you change the topic? When do you decide to break off the interaction? How do you end it? The fact is that our *nonverbal* behaviours very often play these kinds of strategic regulative roles.

Head nods and shakes
Widening of the eyes
Smiles and other facial expressions
Shifting weight from one foot to another
Mutual glances
Glancing at watch
Shuffling feet
Glancing around from time to time
Avoiding eye contact
Flashing eyebrows up suddenly
Twisting your body away from your partner
Folding your arms across your chest
Drumming your fingertips on your desk
A-hemm-ing
Handshakes
Waves
Touches
Hand motions that touch your own body
Blushing
Pursing your lips

Look at the list of behaviours above, and try to decide which ones you would use to communicate the messages below.

"Now wait *just* a minute!"
"Hurry up, I want to speak now."
"I agree."
"I doubt it very much."
"Well—I'm not completely convinced."
"Absolutely correct."
"Is something wrong?"
"I'm bored."
"It was nice meeting you."
"I'm going to have to leave soon."
"Go on, I'm listening."
"Don't interrupt me."
"Don't interrupt me. I *know* what I want to say, but I need a second to gather my thoughts."
"Now that we've finished that point, let's go on to another one."
"I'm ready to interact with you."
"I am not threatening to you. I want to have a friendly interaction."
"I can't hear you."
"I'm finished speaking."
"Am I right or wrong?"
"Don't you agree?"
"Take it easy. I'm on your side."

"The next time we meet, we'll be on good terms."

"I'm going to take this side of the sidewalk, and you take that side, and we won't bump into each other."

"I'm lonely."

"I don't want to speak to you at all."

"I want to speak to you, but make it quick."

"I'm speaking to you only because I have to."

"I'm embarrassed."

"This is getting us nowhere."

"I'm trying to get through to you. Help me."

All of these messages serve to regulate interaction, and all of them can be—and very often are—sent nonverbally.

Regulators grease the wheels of interaction. Without them, we just couldn't get along together. They are that important.

Can you think of reasons why we often prefer to code these kinds of messages nonverbally rather than verbally?

Are there any regulative behaviours, not on the behaviour list above, that you need to "act out" the messages? Which ones?

We have just reviewed three functions of nonverbal information in the process of human interaction: 1) revealing the interactants continuously, efficiently, and in depth; 2) substituting for language; and 3) regulating the interaction. Let's turn now to a comparison of verbal and nonverbal communication systems to see how each works, and how they work together in face-to-face situations.

SECTION FOUR: HOW LANGUAGE AND NONVERBAL SYSTEMS WORK, AND HOW THEY WORK TOGETHER

Language and nonverbal behaviours are obviously quite different, and volumes could be written detailing those differences. In this section, we will be concerned with just two: differences in the *kinds* of meaning each elicits, and differences in the *patternings* of meaning. Understanding these differences will deepen your appreciation of both systems and clarify their roles in face-to-face interaction. In the latter part of this section we will deal briefly with the question of how language and nonverbal systems operate together.

Symbols and Symptoms

The denotative meaning of a word comprises all those characteristics of the thing referred to, which label or identify it as belonging to a certain group or class of things. Dictionaries provide denotative meanings by describing such characteristics. Sometimes pictures help to clarify the denotative meaning. Thus, when you look up the meaning of "lamp" in the dictionary, you will see a description of those characteristics of lamps that *define* "lampness." Anything that fits this description is in the group or class of things labelled "lamp."

Connotative meaning, on the other hand, comprises *all other* characteristics, real or imagined, private or public, attributed to a thing. The connotative meaning does not define a class of things, but people's subjective reactions to them. Often, different people will have similar connotative meanings for a thing simply because their past experiences have been similar. On the other hand, someone may react to a thing in a completely unique way, and so his connotative meaning for it will be unique. For example, perhaps you and I will agree that "rat" has "filthy" connotations, whereas a young child seeing one for the first time may react to it as he would to his pet puppy. His connotative meaning may be closer to "cuddly" or "fun."

Now that you understand the distinction between denotation and connotation, we can move directly to the main point of this section: a large and significant portion of our nonverbal repertoire does not function denotatively, and therefore does not function as language does.

Only symbols can denote. When we say something is a symbol, we mean it stands or substitutes for, or refers to, something else, of which it is not a part (though the symbol may resemble its referent). All words are symbols, which have been deliberately and

ANIMAL: *DENOTATIVE MEANING*   ANIMAL: *CONNOTATIVE MEANING*

artificially created to "stand in" for something else.

A fair number of nonverbal behaviours—in both animals and humans—are symbolic by definition: greeting and departure ritual behaviours such as handshakes, kisses and embraces; head nodding and shaking; obscene gestures; pictorial hand movements; signals used in sporting events; deaf mute signs, and so on. We possess a mostly unwritten "dictionary" of these symbolic behaviours, in much the same fashion as we keep track of the denotative meanings for word symbols by actually writing them down. Almost invariably, when we use symbolic nonverbal behaviours, they are performed quite consciously and deliberately to communicate specific, clearly understood messages.

But there are great numbers of other nonverbal behaviours which do not function as symbols, and do not serve to stand in for other things. Facial expressions such as fear and anger do not stand for fear and anger—they are *part of* fear and anger. Folded limbs do not refer to withdrawal—they are *part of* the withdrawal itself. Dragging feet and sweating brows are symptoms of tiredness and nervousness, and not substitutes for these conditions. When you rub your thighs or scratch an itch, you are not deliberately trying to communicate about something else—you are in fact manifesting a portion of that "something else." The postures we take, the distances we choose when interacting, countless eye and hand movements—these and many other behaviours *express* interior motives, and do not substitute for them. They are symptoms rather than symbols.

It must immediately be said, however, that we can, and often do, take an action and *raise* it to the level of symbol by consciously and deliberately performing it—often in an exaggerated and overblown fashion. For example, we may scratch our head to signal puzzlement when we are not, in fact, feeling an itch. We may mimic helplessness or disgust or anger to a receiver who understands perfectly that we are not really feeling these emotions. We may consciously limp or whimper for some special effect—for instance, to mock another person, or to portray a part in a drama (though in this latter case it is a moot point whether or not symbolic action—acting—may sometimes be, in effect, indistinguishable from genuine, spontaneous behaviour). Deliberate attempts to deceive people by feigning behaviour are symbolic from the sender's point of view, if not always from the receiver's!

Because such a large and important proportion of our nonverbal repertoire is non-symbolic, it is not a very suitable medium for communicating about things that lie outside the immediate time/space dimension of the interactions in which we participate. While a Marcel Marceau may be able (with years of practice under his belt) to conjure up whole worlds of experience, and transport his audiences magically back and forth in time and space, our more pedestrian performances tend to be limited to the task of expressing ourselves—as we are here, and as we are now. To say that nonverbal communication is a language—as in "body language"—is either to have a very loose definition of language, or to ignore the fact that it is a system with a very modest stock of truly symbolic elements which can function in ways similar to words. Furthermore, as we shall see in the following section, nonverbal systems seem to lack complex rules, akin to grammar and syntax rules, which serve in the process of combining word elements into the structures we call sentences.

Discursive and Nondiscursive

Ordinary language, mathematics, the deaf codes, and several other communication systems pattern meanings discursively. That is, they are able to make statements, to ask questions, to describe—and most important —to *discuss*. One plus one equals two ($1 + 1 = 2$) is an example of discursive patterning. Notice that some system of rules for combining elements into a sequential, continuous and connected form is involved. Nonverbal communication systems, however, are able to manage only superficial discussions, because they do not possess rules for elaborate combinations of facial expressions, hand and body movements, etc. They are nondiscursive forms. This is a second major difference between language and so-called body language.

Action and Reaction

How do language and nonverbal behaviours work together during interaction? Very well! As we have seen earlier, nonverbal provides feedback on the verbal, and vice versa. Action and reaction. Each serves to guide and shape the other. Each regulates the other. All in all, though, the nonverbal system appears to be the more complex and efficient feedback system, since it is constantly in operation, even while people are speaking, and since it involves several media —two of which are highly visible and rapid, and possess considerable message capacity: the face and eyes.

Bolstering the Message

Language and nonverbal behaviours can provide you with information about the same "thing," thus clarifying, supporting, underlining and elaborating each other. For example, you can show apprehension and talk about it; you can comfort people by speaking to them and touching them; you can smile and wish someone well. Thus, the two systems are mutually reinforcing. They "bolster" each other. This makes for clearer communication because bolstering reduces the effects of badly coded messages, and the effects of interference in the environment, in the channel, or within the receiver. Bolstering also make for richer, more subtle, communication by providing information "orchestrated" in two or more media modes.

Checking and Balancing

At times, verbal and nonverbal information may contradict each other. "I'm all right, Jack," you may say, but you have a weak, silly smile on your face, and your hands are trembling. We would discount the verbal information here, as in most cases of contradiction, and believe the nonverbal messages. Thus, nonverbal serves the very valuable function of providing a *check* on the verbal stream.

Occasionally the verbal messages may simply be different from the nonverbal ones. Not contradictory, just different. A person, for example, may actually be experiencing both anger and fear—the anger on his face perhaps, and the fear in his words. We obtain a more *balanced* impression of him by taking into account both his words and his face.

What we have discovered in this section is that, while verbal and nonverbal systems are quite different in terms of the kinds and patternings of meaning, they work closely together in human encounters, both contributing to the richness and variety of the face-to-face experience. It is meaningless to ask which is the more important source of information; both are unique, and both are truly invaluable assets in our efforts to learn from and about each other through communication.

SELECTED READINGS

Birdwhistell, R.   *Kinesics and Context.* Philadelphia: University of Pennsylvania Press, 1970.

Eisenberg, A. and R. Smith.   *Nonverbal Communication.* Indianapolis: Bobbs-Merrill Co., Inc., 1971.

Ekman, P. and W. Friesen.   "The repertoire of nonverbal behaviour: categories, origins, usage and coding." *Semiotica.* 1(1), 1969.

Ekman, P., ed.   *Darwin and Facial Expression.* New York: Academic Press, 1973.

Fast, J.   *Body Language.* New York: Pocket Books, 1971.

Feldman, S.   *Mannerisms of Speech and Gestures.* New York: International Universities Press, Inc., 1959.

Goffman, E.   *The Presentation of Self in Everyday Life.* Garden City, New York: Anchor Books, 1959.

—————.   *Behaviour in Public Places.* New York. The Free Press, 1963.

—————.   *Interaction Ritual.* Garden City, New York: Anchor Books, 1967.

Hall, E.   *The Hidden Dimension.* Garden City, New York: Anchor Books, 1969.

Harrison, R.   *Beyond Words.* Englewood Cliffs, New Jersey: Prentice-Hall, 1974.

Hinde, R., ed.   *Non-verbal Communication.* Cambridge, England: Cambridge University Press, 1972.

Knapp, M.   *Nonverbal Communication in Human Interaction.* New York: Holt, Rinehart and Winston, Inc., 1972.

Mehrabian, A.   *Silent Messages.* Belmont, California: Wadsworth Publishing Co., 1971.

—————.   *Nonverbal Communication.* Chicago: Aldine Atherton, 1972.

Morris, D.   *Intimate Behaviour.* London: Jonathan Cape, Ltd., 1971.

Nierenberg, G. and H. Calero.   *How to Read a Person Like a Book.* New York: Cornerstone Library, Inc., 1972.

Scheflen, Albert and Alice Scheflen.   *Body Language and Social Order.* Englewood Cliffs, New Jersey: Prentice-Hall, Inc., 1972.

Sommer, R.   *Personal Space.* Englewood Cliffs, New Jersey: Prentice-Hall, Inc., 1969.

6

IMPROVING NONVERBAL COMMUNICATION SKILLS

Robert M. Soucie

Even if you've never *heard* of nonverbal communication before reading this book, the fact is that you have been doing it all your life. You already possess a great deal of implicit or unconscious knowledge about the subject. You are, as they say, "experienced in the field."

But unfortunately, very few of us come close to *mastering* the art of nonverbal communication. In fact, because nonverbal skills have been acquired and are practised largely out-of-awareness, many of us lack solid, explicit incentives for extending and developing them—and don't. Willy-nilly, we attain a certain level of nonverbal competence, then get stuck there, unable to make significant progress as the years go by.

Among those who *do* continue to learn and advance are some whose life styles place them in situations which practically compel them to improve their communication skills, or suffer the consequences. Salesmen and politicians, for example, if they are to do more than stand still in their professions, learn quickly how vital it is to be able to "size up" people quickly and accurately, and to know how to initiate and maintain comfortable, fruitful interactions. These people live daily in environments that provide them with an abundance of feedback, from a wide variety of persons, on their own performance as a communicator. That's their secret. This experience tends to shape and hone their communication skills, for the good reason that failures to tune into this feedback show up sooner or later in their pocketbooks or at the polls. Nice incentives!

So a key to nonverbal skill development is surely experience. But the right kind of experience: where there is a continual adjusting and modifying of behaviour in the light of plentiful and varied feedback.

The right kinds of experience don't come along for all of us in a neat, timely fashion, and they don't come all at once, or easily. This chapter was written to help you make the most of the communication situations you find yourself in now. It offers an analysis of some of the more common and serious nonverbal communication problems, and advice and suggestions for coping with them. Several exercises are included. Try them. You will find that they will increase your sensitivity to body information, and to the

SALESMEN AND POLITICIANS "SIZE YOU UP" QUICKLY

complexities of the interactional process.

No one ever became an accomplished public speaker, or golfer, or painter—or nonverbal communicator—*simply* by reading a book on the subject. Practice and experience are necessary. But after reading this chapter, you should be equipped to learn faster and more thoroughly the many lessons in communication that life's experiences will teach you as you move from day to day.

PART 1. IMPROVING YOUR SENSITIVITY TO OTHERS' NONVERBAL BEHAVIOUR

Résumé: Several factors, often operating in combination, are responsible for breakdowns in our perception of others' nonverbal behaviour. Obviously, such breakdowns can threaten the stability of the interaction, and the success of the relationship itself. These factors include: 1) ignorance; 2) lack of emotional control; 3) character defects; and 4) faulty habits of perception.

Sensitivity and Ignorance

Simply not knowing. That's what we're speaking of here. If you didn't know the

Chinese or Dutch language "codes" or didn't know them very well, you wouldn't be able to process Chinese or Dutch verbal information properly. You'd be ignorant. The same sort of ignorance occurs with respect to nonverbal codes, despite the fact that body "language" is far more universal than any spoken or written one. Our nonverbal ignorance tends to show up when we deal with cross-cultural "emblems" and space behaviours, and with "illustrators" and "adaptors".

Emblems.   North American and European emblems (see Appendix for definition) tend to overlap to a large extent. It's when we travel elsewhere that we might run into a little difficulty with these language substitutes. There's the story about the late President Lyndon Johnson that illustrates the point well.

The newspapers in Canada and the United States carried a picture of him sitting up in a hospital bed, attended by a young, beautiful nurse. Johnson is lifting his shirt up with one hand, exposing a long, wicked scar—the result of his recent gall bladder operation. But the operation had been a success, and he is smiling broadly at the nurse, while flashing the thumb-to-forefinger, circular "OK" sign. The message was perfectly clear to Canadians and Americans, but not so to the Russians. Apparently the photo they printed in their papers had been broken up pretty badly in transmission, and the scar was barely discernible, if at all. But the problem was really that "OK" emblem. There was the President in bed, smiling at a young woman (who didn't look like a nurse to the Russians because they dress differently over there), pulling up his shirt, and sending a clear, unmistakeable emblem meaning: "I'd like to become—well—'intimate' with you"!

So some advice when you're travelling abroad: though you can usually pick up the meanings of strange emblems quickly, don't be too free, for the first little while, in *making* any. They may well mean something quite different—and offensive—to others!

Space Behaviours.   How far do you stand from someone you're taking to? The distance varies with your mood, your age, your relationship with each other, the topic you're discussing, the location you're in, your personality, and—your culture.

Some people come from "contact" cultures.

SOME PEOPLE COME FROM "CONTACT" CULTURES

They like to stand up close to you, to touch and manipulate your body, to smell your breath, and to stare long and hard into your eyes. A couple of minutes of this, and shock waves start coursing through your rigid, sweating, backward-leaning Canadian frame. You fight to keep that weak, silly smile on your face, and your eyes from crossing any further than they already have behind your fogged glasses. One more step and you know you'll end up in the ditch.

Why, oh why, you ask yourself, do these people have to be so pushy, overbearing and ill-mannered? For the same reason that we "have to be" so stand-offish, distant, cold and impersonal!

But neither culture is really being ill-mannered here at all. It's simply that we use space differently. We prefer different conversational distances and have different attitudes to physical contact, and that's that.

But what do we say when we run into these differences? *"Vive la difference!"*? Unfortunately not. In our ignorance, we tend to become hostile, and begin to attribute all manner of unkind motives and characteristics to them. After all (expletive deleted), they're making us uncomfortable! Well, it's a short, simple step from ignorance to prejudice.

Be very careful that your perfectly normal bias for your own way of handling space and touch don't harden and sicken into racial slurs. Somewhere deep in all of us is the tendency to jump from "He is different" to "There must be something wrong with those people!"

Despite your full awareness that conversational distance varies with culture, you will most likely *continue* to feel uncomfortable when you interact with people from contact or "near-contact" cultures. You may also find yourself at uncomfortable distance for reasons that have nothing to do with culture, but, as we have seen above, with the nature of your relationships, mood, personality, and so on. Don't try your darndest to *love* that uncomfortable distance which your interactional partner seems to favour. That's liable only to lead to frustration, because our spatial preferences are thoroughly ingrained. But do try to *adapt* to it, as best you can, for the good of the cause. In general, it can be said that adapting your behaviour to another's is a politeness that will yield you returns out of all proportion to the effort required to perform it. You will have to get in the habit of making such little gifts to people, if you wish to interact successfully with them.

The easy way—or so it seems to us some-times—is to let the other guy take us as he finds us, or "too bad, Charlie!" The "you do your thing, and I'll do mine" philosophy sounds attractive enough, but it can wreck communication. Like so many other human processes, you get out of communication what you put in.

Illustrators. Remember the Italian bus drivers who weren't allowed to speak to the passengers because they had to keep their hands on the wheel?

There are quite a few people in this world who find it perfectly natural to "talk" freely with their hands. In fact, everybody uses "illustrators" (see Appendix for definition) to a greater or lesser extent. Your ignorance will be showing though, if like many people, you assume that "hand talk" is some kind of second-rate substitute for language which the semi-civilized use as a crutch to make up for their verbal deficiencies.* Far from it. Illustrators *enhance* language, not substitute for it. They underline, qualify, expand, embellish and pictorialize the spoken word, not take its place.

*Don't confuse illustrators with emblems. The latter *are* language substitutes. But even emblems are not viable alternatives to talk, but only to simple isolated words or phrases.

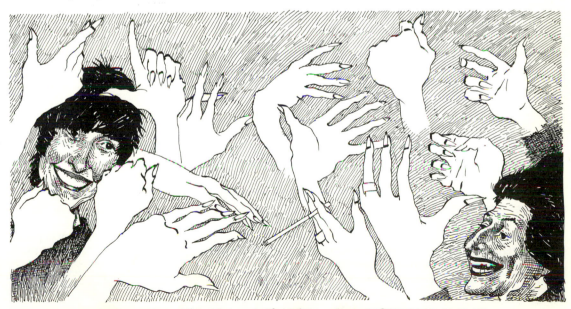

ILLUSTRATORS *ENHANCE* LANGUAGE, NOT SUBSTITUTE FOR IT

If you have a feeling of resentment (the word is not too strong) against those who use illustrators frequently, then try to overcome it. Otherwise, you are very likely to see illustrators as so much *noise* interfering with, and spoiling, your determined efforts to concentrate on the "important" messages—the words.

That would be a mistake. Don't tune them out, tune them in. You'll be amazed at the wealth of information they contain about the speaker's mood, emotion and even personality. Study them. Try turning the sound off your TV set and spending half-hour sessions observing them. If you don't get much hand/arm action, switch to another channel. You will find it helpful to hold a small piece of cardboard in front of you, switching hands from time to time, to cut off the faces; facial expressions will otherwise tend to become confused with the illustrators. Perhaps for the first time in your life, you will be getting the chance to concentrate—really concentrate—on this nonverbal variable, and you're bound to come away from these TV sessions with an increased appreciation of the role they play in revealing people during interaction.

Adaptors. A very interesting and important class of nonverbal variables is "adaptors." These are behaviours, occurring anywhere in the body, which reflect a person's conscious or unconscious attempts to adapt to, or cope with, some pressing interior need /state, or somebody or something in his environment.

For instance, tension may be reflected in a clenched fist or in tightly compressed lips. Fear may be reflected in body twisting, or in backward movements of the trunk or feet. Nervousness may be reflected in rapid eye movements, or in fiddling with keys or a pen. You may cover your eyes with your hand(s) and lower your head when you feel guilty or ashamed.

These behaviours are rather easy to interpret but, as Paul Ekman points out, the meaning of many adaptors is far from obvious.* One reason is that adaptors may reflect things about a person that are intensely personal, or socially unacceptable, in nature. So we learn fairly early in life to inhibit performing them, with the result that they often appear, particularly in public, in a frag-

mented form which offers little clue to their origin, and thus to their function and meaning. They may become under this inhibition process extremely small in form or in duration. They may become disguised or hidden. Let's take a few examples.

1. Touching or rubbing the side or underside of the nose. Possible interpretation: Uncertainty or doubt. Something "smells."
2. Touching the lips, or actually covering the mouth, with your fingers or hand during interaction. Possible interpretation: Insecurity. May be disguised finger sucking. Regret. Futile attempt to "take back" words after they are spoken.
3. Rubbing, picking or scratching forearm or thigh briskly. Possible interpretation: Frustration or resentment is being worked out, or "displaced" in a socially acceptable manner.
4. Rubbing or scratching back of neck briskly after raising arm quickly to neck. Possible interpretation: Another displacement of frustration, except here the emotion is stronger. A disguised punch.
5. Presentation of open hand, palm up, with hand held level or at a slight angle. Possible interpretation: Sincerity.
6. Slight, quick movement of feet towards another, when seated. May be repeated several times, especially when legs are crossed. (Not to be confused with the rhythmical back and forth "bobbing" of the foot, which reveals impatience or boredom.) Possible interpretation: Aggression. Disguised, partial kick.
7. Rubbing, stroking or simply placing hand near genitals. Squeezing thighs together. Moving thighs together and apart quickly when seated with feet on floor. Possible interpretation: Auto-erotic soothing behaviours, usually performed when sexually aroused or when feeling somewhat insecure or rejected.
8. Tugging at ear. Possible interpretation: Signals a desire to interrupt. Disguised,

*See Paul Ekman and Wallace Friesen, "The Repertoire of Nonverbal Behavior—Categories, Origins, Usage and Coding", *Semiotica*, 1969, 1, 49-98. Most of this section on adaptors draws heavily on Ekman's theories.

partial raising of hand, which is socially unacceptable in the context of interaction.

9. Locked ankles. Ankles wrapped around chair legs. Possible interpretation: Tension.

10. Leaning head and/or upper part of body backwards. Sitting back in seat stiffly. Moving feet backwards slightly. Shuffling feet back and forth or lifting and dropping them alternately, as in "cold feet." Possible interpretation: Desire to retreat from the interaction.

You wish to increase your sensitivity to adaptors? You will certainly get some guidance from several of the books listed in the Selected Readings section in Chapter Five, so go and read them carefully. (Most of the authors, though, don't call them "adaptors," which is Paul Ekman's term, so be sure you know how to define them so you'll recognize them when they are being discussed.)

Combine this reading with careful, intense observation of people, wherever you find them—in parks, offices, beaches, classrooms, homes, and in the streets. One of the prime skills you will have to develop, if you are to become much more sensitive to nonverbal behaviour of *all* kinds, is the ability to focus your attention, concentrate it, on one variable at a time, excluding all other "extraneous" ones. You have to learn how to *selectively perceive* a behaviour, and to study it in isolation. Otherwise, the information from a single behavioural class will tend to merge with that from several others, and your impressions of that "target" behaviour will become generalized and less precise—out of focus. So start now to train yourself to see selectively. Zoom in, like a camera lens, on your target, and forget about the rest of the field. You'll be surprised how quickly you can learn to see not people but behaviours, not forests but trees.

The importance of context. Now this is just an *exercise,* mind you, to develop your powers of observation. When it comes to interpreting the *meaning* of any behaviour or group of behaviours, the last thing you want to do is focus on the trees and forget about the forest. The exercise will help you *see* behaviours that you might otherwise fail to see; but when *interpretation* is involved, you have to take the entire context into account.

Don't *ever* attempt to "read" *any* behaviour without assessing it in the light of what's going on, or has gone on previously, in the rest of the body and in the verbal stream. You don't do that with language, and you can't do it with nonverbal behaviour either. For example, if you were asked what the meaning of the word "run" is, you would say it depended on the context, or the way it was used. That's because "run" means different things in different contexts.

Run an office	manage
Run for office	compete
Run into a friend	come across
Run into a friend's car	crash into
Run in the family	prevalent in
Run-in with the family	argument
Run in your stocking	tear
Run-in your car	break in
Run around	move quickly
The old run-around	put-off

Similarly, context plays a crucial role in assessing nonverbal meaning. If a person's level of eye contact drops, and he is at the same time shuffling his feet and leaning away from you and making his verbal replies shorter and shorter, you can be fairly confident that his shuffling feet indicate his desire to withdraw from the conversation. But suppose he was simultaneously smiling and telling you to go on, to continue because he wanted to hear what you were saying? If you were only focused in on that smile and on his words, you would be misled. The adaptors are the trustworthy messages, and the smile is merely a polite piece of facework to harmonize with the spoken words. On the other hand, if you observed *only* the shuffling feet, and none of the other adaptors (but saw the smile and heard the words as before), then you ought to be very, very tentative in your judgment of that shuffling. Though you can't rightly be at all certain that the person wants to withdraw, at least you'd be in a better position than if you'd missed it entirely.

Caution: dangerous assumptions. It is extremely — repeat extremely — important, when you are assessing nonverbal behaviour, not to go beyond the information at your disposal. Our "shuffler" above may have wanted to withdraw because he had an appointment elsewhere to keep, or because he was bored, or tired, or sick, or because—well—his kid-

IT'S ALWAYS POSSIBLE THAT HE WANTED BOTH TO GO AND TO STAY

neys demanded it. The shuffling, in fact, may have revealed only a very temporary desire to withdraw, and if that were the case, you would have to revise your judgment that the smile and words were really not heartfelt. And it's always possible, of course, that he wanted both to go *and* to stay. Under what circumstances would you make this judgment?

A clenched fist signals tension, but it may or may not be the tension of anger, and it may or may not be anger focused on you or anyone else present. Similarly, signs of insecurity—or any other behaviour—do not *in and of themselves* reveal their CAUSE. The cause of a behaviour is an inference you make, it's not a direct perception.

So be sure not to go beyond your information, to "fill-in" another's motives, or to create explanations for behaviours you observe which the evidence doesn't support. Often, of course, you will be able to piece together several items of information, and thus infer the underlying cause of some behaviour. But this process should be a careful, conservative one. Quite bluntly, you can very easily be dead wrong! An old story illustrates just *how* easily.

Two medical doctors were chatting one day on a street corner when an elderly man shuffled by, his body rigid and his feet barely clearing the ground. "Ah," said the first doctor. "A classic case of rheumatoid arthritis!" "Wrong," the second doctor insisted. "That man is suffering from acute muscular hypertension." After arguing bitterly over their different diagnoses and reaching no agreement, the doctors decided to settle the matter by approaching the man himself and asking him why he walked the way he did. The elderly man's answer made perfectly good sense: "Loose rubbers!"

Summary

Improving your sensitivity to others' nonverbal behaviour is fundamental to improving your entire repertoire of nonverbal communication skills. To interact with people successfully, you must be capable of perceiving these behaviours which can provide so much information about them.

We have just explored a few areas where ignorance of alternate nonverbal coding systems in other cultures, and ignorance of the rich information hidden in seemingly unimportant or meaningless behaviours (adaptors), can render you less sensitive to other people and thus reduce your effectiveness as a communicator. We have stressed as well the dangers of what may be termed a "mis-sensitivity" to nonverbal behaviours, where the problem is not a failure to perceive an act, but a failure to exercise sufficient caution in assessing its meaning. Both are problems of ignorance, or not-knowing.

Sensitivity and Emotion

While ignorance certainly can reduce your sensitivity to others' nonverbal behaviour, it is not a terribly serious problem in most daily face-to-face interactions. We suffer far more, in our routine lives, from not perceiving or from mis-perceiving what we know how to perceive, than from not knowing how to perceive at all. The real challenge in improving your sensitivity to others, therefore, is not to learn how to "read" a great many new and wonderful behaviours, but to learn how to focus and consistently apply the knowledge you already possess. In short, the difficulties lie more in the practice than in the theory of nonverbal perception.

One such difficulty—and it is a common, persistent one—is the difficulty of perceiving others accurately when we are under the influence of some strong emotion. Generally speaking, our sensitivity to others tends to go down as our emotions go up. Emotion tends to short-circuit our perceptual system.

Anger opens our mouth, and closes our eyes, say the Chinese. Someone described anger as "a short madness." But *any* of the emotions can so consume our attention with *self-messages* that they render us temporarily out of touch with the reality beyond us, temporarily mad.

So, strong emotion means strong involvement with the self. This can and does dull your sensitivity to the conscious and unconscious messages being sent to you by the other person.

Have you ever been so mad at a restaurant that you cussed out the waiter—until you discovered that he was a customer passing by your table on his way back from the washroom?

Have you ever come on to a friend with a back-slapping, "How the hell are ya' Charlie" routine, when poor Charlie's entire body was fairly screaming for you to either tiptoe past him, or lend him your shoulder to cry on?

Have you ever been in the kind of blue funk where you turn off everybody around you, and to your great, shocked surprise, "suddenly" find even your loving, face-licking dog Fido growling at you?

Have you ever been so absorbed in your newspaper or mashed potatoes that your husband quit trying to tell you the dishwasher was overflowing?

Have you ever been so afraid while giving a speech that you didn't notice that the first twelve rows had fallen asleep?

Merely telling someone to control his emotions is only marginally better than telling an insomniac to get plenty of sleep. Your emotional makeup is a pretty deep-seated part of you, and very difficult to alter. No magic formula is being offered here as a sure-fire antidote to an uncontrolled emotional life. And of course, to control your emotions perfectly and completely is not much of an ideal to strive for. Besides being next to impossible to achieve, it should leave you rather mechanical and predictable, and perhaps not a little frightening to us lesser mortals.

But it *is* suggested that you first try to *identify* troublesome emotions—ones which pull you up or down dramatically at certain times. You'll know better than anyone which emotions these are. And they could be anything from sadness to joy; don't consider only anger or fear.

After you've identified them, the next step is to convince yourself of something. Convince yourself that, whatever other negative or positive consequences they have, these emotions, uncontrolled, will render you something less of a communicator than you really are *normally*, for the reason that they blunt your awareness of the nonverbal signals the other guy is constantly sending you. There may well be other reasons they hinder you as a communicator, but we're not concerned with them here; focus only on your ability to perceive others' nonverbal behaviour.

How do you go about convincing yourself? Catch yourself in the act! At every opportunity over the next few weeks or so, stop suddenly in the middle of one of your emotional binges (when the other guy is talking), and *count to ten*. Then observe the person you are interacting with as closely and calmly as you can. (Don't worry, you can still continue interacting all the while without his knowing it. Just recall how often you daydreamed through boring lectures without the teacher noticing!) Study his face. What's his voice like? What's he doing with his hands and feet? How is he sitting or standing? How close are you?

Next, try to think of the nonverbal information you have picked up from him over the past several minutes.

It's a pretty safe bet that your initial careful observations of your partner will yield all kinds of information you previously were not tuned in to very well, if at all. In fact, a common result is a startling, sudden awareness that you are seeing this person for the first time, that he has just popped into clear focus for you. The feeling is somewhat akin to the one you get when you are driving along the road, daydreaming to beat the band, and a swerving car suddenly snaps you alert. The whole field of view in front of you quickly becomes ultra-real and very much on your mind. You begin to *concentrate*, that's all.

So concentrate. Put the other person in the foreground. Take him out of the background. You'll be amazed at the number of things about him that just weren't getting through to you before. You'll be surprised, too, at how fuzzy your recollection is of the information from a few minutes back in the interaction. No wonder. You weren't paying much attention to it.

Perhaps this sounds like a rather difficult exercise to pull off successfully. It isn't. Try it and see. You may have some trouble remembering to give it a go at the appropriate time—but only if you aren't sincerely interested in the exercise to begin with. Keep it on your mind as often as you can, and you'll find yourself doing it spontaneously.

A marvellous habit to get into is to stop in *any* conversation (not just when you are in some kind of emotional state) and at *any* convenient point, and check out the other person carefully. If you do this often enough you'll start developing an entirely new way of seeing people that will eventually become habitual, so that you'll need fewer and fewer deliberate exercises to hone your sensitivity. After a while, much of your perceptual activity will become unconscious. Which it has to be if you want to be able to follow a conversation! Just try thinking about what your feet are doing as you descend a flight of stairs: you are very likely to trip yourself. So the goal of this exercise is not to get you thinking consciously about nonverbal, but to develop new habits of perception which, after a time, will slip into the lower levels of your consciousness.

OK, you say. So I convince myself that emotion reduces my sensitivity to others' nonverbal behaviour. But now what do I do about my emotions?

As much as you can. If you've achieved a little insight, you've now got to couple it with hard work. There are no magic formulae.

Sensitivity and Character Defects

A number of factors, here loosely termed "character defects," operate to dull and deaden our sensitivity to others' nonverbal behaviour. Because these are treated in one form or another in other parts of this book, they will receive only very brief treatment here. Advice and suggestions for coping with them are likewise found in the other chapters, and so the reader is urged to refer to them, and to make his own applications to the nonverbal area.

Selfishness.   What can be said about a person who simply is too involved with satisfying his own needs and desires to take other people into account? Sensitive to their nonverbal behaviour? Why should he be? Unless, of course, there is something in it for him. This person is not necessarily *incapable* of close and careful observation of others, he is just too busy worrying about himself. The effect is the same; the nonverbal information doesn't register.

Prejudice.   Prejudice puts blinders on you. What you see in another person is what you want or expect to see. So prejudice acts like some kind of malignant perceptual set.

We tend to think of prejudice mainly in terms of race these days. But this peculiar form of blindness hardly stops there. You can be prejudiced against a person because he is a Mormon, or a unionist, or rich, or an athlete.

Prejudice causes us to glide over, to misinterpret, to twist or to fail completely to see things about a person which don't square with our preconceived notions about him.

You can imagine what prejudice does to our nonverbal sensitivity.

SELFISHNESS!   PREJUDICE!   DISTRUST!

Distrust. Interaction is a process of giving and taking. Open, honest communication requires the participants to approach each other without fear of being taken advantage of, or hurt or threatened in some way. In short, open communication demands mutual trust.

Each of us knows, however, that interaction can sometimes have negative consequences, and that we *can* be hurt or threatened psychologically. So we defend ourselves by playing a wait-and-see game, withholding our trust of the other person until we are convinced it will be reciprocated. Some of us go through life always hiding behind our defensive wall, playing it safe. We grow extremely sensitive to the slightest sign of rebuff or rejection, and interaction becomes not an occasion for freely giving and taking, but an ordeal characterized by maneuvering, withholding, second-guessing, and excessively mannered small talk. On occasions, distrust takes the quite different form of senseless and cruel aggression—subtle or otherwise—coupled with an elaborately constructed imperviousness to any counter aggression that is mounted against it. Attempts to penetrate this rock-hard defence by kindness or offers of trust are likewise turned away.

Emotion, selfishness, prejudice and distrust have in common the effect of dulling our nonverbal sensitivity. In each case we become extraordinarily wrapped up and concerned with ourselves, our own viewpoint, and our own needs and desires. We are not ready or willing to approach and take, and so we don't ever get close enough to see others clearly.

Sensitivity and Perceptual Habits

As we noted at the beginning of this chapter, one reason many of us don't make much progress in developing our nonverbal skills is that we never really stop to think about the process of communication at all. It's just something we do. Our skills are acquired and practised out-of-awareness, so we never set ourselves specific goals and objectives calculated to effect improvement.

Another reason is that our nonverbal skills, such as they are, becomes hardened into habits over time, and thus become very resistant to change, even if we want to change them. In this section, let's take a look at a few nonverbal habits which are faulty, and which impair our overall performance as a communicator. Identifying a bad habit is the first step in overcoming it. Once one is aware of a problem, he is ready to take further steps in the direction of change.

Face-struck. You don't have to be told that the face is a crucial source of information about another person. That's why you watch it so much, and assign so much weight to its messages. But keep one thing in mind: the other person *knows* you monitor his face constantly, and he *knows* you put a great deal of stock in what you see there!

Inevitably, therefore, people use their faces to simulate information, to show you what you want or expect to see. They also control their faces to conceal things from you.

Erving Goffman's *Interaction Ritual* contains a marvellous essay which explains how a person's very self is bound up with his face, and the elaborate "facework" he will perform during interaction to maintain a certain image of himself. It's not a Machiavellian thing at all, though. We routinely exercise a great deal of control over our faces, not because we are deceivers and liars, but because the ritual of interaction *demands* we control them—for our own good, and also for the good of others. Pride, honor, dignity, self-respect and consideration are characteristics others expect you to possess (as you do them), and we give evidence of them, says Goffman, in sometimes artificial ways during interaction. A major component of our image as a reliable interactant is our face and body image, and so we manipulate them in accordance with the ritual demands of the situation.

You are most strongly urged to read and study this essay of Goffman's.

The point being made here is a simple one: as important as the face is, do not become "face-struck" and rely on it to the exclusion or neglect of the rest of the body media. People control their faces, but put much less effort into controlling their bodies, for the very good reasons that they are less visible and far less watched.* So watch them! Though the body is capable of providing far fewer messages, and these messages are generally less precise and clear, they are generally more *reliable*, and thus can provide a vital check on facial information.

Smile-struck.   The smile is a super-potent stimulus. We like them.** They turn us on

*See Paul Ekman and Wallace Friesen, "Non-verbal leakage and clues to deception," *Psychiatry*, February 1969, 32 (1), 88-105.

**Of course, there are smiles and there are smiles. We're speaking here of friendly smiles, not silly grins, sick or sarcastic smiles, smirks, etc.

since they tell us—the smilee—that the smiler is friendly towards us. Flattering, eh?

Smiles can cover multitudes of sins, as it were, because once smile-struck, brother, you're on *his* side! Smiles can turn your head —which puts you in a poor position indeed to observe his nonverbal behaviour.

What Isn't There.   This section would run for pages and pages if length were proportionate to the importance of the topic. Fortunately the point can be made in a much shorter space.

Have you got into the habit of watching only what people *do*? Are you sensitive to what people *don't do* during interaction? Sensitive to behaviours they would normally be expected to perform, but do not? Omitted behaviours can be clues that some sort of deception is going on, or simply that the person, for any number of reasons, is self-conscious.

You may notice that he seems "frozen" and that the rate of one or more of his behaviours —facial expressions, eye, hand and feet motions, etc.—drops off drastically. Or you may notice a sizeable increase in behaviours in one part of the body—say the hands—while in the other parts there is hardly any activity at all. Sometimes, of course, the behaviours you do see lose their usual smoothness and

EACH PERSON'S BEHAVIOURAL REPERTOIRE IS UNIQUE

appear somewhat clumsy, forced or mechanical-looking, or hurried and nervous-looking. These latter differences are rather easy to spot.

It takes imagination and a fair amount of deliberate practice to "fill-in" missing behaviours when the pattern is not too different from normal. We find this relatively easier to do when we know the other person well. With close friends, for example, very subtle omissions (or changes) may leap out at us, whereas a stranger would see nothing unusual. This is partly because each person's behavioural repertoire is to some extent unique, and known only to his closest associates. The real trick is to sensitize yourself to the subtleties of the behaviour patterns which are distributed fairly commonly across a population of people. When you are able to read strangers with half the accuracy that you can read your friends, then you will be getting somewhere!

As you build up hours of experience in careful, concentrated "people watching" sessions, you will become attuned to the shape of these common behaviour patterns, and discover yourself acquiring a fair degree of skill in seeing what isn't there.

PART II.   IMPROVING YOUR SENSITIVITY TO YOUR OWN NONVERBAL BEHAVIOUR

Résumé: The factors of ignorance, emotion, character defects and faulty habits of perception all bear on the issue of improving your sensitivity to your own nonverbal behaviour. But there is a further, more important factor: the lack or mis-use of feedback, both internal and external, on your behaviour. This factor will be examined below.

Oh wad some power the giftie gie us
To see oursels as others see us!
                                        Robert Burns

There is nothing very complicated about the notion of feedback. Feedback is information which informs us about our behaviour. It can originate with us (internal feedback) or come to us from beyond ourselves (external feedback). You totally depend upon feedback to keep yourself informed about your behaviour. There is nothing more important for your success in face-to-face interaction than a steady, accurate flow of feedback informing you of what you are doing, and how others are perceiving what you are doing.

Internal Feedback

Internal feedback mechanisms are constantly monitoring the functioning of your body and reporting back to it, and sometimes to your conscious mind, "how you're getting along," in order that your body can regulate and maintain itself. Your muscles, organs and nervous system are all cared for in this way, even though you are totally unaware of much of this activity going on within you. Sometimes, of course, you *can* tune in, as when you feel some internal pain.

Our external senses of sight, hearing and so on are two-way feedback mechanisms, in that you use them to monitor yourself and to gather information about yourself from sources beyond you. As you sit, or walk, or eat—or perform any bodily activity—your feedback mechanisms supply your nervous system with millions of pieces of information. Just step into a pothole unexpectedly, or miss the seat of your chair, or plug your ears tightly when you speak—and you'll quickly discover just how important these mechanisms are in regulating your behaviour. You'll suddenly find you can't do anything without them. Your foot needs 'information' from the ground in order to walk, your rear-end needs 'information' from the seat of the chair to sit down, and you have to hear yourself in order to speak. What we will be considering in this second part of the chapter are the kinds and quality of information you need in order to interact successfully face-to-face.

Earlier it was suggested that you could improve your sensitivity to others' nonverbal behaviour by deliberately pausing during conversation and focusing your attention carefully on one or more body parts. Isolate and focus. Screen out competing informa-

FREEZE, AND ANALYZE YOUR POSTURE

tion. Exactly the same advice is offered here again, only make your own body the subject of your observations. It may sound ridiculously simple, but this exercise in self-monitoring can yield you a great deal of insight into yourself which can significantly alter your approach to the interactions you have with others.

Monitor your behaviour in as many different kinds of situations as possible, and as often as you can. Monitor yourself when you are alone too. Freeze, and analyze your posture, where your hands and feet are, and the expression on your face. You don't have to spend long hours doing this. A few seconds or minutes of reflection each time will do. Ask yourself—always—what impressions are likely being formed of you on the basis of how you look and act. Or, if you are alone—what impressions *would* your appearance and behaviour likely elicit.

If you perform this exercise sufficiently often, over a period of time you should notice some shift in your self image. You should have a clearer idea of how you look to other people, the way you normally hold and move your body, and your characteristic range of facial expressions. You will have gotten "out of your skin," and put that distance between your mind and body that allows you the perspective to see your body more objectively.

Something like looking into a mirror, except that a mirror reflects only what you wish it to because you *set yourself* to look into a mirror. But have you ever walked past a mirror and *unexpectedly* caught a glimpse of yourself? That's more the person that others see, and that's something like the view of yourself this exercise is designed to give you. But you have to "catch yourself in the act"; don't dispose your face and body "appropriately," *then* start your analysis. That would be like looking in a mirror, and it's cheating!

Do you think you already know all about your own image? Well, perhaps you do, and if so, you've probably seen yourself on television over and over again, in countless and different kinds of situations. Otherwise, you are a rare bird indeed. The fact is, as Robert Burns knew well, the vast majority of us do *not* have "the giftie" to "see ourselves as other see us." And the damnable shame about it is that they aren't telling!

External Feedback

That last sentence is not quite accurate. People *do* provide us with a lot of feedback about ourselves, but rarely in so many words; their feedback on our nonverbal behaviour is itself mainly nonverbal. And the rules of the ritual of interaction are such that a sizeable proportion of this feedback is polite drivel. If you could find out what people say behind your back, you'd have something! And there is a further problem: when valuable feedback *does* come our way, we have a maddening tendency to discount it, ignore it, or rationalize it out of existence. You are referred to other chapters for a rundown on all the crazy things we do to protect that ideal image we have of ourselves, no matter how badly out of whack with reality it really is. A final stumbling block is simply our lack of sensitivity: we don't recognize feedback for what it is—or, we just don't see it at all.

Not a very rosy picture, is it? Here are some suggestions for increasing the amount and quality of feedback on your nonverbal behaviour. You probably won't be able to try them all, but if you can, so much the better.

1. Get yourself videotaped interacting with other people in as many different kinds of situations as possible. Tape yourself giving a speech, conducting a seminar, participating in a group discussion, acting in a play—

whatever. Deliberately try to get lots of footage of yourself "letting go" emotionally—and not just one or two emotions either, but the whole range from happiness to sadness. There is absolutely no better way to put yourself in other people's shoes, and to gain a comprehensive, objective view of yourself than television. Take these tapes and watch them till you can anticipate every word and every action. If possible, have the cameraman zoom in on different parts of your body. Television is the closest thing to Burns' "giftie" we have. If you have access to the equipment, using it in this manner will yield you mountains of feedback you simply can't get in any other way.

2. Ask every person you think will go along with it to fill out the "Personality Perception Test" on page 96. They are to put a single "X" in one of the seven spaces, making sure to mark all the scales, or adjective pairings. They mark the number 3 spot (left) if they feel you, for example, are *extremely* energetic; the number 2 spot if they feel you are *fairly* energetic; the number 1 spot if they feel you are *moderately* energetic; the 0 spot if they feel you are neither energetic nor lazy, but sort of in-between; *or* if they cannot truly make up their minds about it. (But insist that they give you their *first* impression, and work quickly, but not sloppily; this goes for all the scales they complete.) If *moderately* lazy, a 1 on the other side of the scale; if *fairly* lazy, a number 2 mark; and finally, a number 3 mark if they feel you are *extremely* lazy. What do you do with these scales once you get them back? Well, you can perform all kinds of fancy analyses, and if you want to, go ahead. All you really need to do is go over each one carefully with your eyeballs, and when you're finished, you should have—well—a heck of a lot of feedback on yourself that you never had before, in quite this form anyway.

If possible, ask all the people to "do" you again a month or so afterwards, and compare the results. Pay particular attention both times to those people who know you well.

3. Ask every friend you have to tell you what they like about your appearance and the way you use your face and body during interaction, and what they don't like. Get them to explain themselves. *Listen!!*

4. When you're talking, pay particular attention to the other person's eyes and voice qualities. The eyes and voice are the richest source of feedback of all the nonverbal media.

5. A person's attitudes are also reflected eloquently in his posture and in the conversational distance he prefers. He usually doesn't manipulate these aspects of his behaviour deliberately, so they provide feedback for you that is fairly reliable.

6. Take every opportunity that comes along to meet new people and to involve yourself in new kinds of activities. If you are always interacting with the same people, and follow the same old routine, how are you going to learn about other facets of your personality? You need the stimulation of novel situations to discover and develop yourself. So take the trouble to find out how you can cope in circumstances different from the ones that are familiar and easy for you. In short, get some experience. There are things about yourself you'll never find out about otherwise.

7. When negative feedback *is* laid on you, try to resist that powerful temptation to dismiss it out of hand, or to rationalize it away. It's tough; but you can't go through life clinging to your own, subjective image of yourself. Chances are that negative feedback will be closer to the truth than nine-tenths of the positive feedback you so eagerly swallow.

8. Pay attention to the adaptors other people perform. Sometimes their attitudes to you are disguised and hidden in these seemingly random behaviours. They can therefore be a valuable source of feedback for you of a kind you're not likely to get in a verbalized form.

Summary

Paradoxically, there are many people in this world who are more sensitive to other's nonverbal behaviour than they are to their own. Oh, we all form a very comprehensive and clear picture in our minds of what we are like, but just how accurate that picture is, is another matter. For quite understandable human reasons, we suffer from a strong tendency to tune out the more objective evaluations others provide us whenever this external feedback threatens to force us to revise our precious self-images. So we seem to develop certain blind spots, certain gaps in our self-knowledge, into which the truth seeps very slowly indeed.

The second part of this chapter suggests you try to open up these blind spots by embarking on a deliberate program calculated to increase the quantity and quality of the flow of external feedback. It also suggests that our inadequate self-images derive in part from our general lack of sensitivity to internal feedback—information generated by our own bodies. Accordingly, you were advised to apply the techniques of observation and analysis, discussed in the first part of this chapter, to your own nonverbal behaviour as it can be perceived directly by you.

	3	2	1	0	1	2	3	
Nervous	__	__	__	__	__	__	__	Relaxed
Dynamic	__	__	__	__	__	__	__	Sluggish
Trustworthy	__	__	__	__	__	__	__	Untrustworthy
Skinny	__	__	__	__	__	__	__	Fat
Unattractive	__	__	__	__	__	__	__	Attractive
Passive	__	__	__	__	__	__	__	Active
Careful	__	__	__	__	__	__	__	Careless
Confident	__	__	__	__	__	__	__	Unsure of self
Feminine	__	__	__	__	__	__	__	Masculine
Introverted	__	__	__	__	__	__	__	Extroverted
Tight	__	__	__	__	__	__	__	Loose
Self-respecting	__	__	__	__	__	__	__	Servile
Warm	__	__	__	__	__	__	__	Cold
Neat	__	__	__	__	__	__	__	Sloppy
Insincere	__	__	__	__	__	__	__	Sincere
Strong-willed	__	__	__	__	__	__	__	Weak-willed
Interesting	__	__	__	__	__	__	__	Uninteresting
Emotional	__	__	__	__	__	__	__	Unemotional
Sophisticated	__	__	__	__	__	__	__	Naive
Jovial	__	__	__	__	__	__	__	Morose

Unenthusiastic	__:__:__:__:__:__:__	Enthusiastic
	3 2 1 0 1 2 3	
Graceful	__:__:__:__:__:__:__	Clumsy
	3 2 1 0 1 2 3	
Mature	__:__:__:__:__:__:__	Immature
	3 2 1 0 1 2 3	
Boorish	__:__:__:__:__:__:__	Polite
	3 2 1 0 1 2 3	
Conventional	__:__:__:__:__:__:__	Unconventional
	3 2 1 0 1 2 3	

7

THE PSYCHOLOGICAL STRUCTURE OF INTERPERSONAL COMMUNICATION

Carl J. Hartleib

Each person is born a unique individual with his own innate capabilities, limitations, and potentials, which create his range of endeavour. Within this range, he may become a significant, thinking, feeling, aware and creatively expressive person and respond to his environment genuinely. He has, so to speak, a clean internal slate upon which he will write his personal identity as he learns it; for all his behaviour will be learned via his experiences in life.

How does a person develop his personal identity or psychological positions around himself and others?

From his learnings, what is written upon his internal slate? How is this identity reflected or communicated to himself and others?

I will attempt to offer the reader a psychological framework to view conceptually both personality development factors and an ego-state personality structure which results in an innovative mode of analyzing an interpersonal communication system. Most of the concepts of personality development factors and the ego-state personality structure presented here are drawn from Dr. Eric Berne's work on Transactional Analysis, and we gratefully acknowledge this theory.

A FRAMEWORK OF HUMAN DEVELOPMENT

As a person, you the reader have taken psychological positions around yourself and others with which you were not born, but through your experiences have learned. Let us complete a simple exercise to illustrate to you some of your psychological positions.

Exercise:

Draw on a piece of paper, a continuum such as below:

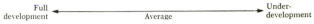

Full development ← Average → Under-development

Now rate yourself by inserting an "X" somewhere along the continuum, judging from how you feel about yourself under the following characteristics:
- (a) How do you feel about yourself?
- (b) How do you feel about what you have accomplished in your life?
- (c) How do you feel about your interpersonal relationships?
- (d) How do you feel about your career development?

YOUR "X"ES HAVE FALLEN PREDOMINANTLY TO THE RIGHT OF THE AVERAGE

FULL DEVELOPMENT   AVERAGE   UNDER-DEVELOPMENT

(e) How do you feel about your educational achievements?

(f) How do you feel about your family life and relationships?

(g) How do you feel about your masculinity or femininity?

(h) How do you feel about your money-making potential?

(i) How do you feel about the use of your time?

(j) How do you feel about your athletic prowess?

(k) How do you feel about your sexual relationships?

(l) How do you feel about your body physically?

(m) How do you feel about your mental capacities?

(n) How do you feel about the development of your talents?

If you have answered these questions honestly you will see that your "X"es have fallen predominantly to the left or to the right of the average, and that there is a definite pattern manifested in how you feel about your self-development. Perhaps you feel very good about yourself and the majority of your "X"es were towards the fully-developed end of the continuum. Perhaps, due to your circumstances, you feel very much underdeveloped in the majority of items, and you find your "X"es forming a pattern towards that end. Regardless of the particular pattern you developed, it is important to note that you do have psychological positions that you have adopted. Not only have you adopted these positions but, more important, you act them out in your daily behaviour and communications patterns with yourself and others.

OVERVIEW OF PERSONALITY DEVELOPMENT

Birth ——————▶ life experiences ——————▶ life decisions ——————▶

psychological positions ——————▶

reinforcing behaviour and communication pattern

The diagram above illustrates a psychological overview to help in understanding one's developing personality structure, and the psychological positions people have learned to adopt via their experiences.

Everyone is born void of human behaviour characteristics, but as the child grows, he develops a concept of his own worth and the worth of others. As he interacts with his environment, he makes decisions about what life means to him and he commits himself to acting in certain ways, which become part of his character. Let me illustrate the above principle with a few examples.

Emotionally, if through infancy and childhood a person is frequently neglected and not loved, and even rejected, he will begin to develop a position that he is unloveable. This position in later life will be reflected in how he feels about himself and how he transmits this to others via his communication process. He just feels that he can't be loved and therefore reflects this in his actions and love relationships, if indeed any develop.

Intellectually, if a child is ridiculed and frequently called stupid and dumb, he will decide eventually that he is unintelligent and begin to act out this role. When he goes to school he may fail, because he has decided he has limited capacities to demonstrate.

The above-mentioned behaviours will, in both cases, reinforce the original psychological position (unloved and stupid) adopted by the child from his early life experiences.

Dr. Eric Berne, in his Transactional Analysis theory, has developed four basic positions that a person can take around himself and others. For our purposes we will adapt and modify the four position concept to increase our understanding of life positions and resulting communication. It is not the scope of this chapter to explain Berne's views of psychology, but more to utilize concepts developed in Transactional Analysis to increase our understanding of psychological communication.

When taking positions about themselves, people may conclude:

—No matter what I try, nothing works out!
  or
—I do many things right.

—I don't deserve to have anything or anyone!
  or
—I'm as good as anybody else.

FOUR BASIC LIFE POSITIONS — O.K.?

—I need help to think this out.
   or
—I can solve my own problems very well.

—I'm a bum!
   or
—I'm O.K.

—I'll never do anything good enough!
   or
—I can do whatever I decide to do.

When taking positions about others, a person may conclude:
—Don't trust anyone!
   or
—People are basically honest.

—People are out to get me!
   or
—People are very helpful.

—People just don't give a damn!
   or
—People are terrific!

The above statements reflect a generalized position that these people have taken in regard to themselves and others, and all communication about yourself and others can be summarized into the following four basic life positions. These are described for our purposes primarily, and not as a full description of life positions developed by Dr. Eric Berne, whose concept we are adopting.

First Position—I'm O.K.—You're O.K.
   This is a mentally healthy position; the person taking this position feels worthwhile and constructive and his expectations about himself will be valid. He cares for people and sees the significance of each individual. He will form interpersonal relationships well and live a productive, creative life.

Second Position—I'm O.K.—You're Not O.K.
   This person feels victimized and often persecuted by others. He blames others for his miseries and often projects and strikes out at people from his paranoid position.

Third Position—I'm Not O.K.—You're O.K.
   This person feels powerless and inadequate and often withdraws to experience depression and sadness. He introjects his failures and feels inferior when compared to others.

Fourth Position—I'm Not O.K.—You're Not O.K.
   This person is unhealthy and has lost interest in life and people, and often exhibits schizoid behaviour.

Consider the four psychological positions described and do as many positions as you can by completing the chart on page 102. One descriptive word has been given in each case as an example.

So, as an individual, you have learned via your family, subculture and social culture the psychological positions you hold about yourself and people. With this realization, consider the ways that these positions must be reflected in your communication with others.

Exercise:
What verbal and nonverbal messages do you

	1. I'm O.K.— You're O.K.	2. I'm O.K.— You're Not O.K.	3. I'm Not O.K.— You're O.K.	4. I'm Not O.K.— You're Not O.K.
Adjectives that describe person	Aware	Critical	Insecure	Disoriented
Verbs that describe person's actions	Expressing	Initiating	Following	Hallucinating
Feelings most likely to have	Happiness	Superior	Unworthy	Depressed
Approach to handling relationships (conflict, love, etc.)	Cooperative	Dominating	Passively	Inconsistently
Ways of giving	Freely	Reluctantly	Adoringly	Desperately
Ways of receiving	Gratefully	Patronizingly	Undeservedly	Mistrustingly

send about yourself? Try to fill in some descriptive messages on each of the following topics:

Topic	Messages sent
Your worth	_____
Your looks	_____
Your abilities	_____
Your intelligence	_____
Your morals	_____
Your health	_____
Your sexuality	_____
Your future	_____

Summary

1. People learn and develop psychological positions about themselves and others.
2. These positions take a definite form— I'm O.K., etc.
3. These psychological attitudes are reflected in one's communication pattern.

A PSYCHOLOGICAL STRUCTURE OF COMMUNICATION

To help us understand the communication process in human beings, we will present a structure of human ego states in which a person thinks, feels and acts. The three ego states, for our purposes of communication, have been labelled Emotional, Rational, and Societal. These ego states are distinct sources of functional behaviour; that is to say, when one is crying or laughing, or expressing feelings in some way, he is coming from his *emotional* ego state. When one is dealing with decision making, he is coming from his *rational* ego state, and when one is obeying the law and stopping at a red light, he is coming from his *societal* ego state. These three ego states form the structure of a personality and the sources of communication with oneself and with others. The state of being in

STRUCTURE OF A PERSON'S EGO STATES

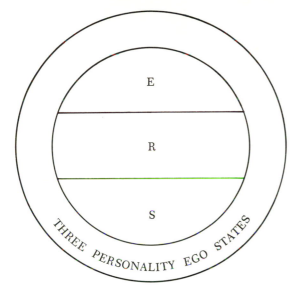

Emotional Ego State   (E)
(learned expressions of feel-
ings and natural impulses)

Rational Ego State   (R)
(objective computing of in-
formation towards decision
making)

Societal Ego State   (S)
(attitudes, norms of behaviour
learned from external sources
of authority expressed in a
parenting style)

which one finds oneself dictates what ego state it is most appropriate to activate and utilize, to result in appropriate behaviour and communication patterns.

FUNCTION AND DESCRIPTION OF EGO STATES

A person can sense his real self in any of his ego states, and it is useful to think of each ego state as having boundaries and different functions. One's psychic energy flows from one ego state to another, depending on the function that is required of one's thinking. A healthy development requires the inclusion of all three ego states and the proportionately equal development of all three ego states so that one ego state is not operating exclusively. There is a harmony between all ego states and the person is in touch with all three ego states when the need arises. We draw upon the skills and experiences that are in each of our different ego states.

EMOTIONAL EGO STATE

When one is operating from the emotional ego state, whether he is acting, thinking, feeling, or communicating, he is doing so as he has learned, primarily from childhood. Our early childlike natural impulses have developed into emotional learnings which are expressed in a fashion or style which was adopted in childhood but are now adapted to reflect adult behaviour as much as possible.

The emotional ego state is affectionate, impulsive, sensuous, curious, angry, fearful, self-indulgent, rebellious, aggressive, intuitive, creative, manipulative, hurting, playful, etc. These are natural impulses that stem back into childhood and if there were no restrictions, the child would act out spontaneously and freely. Strong basic drives related to physical survival are centred in the emotional ego state. Uncensored, one reacts in a natural fashion, emotionally, but the expression of that natural reaction is learned and expressed in appropriate ways. Everyone had within himself, at one time, a natural freeness and spontaneity in expressions of emotions and feelings to which one can return when he is uninhibited and natural.

SOCIETAL EGO STATE

When one is operating from the societal ego state his actions contain the attitudes and behaviour incorporated from external authority sources. External authority sources are parents and significant others, such as

EGO STATES

teachers, priests, policemen, etc. Through these sources, the individual learns what society regards as right and wrong, and inwardly this is known as one's conscience. The societal rules, ethics, laws, and morals, the "should's" and the "should not's" of expected behaviour are all bound up in the societal ego state,

Parents are the main figures in developing the societal ego state, for they establish an emotional climate in which you learn to copy their behaviour.

The outward expression of the societal ego state can be influenced in two directions by the parent—towards a nurturing, or towards a prejudicial or critical societal ego state. A nurturing societal ego state develops in people whose parents were sympathetic, protective and nurturing most of the time. A prejudicial or critical societal ego state develops where the parents' opinions about religion, politics, sex, life styles, proper dress and speech may often be irrational and erroneous, and set standards of behaviour not based on facts. These standards are imposed by the parents for the children to learn and imitate in a style that comes from criticism and judgments. A fully developed societal ego state has a mixture of both nurturing and critical expression.

RATIONAL EGO STATE

When one is operating from his rational ego state, one is dealing with reality and the objective gathering of information. The rational ego state is organized, adaptable, intelligent, and is the computer of a person's thinking. The decision-making process is the main function of the rational ego state by virtue of collecting, evaluating, estimating, studying, and objectively appraising all realities that can be perceived by the individual. The rational ego state can be seen as the executive of the personality in that a person learns to receive more and more data from the objective world and is not trapped by his conscience (societal ego state) or his feelings (emotional ego state), but considers both before he decides. Making a conscious choice involves shifting from one ego state to another so that one's feelings and societal messages are taken into consideration with all other objective data.

Exercise:
Identify each verbal reaction to the situation given as either emotional, rational, or societal. Because you cannot see gestures or other nonverbal language, nor can you hear the intonation, your answers will be educated guesses.

1. An 18-year-old, celebrating his birthday by having a few drinks, has a few too many and gets sick.
   (a) "Isn't that disgusting!"
   (b) "They never should have lowered the drinking-age."
   (c) "Most people need to learn through their experiences what their drinking capacity is. He'll learn too; just give him a chance."

2. A very well-proportioned girl wears a scant bikini on the beach.
   (a) "There ought to be a law against that sort of dress!"
   (b) "She is certainly getting an overall tan."
   (c) "Woo-eee!"

3. A foursome at a resort, having dinner in the classy dining room, are making no attempt to subdue their gaiety and laughter.
   (a) "I wonder if they met here?"
   (b) "Look at those people—behaving like children! You'd think this was their own private dining room!"
   (c) "How come we never have any fun like that?"

4. A husband arrives home two hours late for a formal dinner party.
   (a) "Thanks a lot for being here when I needed you!"
   (b) "Your company just shouldn't expect you to work such long hours."
   (c) "Is everything O.K. at the office?"

5. A husband arrives home, hot and exhausted, after a long day at work, goes to fix his favourite drink, but there is no mix.
   (a) "You should have a more efficient method of preparing your shopping list."
   (b) "Let's send Bobbie to the store for a few cans of Pepsi."
   (c) "For crying out loud can't you even buy groceries when we need them!"

6. A promotion is given to an employee with an obvious lack of experience and knowledge.
   (a) "Perhaps he'll do a better job than anyone would expect if we give him the opportunity and our support."
   (b) "There's no way I'm taking orders from that jerk!"
   (c) "This company shouldn't have given a promotion to an inexperienced person."

7. An order clerk has ordered an insufficient quantity of an item urgently needed.
   (a) "Phone the supplier and explain that there was an error in our order and see if he can rush the remainder to us."
   (b) "Oh that's just great! Well you can go tell the Sales Department you goofed up their order!"
   (c) "I knew I should have checked your work."

8. A typewriter is broken again.
   (a) "My typewriter is broken. Could I use this one until the repairman gets here?"
   (b) "Oh this stupid typewriter is good for nothing!"
   (c) "We shouldn't have to suffer these breakdowns all the time. I'm going to tell the company we'll buy from a competitor if they can't fix it once and for all this time."

(See page 111 for the answer key to this exercise.)

EGO PORTRAITS

The development of your ego portrait is related directly to your past experience, but your present portrait can be changed as you become more aware of your ego states. Perhaps at this point we could examine a healthy ego portrait.

HEALTHY EGO PORTRAIT

1. Each ego state is of equal size.
2. The flow of psychic energy between ego states is fluid and not biased or blocked.

BIASED EGO PORTRAITS

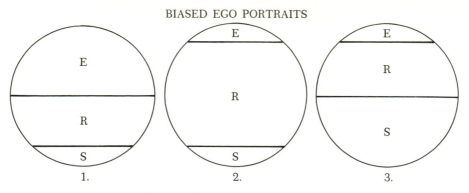

1.   2.   3.

The first biased ego portrait shows a large emotional ego state which depicts a person who lives too much in his feelings and acts impulsively and overemotionally.

The small societal ego state indicates poor development of restrictive controls and conscience.

The second biased ego portrait shows that a large rational ego state has developed, with this person being mainly a decision maker, indicating that he lives in his head too much and does not have access to his emotions or societal norms.

This person probably could not develop good interpersonal relationships.

The third biased ego portrait shows a large societal ego state which indicates a person who has developed a super-conscience and is very much controlled internally, being very restrictive, moralistic and prejudicial.

He would be unable to make proper decisions or express his feelings without internal conflict with his rules and regulations.

The above portraits would indicate that an overdeveloped ego state would lead to an unbalanced personality. With a biased ego portrait the person's ability to communicate would be limited in those ego states which were not fully developed. His conversations with individuals would be greatly influenced by his tendency to move into his overdeveloped ego state. With accessibility to all ego

BIASED   EGO   PEOPLE

states of equal development, the individual could draw upon those human resources necessary to meet the circumstances in which he found himself. He would be more free to respond to others who might be drawing upon any of his three ego states at the time.

Exercises on Ego Portraits:
Draw your ego portrait in the following different circumstances and indicate the types of conversations that would likely occur in each circumstance. Illustrate which ego state would be predominant: which of "E," "R," or "S" would be graphically larger in each circumstance.
(a) A swinging party with many good friends.
(b) A serious discussion with one's supervisor concerning one's demotion.
(c) Playing naturally with your small two-year-old son.
(d) Discussing a decision on which automobile to buy.
(e) Having received too much change from a cashier.

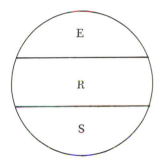

Summary
1. A person's thoughts and actions are drawn from his three ego states:
   (a) Emotional (feelings)
   (b) Rational (decisions)
   (c) Societal (attitudes)
2. Access to all three ego states is necessary for a healthy personality.
3. The skills, knowledge and function of each ego state are different, but proportionate combinations in a healthy personality result in effective living.

EXAMINING DYADIC TRANSACTIONS

If we are to think of individuals in terms of ego portraits it becomes clear that the sources of communication would be between the ego states of conversing individuals. When one person sends a message from one of his ego states to another person, he expects a response from one of their ego states. These are interpersonal transactions occurring between one or more ego states of one person and one or more ego states of another. For our purposes all transactions can be classified as:
(a) predictable,
(b) unpredicted,
(c) double.
To fully understand a message both the sender and the receiver must take into consideration both the verbal and nonverbal aspects. Gestures, facial expressions, body posture and tone of voice all contribute to the meaning of transactions.

Thus, by conceptualizing a communication process in ego-state terms, one is able to understand another person's meaning more easily. Let us increase our awareness by examining the three types of transactions.

PREDICTABLE TRANSACTIONS

Have you ever observed two people talking to each other on the same wave length? The lines of communication are open and flowing between the sender and the responder, whose positions alternate. In thise case predictable transactions are occurring in that the initiator, via one of his ego states, sends a message to which the responder responds in a predictable way from his expected ego state. For example:

1. "Do you know what time it is?"
2. "It is 7:30."
In this case a message from the rational ego state of the initiator was responded to via the rational ego state of the responder, which was the expected response. In all predictable transactions the response expected comes from the anticipated appropriate ego state. For example, the same initial question "Do

PREDICTABLE TRANSACTIONS

you know what time it is?" asked with a very worried and harried look and gesture would be diagramed as follows:

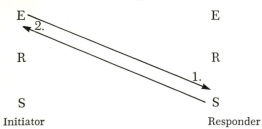

Initiator   Responder

1. "Do you know what time it is?"
2. "Now don't you worry, it's only 7:30."

In the above example the initiator's emotional ego state was responded to via the responder's societal ego state in a nurturing, sympathetic, parenting style which was predicted and needed by the initiator. These transactions are smooth and uncomplicated and flow between the expected ego states of the two people involved.

UNPREDICTED RESPONSES

Unpredicted responses are a frequent source of pain and resentment between people. Unpredicted transactions occur when-

ever the initiator experiences an unpredicted response from the responder. That is, the initiator activates an unexpected or unpredicted ego state in the responder, which catches him by surprise and more often leaves him feeling confused or hurt or puzzled by what has just occurred between them. For example:

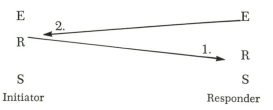

Initiator   Responder

1. "Hey, Mary, do you know where my keys are?"
2. (Sarcastically) "Did you ever think to look where you left them? I'm tired of waiting on you!"

In thise case the sender was looking for some information from the rational ego state, but unexpectedly activated some feelings and received an unpredicted emotional ego state response. At this point an unpredicted transaction has occurred and the initiator has the choice of responding to the emotional ego state of the responder or terminating the transaction.

Another example:

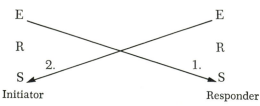

Initiator   Responder

1. "Mary, can you please help me find my keys; I'm tired of looking for them."
2. "I'm just as tired as you—I've been looking after the kids all day!"

In this case the initiator was expecting a response of a nurturing, helpful nature from the societal ego state of the responder. However, the responder unexpectedly responded from her emotional ego state which switched the conversation in another direction, to which the initiator may choose to respond or not. Unexpected transactions usually can become expected transactions if both people

AN UNPREDICTED RESPONSE

take care in responding in expected or needed ways which are usually identifiable.

DOUBLE TRANSACTIONS

Double transactions occur when the initiator sends a double message that could initiate a response from one of two ego states. On the surface it appears that a rational-to-rational ego state exchange could occur, but the message also holds a hidden meaning which could hook the emotional or societal ego state of the responder. These double messages are usually disguised in socially acceptable ways, and the responder has the choice, if he is aware of the double message, of responding to the one that appeals to him. Quite often the initiator and the responder are quite aware of the double messages, even though others may not be. For example:

1. (With a smile), "Hey, Mary, do you think you'll be able to come over to my

place tonight and help me with my assignment?"
2. "Sure, Harry, I enjoyed helping you last time."

In the above case, the initiator and responder are both aware of the double message transaction. On the surface it would appear the initiator is asking for some information and that that information is provided; a straight rational-to-rational transaction. However, the hidden meaning is one in which Harry is asking Mary to come to his place for other reasons, and Mary is responding to those reasons quite cheerfully.

In other cases, the initiator may be attempting to trap the responder into a response by sending a double message which the responder could deal with from one of two ego states. For example:

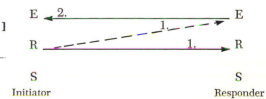

1. A saleswoman says to her customer with a sneer, "This is our finest blouse,

A DOUBLE TRANSACTION

but it is probably too expensive for you."

2. "It certainly isn't too expensive for me! I'll take it!"

In this example, the saleswoman is presenting information, but her ulterior motive is to hook an emotional response of pride from her customer. The customer reacts to the hidden message and responds from her emotional ego state to show that the saleswoman is wrong, and that she *can* afford this blouse.

Exercise:

Diagram the following transactions using the ego state diagram. Name the type of transaction.

E		E
R		R
S		S
Initiator		Responder

Example A
1. BOSS: "What time is my next appointment?"

2. SECRETARY: "Your next appointment is at 2:15."

Example B
1. DICK: "Let's have another drink and have some fun, Mary."
2. MARY: "We have a decision to make Dick, can't you ever be serious?"

Example C
1. SUPERVISOR: "Be at your desk promptly at 8:30."
2. EMPLOYEE: "Yes sir, I'll be very prompt from now on."

Example D
1. MAN: "As a woman, do you think you could understand this communication process?"
2. WOMAN: "Whether I'm a woman or not doesn't impede my understanding of this communication process."

Example E
1. TEACHER: "Do you have your assignment ready, Miss Smith?"
2. MISS SMITH: "If you taught us the way you're supposed to, I would have another week for this assignment."

Example F
1. WOMAN: "You'd never catch a 'man' crying in this situation!"
2. MAN: (Wiping his tears) "You're right, I'm acting foolishly."

(See page 111 for the answer key to these examples.)

SUMMARY

Towards an Authentic Communication Style

I have attempted, in this chapter, to give the reader an opportunity to view interpersonal communication within a particular psychological framework. Three major concepts which the reader should comprehend in this endeavour would be:

(a) to realize that people adopt phychological positions around their identity which greatly influence their style of personal communication;

(b) that within the concepts developed in this chapter, one can view a functioning personality via an ego state structure, and that the understanding of this ego state structure allows the reader to better comprehend himself and others and the resulting interpersonal communication system; and

(c) to allow the reader a system for analyzing the communication transactions between two people in order to increase the flow and harmony of these transactions.

If the reader, through this chapter, has developed more acute awareness of his psychological functioning in his communication process, he has increased his ability to listen to the messages of his own body and of other people. An aware person knows what is happening now in his interpersonal communication with others. He is more in touch with his inner world via his emotional, rational, and societal ego states and makes genuine contact with other persons by demonstrating the skills of both talking and listening.

By becoming aware of the communication transactions between people, the reader has become aware of his involvement in either predictable, unpredicted, or double transactions and now has the appropriate knowledge to improve his personal communication patterns.

Answer keys to Exercises:

Page 105:

1. (a) Emotional
   (b) Societal
   (c) Rational

2. (a) Societal
   (b) Rational
   (c) Emotional

3. (a) Rational
   (b) Societal
   (c) Emotional

4. (a) Emotional
   (b) Societal
   (c) Rational

5. (a) Societal
   (b) Rational
   (c) Emotional

6. (a) Rational
   (b) Emotional
   (c) Societal

7. (a) Rational
   (b) Emotional
   (c) Societal

8. (a) Rational
   (b) Emotional
   (c) Societal

Pages 110 and 111:

A. 1. R to R
   2. R to R
   Predictable

B. 1. E to E
   2. S to E
   Unpredicted

C. 1. S to E
   2. E to S
   Predictable

D. 1. R to R
      R to E ----
   2. R to R
   Double

E. 1. R to R
   2. S to E
   Unpredicted

F. 1. S to R
      S to E ----
   2. E to S
   Double

SELECTED READINGS

Harris, T.   *I'm O.K.—You're O.K.: A Practical Guide to Transactional Analysis.*
New York: Harper and Row, 1969.

McCormick, P., and L. Campos.   *Introduce Yourself to Transactional Analysis.*
Stockton, California: San Joaquin Transactional Analysis Study Group, 1969.

James and Jongeward.   *Born to Win.* Don Mills, Ontario: Addison-Wesley Publishing Co., 1971.

—————.   *Winning with People* (Workbook). Don Mills, Ontario: Addison-Wesley Publishing Co., 1973.

8

PUBLIC SPEAKING

Ronald F. G. Campbell

The ability to communicate ideas clearly and effectively is an important asset in these sophisticated times. So many excellent and timely ideas are lost simply because the originator is not able to present his projects with sufficient force and clarity to convince others. No matter what your occupation is you are called upon to discuss your thoughts in face-to-face situations. You may find yourself expressing your ideas on a particular subject to a single colleague or to a large group of people. You will soon discover that technical expertise is not sufficient in itself, and that you must develop skill in oral communication if you are to reach your maximum potential. A friend of mine, for instance, spent three years earning a diploma as an electronics technologist. After an indoctrination period of six months with his new company, he became part of a team of specialists made up of engineers from a number of branches of engineering. The task of this group was to solve a particular engineering problem presented by a client. My friend soon discovered that as much of his working time was spent in presenting his ideas orally to his colleagues as in using the technical skills he had developed at college. He said to me, "Why didn't I spend some time in school learning how to get my ideas across to others orally?"

The purpose of this chapter is to assist you to become more effective in your chosen career through the study and practice of public speaking. In this process, at the same time, you will understand yourself and others better as ideas and feelings are exchanged.

To begin, let us suppose that you are a student who has been asked to be one of a panel of speakers presenting a variety of views on the subject of the fluoridation of the town water system. For some unknown reason you have accepted! Now, what do you do?

Let me suggest that once you have restrained your initial panic, there is help available for you. The act of speechmaking has been studied for many centuries. In fact, there is a large body of knowledge in existence from which many practical suggestions may be derived. In an extremely simplistic fashion this information may be summarized under five main headings. The five general elements of speechmaking that we should

MAKING A POINT ABOUT FLUORIDATION

talk about are: subject matter, audience, occasion, speaker and the desired end result.

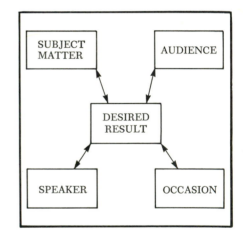

Your success as a speaker will depend to a large extent on how skillful you become in using these five characteristics of speechmaking. You must not only understand thoroughly each individual characteristic, but must also grasp fully how they are interrelated. If you are a person who really wants to come to grips with the challenge of a speaking occasion, you must learn to ask questions about each of these five elements of speech making as they relate to your specific speaking engagement. As an extended example, let us use these five headings to see how you would employ them to help you in the preparation of your talk on fluoridation.

SUBJECT MATTER

In this case the topic in the broadest sense has been assigned. Your first task, then, is to examine your present views on the subject. You may discover to your complete horror that you lack practically any understanding of the issues surrounding the matter of fluoridation of water. You must get to work immediately. Search out information on the subject. You need to do some research. You can ask people in the community their views on fluoridation. You have to search out newspaper and magazine articles. An examination of the situation of a nearby town that has already faced this issue may prove of value to you. You discover in this research that the issue of fluoridation of water in your community has developed into a controversial one and has divided the community into several factions. You finally decide on the basis of careful consideration of all the information you have been able to gather in the time available that you are in favour of the fluoridation of water to reduce tooth decay. This decision has been made because you believe that it has been demonstrated in other areas that cavities have been reduced by adding fluoride to the town's water system. Furthermore, you have come to believe that the process of fluoridation is relatively simple and inexpensive, and that it does not result in any side effects. Finally, you have discovered that the benefits of fluoridation become available to the largest segment of the population if it is added to the drinking water. However, you are aware that other speakers will present opposing views. Things look a little brighter, don't they? It is time now to ask yourself some questions about the audience.

AUDIENCE

It is important to find out about the nature of the audience who will be listening when you make your presentation. How many people will be present? What is their interest in the topic? Will a majority of the audience be in favour of fluoridation of their water supply or against it? Do the members of the audience have sufficient information about all aspects of the topic? Has the audience been influenced by arguments based on fact or on other considerations? Will there be any experts on the subject in the audience? You can find the answers to these and other questions by talking to people who may be expected to attend and by reading typical comments from community members. You discover, for instance, that the audience will likely have no common ground of belief when you speak to them. Now you are ready to think about the influence that the occasion itself will have on your talk.

OCCASION

So many times speakers neglect this important element of speech making! Again, you must ask yourself a number of questions. Why is the discussion on this topic taking place at this particular time? Who is sponsoring this event? How many will be present? What is the format of the program? How many speakers will there be? How should I be dressed? What will the setup on the speakers' platform be? The significance of these questions was impressed upon me one day at Cornell University in Ithaca, New York. It was announced by the President of the University that a most distinguished guest was going to visit Cornell on the Thursday of the next week. General Dwight D. Eisenhower, the former President of the United States, was to visit the University and address the Cornell community in the morning. Classes were to be cancelled and everyone was to gather in the 10,000-seat armoury known as Barton Hall. Can you imagine the sense of expectation that built up as the day approached! An American General, the supreme Allied Commander in the Second World War, and the thirty-fourth President of the United States was coming to this small New York town! As one entered Barton Hall on that occasion, it was evident that elaborate preparations had been made to suitably greet this important dignitary. Anyone who could legitimately muster a uniform did so. The police were dressed in their best outfits and each one wore his military medals. The

University Officers' Training Corps, representing the three services—Army, Navy and Air Force—were paraded together with any military equipment that could be gathered. The University Band was in attendance and played martial music. American flags decorated the armory and the streets leading from the airport to the University. The platform itself was tastefully decorated with American flags and red and white flowers. When the platform party arrived everyone again was in uniform—except Mr. Eisenhower himself. The meeting began with the singing of the national anthem. The whole auditorium shook with emotion as the assembled audience sang "The Star Spangled Banner." The President of the University introduced the esteemed guest in one sentence, "Ladies and gentlemen, the former President of the United States of America!" There was a deafening roar as the audience gave a standing ovation of perhaps three minutes duration. In the midst of all this emotional build-up Mr. Eisenhower delivered what many people thought to be a disappointing speech. He stepped away from the microphone. He faltered. He quoted incorrect dates from American history. His speech was not organized and did not have any point to it. His attempts at humour were disastrous. Everyone was relieved when he finally sat down after about fifteen calamitous minutes. It turned out later that the former President of the United States had only planned to drop in informally on his relative, the wife of the President of the University. He did not look upon his visit as an official occasion to deliver a major address to ten thousand people. The President's poorly prepared impromptu remarks delivered in an inadequate manner did not meet the requirements of the occasion.

Other questions that could be asked about the occasion of your speech come to mind. Will I be able to use audio-visual aids? Will there be time for questions? Will there be facilities for radio and television broadcasting? Is there any other matter on the program, before or after the speakers? These questions and others will help you make decisions about your speech and your delivery of it. Let us suppose that you discover that the occasion is an open town meeting and that the subject will be discussed fully by those present and that it will be voted on. The vote,

it is hoped, will guide the town council in making the policy on fluoridation. Additional questions may be asked regarding the speaker.

SPEAKER

You might ask yourself such questions as: "Why was I chosen to speak? What will the audience think of my competency to speak on this matter? Am I to 'represent' any segment of the community?" Your research shows that you have been chosen because you are president of your student body and are looked upon as a "typical" young person whose views should be considered. Under these circumstances you should take some time in your speech to indicate how you have come to hold the views you presently do on fluoridation. Perhaps you need to survey the thoughts of some of your contemporaries on the subject.

DESIRED END RESULT

Having completed your research on the topic, examined the kind of audience expected, and looked at the nature of the occasion and the audience's view of you as the speaker, you are now ready to ask yourself what you want to accomplish with this speech. What influence do you want to have on the beliefs and behaviour of the audience? What is the desired end result? As part of your research you found out that the community is sharply split over the issue. Now you discover that this division is not based on the facts of the matter, but rather on the allegiance to some leaders who have differing opinions based on political considerations. You decide that in your speech you will try and bring these varying opinions together in favour of fluoridation by providing the audience with the basic information which they seem to be lacking.

As you ask yourself these questions about the five basic elements of speech making, you will begin to see the dynamic nature of their relationship. You will observe that on every new speech occasion each of the elements will have varying weights of importance or significance. However, a serious investigation of these five basic elements before a speech, during the speech occasion itself, and after it as a review, will help

PUBLIC SPEAKING: THE PURPOSEFUL EXCHANGE OF INFORMATION AND FEELING

you become a better communicator. This improvement will be evident not only at formal speaking times, but also on less formal occasions when the exchange of ideas and feelings takes place. Your study and concern will also help you understand how others make their decisions on these matters. As a result you will have a better appreciation of how human nature operates. All these observations will help you operate more effectively as an individual in relationship with others.

Summary

The person who wants to be an effective public speaker has to consider the five basic elements of speech—the audience, subject matter, speaker, occasion and the desired end result. A review of these five basic characteristics will assist the speaker in the development of a speech which is suited to the audience and which succeeds in attaining the chosen purpose.

Of course, there are many other matters to consider before you present your ideas to the audience, such as: choosing the main ideas, selecting relevant support materials, developing the appropriate structure, finding the suitable words, preparing the speech for delivery and evaluating the success of your presentation. However, it would be beneficial

at this point to pause and consolidate the information already presented by completing the following exercises:

Exercises

1. *Written*

   The head of your institution (principal, president), has called the first-year students together in the auditorium to welcome them. Before he speaks to them he must ask himself a number of questions. Write a brief essay describing some of the answers he might give under the headings of subject matter, audience, occasion, speaker and end result.

2. *Oral*

   Prepare and present a two-minute talk introducing yourself to your classmates. At the end of your talk be prepared to discuss the decisions you made concerning the five basic elements of speech making as outlined in the text: subject matter, audience, occasion, speaker and desired end result.

DEFINITION OF PUBLIC SPEAKING

Before moving on to the next steps in the preparation and presentation of oral messages, it is necessary to show how the art of speech making relates to the communication theory described in this book. The definition of public speaking that is used as the basis for the practice and theory in this section is: "The purposeful exchange of information and feeling." The element of purpose pervades all the instructions given in this part of the book. This does not mean that I do not recognize that the speaker unconsciously sends messages which sometimes are contradictory to his main purpose. What I am saying is that a public speaker is mainly interested in developing messages that contribute to his principal intention. The listener is assisted by everything that the speaker does to understand, and interact with, the desired end result of the message.

The second part of the definition to stress at this point is that public speaking is a process involving exchange of information. Too often public speakers think of oral communication as a one-way street. Under these circumstances the speaker is only interested in "delivering a talk." He is not concerned with the effect the thoughts have on the listener, or the receiver's response. This type of speaker is not anxious to interact with the listener.

The definition contains a third significant concept. A speaker reveals not only his thoughts but also his feelings. During his presentation the speaker indicates what he thinks of himself, the subject he is presenting, the audience and the occasion itself.

From the explanation given above, then, it is evident that public speaking is "the purposeful exchange of information and feeling." This definition is amplified by the following diagram:

This sketch illustrates the various aspects of the speaking act. The speaker decides to communicate with a listener concerning an event or an idea. The dotted line between the idea/event and the listener indicates that the listener may or may not be acquainted with the idea/event in the same way that the speaker is. It is important for the communicator to discover as far as possible the receiver's understanding of the main topic presented. The speaker decides on the content of his message and formulates it in words and gestures. These words and gestures are chosen with the listener in mind. The speaker must do his best to formulate his ideas in terms which are understood by the listener. The verbal and nonverbal signals are sent through the channel of the air waves toward the listener. This channel may be blocked partially or completely by various forms of interference which prevent the message being received in the form in which it was sent. The audience, for instance, may be distracted by the arrival of latecomers, and fail to hear the entire message. Or again, perhaps a few of the members of the audience are worried about some serious decisions which have to be made the next day and are not therefore giving the speaker their undivided attention. In any event, the message is received only in part. When the message is received through the listener's senses, he interprets it according to his past experiences and his present framework of values and beliefs. The listener then responds and offers feedback to the speaker. This feedback may be an oral response or it may take the form of signs which display agreement or boredom, etc. The

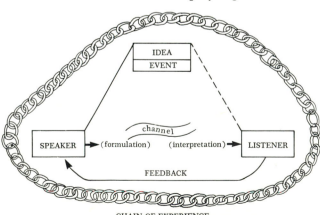

CHAIN OF EXPERIENCE

speaker then realizes how successful or unsuccessful he has been in matching his understanding of the topic discussed with that of the listener. The degree of success depends on the speaker's ability to match his images and ideas to the experience of the listener. The greater the similarity in the experiences of the speaker and the listener, the greater the opportunity for the successful exchange of thoughts and feelings between the speaker and the listener.

Summary

The definition of public speaking offered in this chapter is, "The purposeful exchange of information and feeling." This definition is framed in such a way as to remind the speaker that oral communication is a complex process involving the entire being of both the speaker and the listener.

Exercises
1. *Written*
   Write your own definition of public speaking. In a short paragraph compare your definition with that presented in this book.
2. *Oral*
   Prepare and present to your class a three-minute talk on an important event that has influenced your life.

THE PROCESS OF SPEECH PREPARATION

Now that we have reviewed the five basic elements of speech making and have put the act of speaking into the general framework of a communication model, it is now appropriate to consider at length the steps to be taken in order to produce the best communication effort. We will review what you have to do between the time you have decided to speak and the actual hour you present your thoughts and feelings to an audience.

As part of the learning process, you will be asked to give speeches in class. The classroom speech is an important part of your development as an effective communicator. Some may look upon the speech in class as only a simulation exercise. "After all," they say, "my classmates are hardly the typical audience I will meet in my daily work!"

I realize the classroom is more like a green-house than a "real-life" situation. However, I suggest that you consider the classroom speech as important as any speech you will ever make. After all, the classroom speech contains all the ingredients of the usual speaking occasion. An audience, for instance, is gathered to hear you present ideas that are important to you. This audience has a lot in common with the groups you will speak to later on in life. The members of an audience react favourably to an idea that meets their needs or wants. Some of your listeners will demonstrate interest in your choice of subject, while others will be completely bored. Some will have a great deal of information on the topic, while others will know practically nothing. Some will give you their undivided attention, while others will be primarily worried about matters that have nothing to do with your talk. An excellent technique to use in proving just how often our minds wander is to pause after speaking for two or three minutes and ask your listeners what they have been thinking about *other than the topic being discussed*. Be prepared for such answers as: "I am concerned about arrangements I have to make to get a student loan." "I was thinking how tight these new shoes are." Or, "I am worried about my mother who is ill in the hospital."

It will help you in your speaking to analyze your audience with other characteristics in mind, such as age, socioeconomic level and education; and also the authorities they accept. A person seeking excellence as a speaker studies these characteristics carefully since the acceptance of ideas is influenced by them. The age of your audience, for instance, is a significant factor to consider. The young person has a different outlook on life than a senior citizen. You should take into consideration that all stages of life have their unique desires. You should also recognize that listeners are deeply affected by their cultural, social and economic experiences. You will be less effective in your speaking efforts if you fail to investigate the viewpoints and values held by your audience as a result of their socioeconomic experiences.

Another variable to consider in the investigation of your audience is the level of education of its members. In the college classroom situation the educational level tends to be more uniform, you will find, than in the

THE AGE OF YOUR AUDIENCE IS A SIGNIFICANT FACTOR

nonacademic world. It is generally true that the more educational experience a person has had the more he will be open to new ideas and experiences. As you gain experience as a speaker, your ability to adjust the content of your message to the knowledge held by your audience will be of great value to you.

Your audience analysis also ought to reveal to you the acknowledged authorities accepted by your listeners. You must relate your persuasive arguments to the public statements and actions of these recognized experts. For example, if you are speaking to a group made up predominantly of businessmen, the acceptance of your proposal will be strengthened when you demonstrate that some of the outstanding business leaders have already expressed support for it.

A careful review of the characteristics of your audience, within the classroom and outside it, will pay high dividends in your speech making efforts. The classroom speech also affords the opportunity to consider other parts of speech making which are common with a talk given in the nonacademic situation. These elements include: the need to communicate ideas and feelings to gain some predetermined end; the opportunity to research an issue in order to have an enlightened position on it; the obligation to organize

the material in a helpful manner; and the requirement to present your ideas, through words and gestures, in an interesting fashion.

The classroom does offer some advantages over the situations created by your work opportunities. Giving a speech in class is recognized as a learning situation. Mistakes are recognized as such and are tolerated. The speaker is expected to develop as a person and as a communicator during this period. All your listeners are in the same situation and therefore are more sympathetic to your attempts at innovation. It is a time for frank evaluation, where strengths and weaknesses are assessed and constructive suggestions are made for improvement. On the other hand, the commercial scene has little time to offer such assistance. Competent communicators are expected, and the incompetent rejected.

In the classroom the student of speech is usually given a variety of speaking opportunities. Each successive occasion is marked by increasing complexity and intensified criticism. Permit me to use my own teaching experience to demonstrate what I mean. Each member of a beginning class is usually asked to give a two-minute talk introducing himself to his colleagues. I, as the instructor, offer a few comments on the strengths and weaknesses of the speeches as a whole. Each class member is allowed to apply these criticisms to his own efforts. The comments on these speeches usually include such statements as: "You did not have good eye contact with the members of your audience." "You did not know what to do with your hands." "You did not make use of appropriate illustrations to help your audience maintain their interest." "We couldn't see where you were going in your talk." And, "We didn't know you were finished until you sat down."

This introductory assignment is followed by one which specifies a three-minute speech based on some experience in the speaker's life that has been of great influence. This speech does not require much research since it is based on personal experience. This talk is recorded on audio tape. The speaker listens to the tape with the instructor. The speaker is usually encouraged to listen for distracting voice characteristics. He is also instructed to approach the audience with a "conversational tone" of voice. The instructor generally emphasizes the need for a demonstrated sense of direction within the speech.

The next assignment is to present an eight- to ten-minute speech of information. This talk is recorded on video tape and reviewed by the teacher and student together. The student is also asked to hand in a written critical review of the speech as he saw it on the video tape. In this evaluation the teacher is ordinarily called upon to emphasize the need for a recognizable structure, and the importance of the material in the speech for presentation to the audience.

The next speech, depending on the number of students in the class and the length of the college year, may be the final one. It is the most complex of all because the listeners will expect the greatest improvement to take place. After all, the theory taught in class, the opportunities given for practice and the amount of concerned criticism offered your colleagues, a polished and effective presentation is expected—and usually given! This is usually an eight- to ten-minute persuasive speech. The speaker is asked to convince the members of the audience to accept a point of view or to chart a course of action. Time is left at the end for questions on the topic from the audience. All forms of evaluation mentioned earlier are open for use. Usually the criticism involves the need for the choice of illustrations and examples that are relevant to the experience of the audience, and are of such a nature as to draw the listeners' attention and interest.

After the speeches of information and persuasion, the speaker receives oral and written

"YOU DID NOT HAVE GOOD EYE CONTACT WITH YOUR AUDIENCE"

feedback from his fellow students. A useful form to assist in this evaluation follows:

Speaker's Name: Date:
Topic:
                                    No   Yes
Subject:
  Suited to Audience
  Interesting
  Helpful
  Specific
Organization:
  Introduction
    Get attention
    Sufficient background
      information
    Purpose clear
  Body
    Well organized
    Sense of direction
    Transitions and internal
      summaries effective
    Illustrative material
      effective
  Conclusion
    Thoughts summarized
    Clear ending
Delivery:
  Sufficient eye contact
  Mastery of material
  Vocal variety
  Complimentary gestures
  Fluency of speech

This criticism helps him assess his own progress in reaching his peers with his ideas. The criticism of his fellow students grows in its helpfulness as the term progresses. In my classes, marks are assigned based on the demonstrated progress of the speaker over the whole year. The willingness of the student to master the theoretical material is also considered in the marking scheme. Some teachers do not approve of the assignment of grades to such a subject as speech. However, I feel that the student requires some indication of his progress in the course. He also needs some form of reward mechanism to maintain his sense of motivation.

Summary

The classroom speech presents the beginning speaker with a laboratory situation in which all the characteristics of a normal speech situation are present without the usual risks. The audience for the classroom speech, for instance, is a group of peers brought together for the purpose of studying all aspects of the speech-making act. In this situation, constructive evaluation is presented and considered.

STEPS IN SPEECH PREPARATION
(from initial shock to final evaluation!)

1. *Choice of a Topic*

For many people the choice of the topic is the most difficult step in the whole process of speech making. With all the possible topics in the whole wide world, it seems almost impossible to focus on one particular subject. Suggestions can be made, however, to assist you in this dilemma. It helps if you choose a subject in which you are interested, or one that springs from your own experience. Even a superficial acquaintance with a particular subject may encourage you to do a great deal of research in order to enable you to speak with confidence. You may find a suitable topic from newspaper or magazine articles. Your preferred topic could come from discussions currently taking place among your friends. A recent popular novel may form the basis of ideas to be shared with your listeners.

Your subject may be found in the analysis you make of the needs, characteristics and interests of your audience. You may be invited, for instance, to speak to a service club in your community interested in donating scholarships to your school. You may discover an appropriate subject by reading the literature published by the group or by talking to some of the members of the organization about why they belong.

The occasion itself may provide the seed idea for your talk. For example, you may be asked to make a presentation to someone who has won an achievement award.

The element of time has a large part to play in the choice of a topic. You must decide on your topic as far ahead as possible. The closer you come to the speaking date, the more your panic increases, and the less creative and imaginative your choice may be.

In the classroom speech occasion you should be given notice early in the course about the number and nature of the speeches to be given. At that point I would look out for topics which meet these criteria. It would help if you kept an index card for each subject and added ideas as they occurred, day by day. This system would provide you with an abundant stockpile of information from which to draw. Not incidentally, it would also reduce considerably your anxiety as you approach your speaking engagement. People who are frequently called upon to address audiences soon learn to develop a topical filing system. Interesting examples together with seed thoughts for possible talks are placed into this catalogue of ideas.

Finally, your topic may be assigned directly. Some speech teachers use this tactic of assigning subjects to students in order to make certain that the class considers a variety of worthwhile topics during the term. An organization may also ask a speaker to present his views on a particular subject currently of interest to its membership. You may consider that this is a handicap to you, but if the subject is of concern to the listeners, then you will be assisted in your presentation of it. The discovery of the reasons for the interest of the audience may help you in the development of your speech. You may be invited, for example, to address the Environmental Committee of your town council because your school has successfully mobilized the student body to collect bottles, tin and paper for recycling. The Committee is interested in your efforts because they have been assigned a similar task for the entire community and they are looking at a number of efforts in recycling in order to develop the most effective program. In telling this group of your success you can be assured of their undivided attention. If you deliver what the Committee expects, your success as a guest speaker is almost guaranteed. Groups also invite speakers to address them because they are the acknowledged authorities in their field. A local psychologist, for instance, is continually invited to speak on nudist colonies because he is recognized as the one who understands the psychological and sociological needs of people who belong to such organizations.

Summary

Ideas for speeches, then, come from a variety of sources. They may be derived from the interests and expertise of the speaker. Subjects may be suggested by an analysis of the needs and interests of the audience. The occasion where you are asked to speak may provide the suitable material. Finally, the speech topic may be assigned by the group inviting you to speak. In any event, the choice of subject is only one step of many in the process of developing a successful presentation.

2. *Researching the Topic or Gathering the Material*

Once you have decided upon the general scope of your subject, you must be prepared to spend considerable time on researching it. You will happily discover, for instance, as you read varying opinions on the chosen issue, that your ideas will grow and change. This developing knowledge will help you to become confident in your ability and your right to offer your own views on the subject. Mastery of the theme takes place when you open your mind to articles, books, and the views of experts and friends. It will be of benefit to you in searching out relevant material to consult your local research librarian. Make extensive notes so that the development of your thoughts on the subject can be traced. Isolate insights you have which may be suitable for the speech itself. Make note especially of relevant illustrations and quotations which may be of value to you later. Record the source of these items by author, title and page.

It is necessary to pause in this review of the process of gathering materials to comment on the necessity to produce original points of view and substance for your speech. You should aim at developing a fresh approach or a unique attack on your subject. In other words, attempt to be original! I suppose it is true that there is "nothing new under the sun." Completely innovative ideas are rare indeed. Nevertheless, you must do your best to put your own brand of originality on the material that you are shaping. A regurgitation of a single author's point of view is not a satisfactory approach. This will not attain the desired impact on the audience. It is necessary to discover as much material as time will allow from as many divergent

ATTEMPT TO BE ORIGINAL

sources as possible before reaching your own conclusions on the topic and identifying your own position.

3. *Narrowing Down the Topic*

If you research your topic according to the suggestions above, you will be pleased to discover sufficient material for a series of major speeches on the topic. Your task now is to narrow the topic down to manageable proportions which can reasonably be presented within the time limit you have been given. The audience, too, has a limited capacity to digest material in a restricted period of time. How are you going to limit the amount of material that you are to present? Firstly, you must determine the background information your audience already will have when you speak to them. You can do this best of all by speaking to a wide range of representative people who will be present. Ascertain also the beliefs of the audience regarding the chosen topic. Again, you may find that you are not capable of speaking on certain aspects of the subject because of their technical nature. When you speak on subjects beyond your comprehension, there is danger that experts who are present may readily judge that you are totally incompetent to

speak on the topic at all. Under these circumstances, a question period at the end of your talk could prove disastrous. The occasion itself may also limit what you wish to say. Nothing will be gained at a retirement reception for a long-term employee, for instance, by reviewing all the mistakes in judgment he made over a span of twenty-five years. The occasion almost demands that the speaker review the accomplishments which the individual made to the company during that time, and offer best wishes for a happy retirement.

When you have worked through these general considerations, there are certain particular steps that can be taken to assist in the limitation of the topic. You need to identify your *general purpose* for speaking. You may wish to *inform* your audience about a particular issue. For instance, you may decide to explain to your audience "the five main issues in the present federal election." On the other hand, you may wish to *persuade* your audience to accept a certain belief or to undertake a particular action. For example, you may set out "to persuade the audience to vote for John Smith as their representative in Ottawa". Or again, your general purpose may be to *entertain* your listeners with "the outstanding humorous anecdotes of the present campaign." Or *enquiry* may be your general purpose as you present the subject of "weighing the issues in the current election". Or finally, you may choose to assume a general purpose of *reinforcement* while speaking on "the privilege all Canadians enjoy in voting for the federal government." When you choose one of these five general purposes, you will help yourself in restricting the development of your subject matter. The ability to do so will also assist your audience in the comprehension of your point of view. Early in their planning of a speech I usually ask my students to submit a statement to me indicating their general purpose for speaking. In response, I get such answers as: "Rowing," or "The United Fund," or "The Snakes of Northern Ontario." Of course, these responses are not satisfactory. To overcome this tendency toward generality I encourage my students to frame a statement of the *central idea* of the speech. This expression of the main theme is stated in a *subject sentence* which contains the general purpose (to inform, etc.) and the desired end result of the speech. As indicated early in this section of the book, the desired end result indicates what the speaker expects the audience to do after listening to the speech. With this requirement in mind the three topics listed above are usually changed as follows: "I want to inform my audience about the fantastic sport of rowing so at the next meet they will be able to sit on the bank of the river and understand what is going on"; "I am going to persuade my listeners that their gift to the United Fund will benefit the entire community"; "I am going to speak on the identification of the poisonous snakes of Ontario so that my listeners will be able to enjoy their stay in the North without being concerned about harmful snake bites."

Let me remind you that the development of a subject sentence which contains the general purpose and the desired end result is an important exercise. A disregard for specificity is the major weakness demonstrated by speakers generally. As a further illustration of the narrowing down process, study the development of the following subject sentence. You have been asked to speak on "the preservation of our natural resources." As you recognize by now, this topic is far too broad. However, based on your own experience, your reading that you have undertaken and the advice of experts, you decide to propose in your speech a program to preserve the natural resources of the North. You further decide that this preservation program is designed to promote the utilization of the northern resources by the largest possible number of people. You conclude that you will include in your general purpose an attempt to move the members of the audience to adopt some form of action in support of your thesis.

So now you must write a subject sentence. It might look like this: "The purpose of my talk is to persuade the members of my audience to accept the necessity for a new program for the protection of the natural resources of the North, and to demonstrate their acceptance of the idea by personally signing a petition to be sent to the Ministry of Natural Resources supporting this program."

This subject sentence includes the general purpose (to persuade) and the desired end result (to sign a petition). It is now time to convert your research and thinking and statement of purpose into a general outline.

Summary

Once the topic has been selected and appropriate research has been completed, enabling the speaker to put together a fresh approach to it, the speaker must narrow down the subject to manageable proportions. The speaker must choose the general purpose —to inform, to persuade, to entertain, to enquire or to reinforce. Then a subject sentence outlining the general purpose and the desired end of the speech must be framed.

4. *Developing a General Outline*

The development of a general outline is the next step in the speech preparation process. The purpose of the outline is to produce the entire speech in skeleton form. This outline should communicate to a reader the general form and direction that the speech is going to take. To aid in this process of structure it is helpful to divide the outline into three sections—the introduction, the body and the conclusion. Each part has a unique function. One purpose of the introduction is to attract the listeners' attention and interest in the topic. This can be accomplished, for instance, by giving an illustration which is relevant to the interests and concerns of the audience. In a talk designed to recruit subscribers to a Foster Parents of Viet Nam program, a speaker gained the attention of his audience in the introduction by presenting in vivid fashion the plight of one orphaned victim of the war and contrasting that disastrous situation with the relatively secure and comfortable life of a local child. Attention may also be won by opening with a startling quotation or statistic. One speaker concerned with the lack of support for a community mental health program opened her speech by saying: "Did you know that reliable statistics on mental health demonstrate beyond any doubt whatsoever that seven out of ten people across this national will suffer from some form of mental illness in their lives?" Humour is often used to draw attention in the introduction of a speech. With all these attempts mentioned to gain attention,

SOMETIMES HUMOUR IS WELL RECEIVED...

BOO!

BOO!

LYNCH 'IM!

BANG!
BANG!
BANG!
BANG!
BANG!
BANG!

HISS! HISSS!

--- AND SOMETIMES IT ISN'T

be certain that your introductory remarks do lead naturally into the topic under discussion. Otherwise, you will lose your audience as they try to figure out how you could logically jump from your opening comments to the substance of the subject. Use variety in your method of introducing your topic. One speaker always opened his talk with a humorous story. Sometimes the humour was well received and sometimes it wasn't. But the audience expected the opening on every occasion. If they were disappointed, the main theme of the speech could be lost entirely. On the contrary, sometimes the opening anecdote was so funny that many in the audience didn't listen any further as they tried to rehearse the story in their minds to tell it to their friends at the earliest opportunity.

A second function of the introduction is to reveal the purpose of the speech. This is a significant requirement of an introduction which is often neglected by a speaker. Under these circumstances communication is inhibited because the listener is spending all his energy trying to discover the point of the speech. Many times he just gives up and amuses himself with his own thoughts, thereby ignoring entirely the substance of the talk. As you gain experience as a speaker, you will learn to state your purpose in inter-

esting ways, but in the beginning state in bold terms your intention, even as bluntly as: "This morning I intend to persuade you to join the athletic association of the school and donate your $5.00 membership fee." Later on in your speech making, however, you may develop your speaking skills so as to reveal your purpose in a more subtle way. But whatever you do, make certain that you show your audience what your intention is in addressing them.

The introduction, finally, is the place in the speech to introduce any background information on the subject which may help your listeners understand what you are talking about. The amount of information you need to supply varies, of course, and depends on the knowledge held by the audience. If you were trying to increase the knowledge of a group of veterinarians about the work of a local society devoted to the improvement of the care of stray animals, it would be foolish for you to spend a lot of time talking about the nutritional needs of the modern canine. The doctors already know this and are more interested in the services your organization provides.

The body of the speech is the second major part of the general outline. Here two or three main points ought to be selected and arranged in logical order. The number of main ideas offered is dependent, of course, on the audience's knowledge of the subject, the purpose of the speech and the time limit imposed. Speakers generally try to cram too many ideas into one speech. The audience cannot digest the material and in response turns off the receiving mechanism and ignores the message.

The conclusion is the third division of a speech. In this section the principal emphasis of the talk is reviewed and summarized. Research results into the investigation of the retention of information indicates that a clear concluding statement assists the listener immensely in his attempt to appropriate the speaker's message. The speaker also ought to indicate through the conclusion that he has completed his comments on the subject. The conclusion is not the section in which to introduce any new material. This move only confuses the listener. A vivid illustration summarizing the ideas presented and referring back to the introduction is an excellent technique to use in the conclusion of a speech. This method will also achieve the sense of completion which a good conclusion requires.

In the preparation of a speech it has been found advantageous to write the introduction and conclusion after the body has been developed. Only when the ideas have taken final shape is the speaker in a position to frame an interesting opening and a useful closing.

Although the introduction, the body and the conclusion have been presented as the three main sections of a speech, there are two other components of the structure of an outline which should be stressed, namely transitions and internal summaries. One of the weaknesses usually found in a poor speech is the lack of transitions or bridges between ideas. No sooner does a listener find himself in the point being discussed when, without any warning whatsoever, the speaker jumps to another point. The listener quickly becomes lost and stops following the speaker's thought. Give the listener a chance. Provide him with an indication that you are now moving on to another idea.

A second way to aid comprehension is found in the internal summary. The internal summary indicates to the listener the progress of the speaker's thought to that point in the speech and signals the speaker's intention to move on from there to some new aspect of the topic. Both the transition and the internal summary help the listener to trace the development of the speaker's ideas. Examples of transitions and internal summaries will be found in the sample outline which follows. You will also notice some other useful characteristics usually employed in developing general outlines. A consistent system of symbolization and indentation is employed. This indicates the relative relationship of the ideas to be presented. Ideas with similar symbols bear the same amount of significance. Subordinate ideas are indicated by suitable indentation. By following such a scheme a speaker is able to develop ideas in a logical way. When you study this sample outline, you will become aware that the ideas are expressed in sentences and not in fragments or phrases. This technique helps the speaker to shape his specific ideas early in his speech preparation.

SAMPLE OUTLINE

Title: Preserving The Natural Resources of The North.
Subject Sentence: The purpose of this speech is to persuade the audience to demonstrate their acceptance of a new program designed to preserve the resources of the North by signing a petition to be sent to the Minister of Natural Resources.

I. INTRODUCTION
A. Do you enjoy visiting the North?
B. Do you realize that the resources of the North are threatened because of the lack of a comprehensive government plan?
1. The many agencies involved prevent proper coordination.
2. An example of the result is the declining population of many animals.
(a) The deer population is dwindling.
(b) Wolves have almost been exterminated.
C. The purpose: Let me explain to you the problem as I see it and ask for your support for a new program to correct the deficiencies before it is too late.

II. BODY
A. The present situation in the North, if allowed to persist, will result in the complete destruction of an important part of our natural resources.
1. Uncontrolled growth of the cottage country will pollute lakes and rivers.
(a) For example, there are no regulations governing waste systems.
(b) Pollution Probe in its survey in 1970 uncovered some interesting trends.
2. The popularity of camping if not managed properly will result in the further deterioration of the northern resources.

Transition and Internal Summary:
It is evident then from what I have

said about the new demands made on our northern resources by the rush of city people to the country, that a new program of resource protection is required. What would be the nature of my recommended program?

B. The solution to the problem is for the Ministry of Natural Resources to develop a comprehensive program leading to the preservation of the natural resources of the North.

  1. Regulation for the development of cottage lots must include such items as: size of lot and type of sewage system.

  2. A system of public and private camp sites should be developed.

  3. A plan for the replacement of consumable resources should be introduced.

    (a) The stocking of lakes is necessary.

    (b) Action to plant seedlings must begin.

  4. Your interest can be demonstrated this evening when you sign a copy of this petition.

III. CONCLUSION

A. It is obvious from what I have said that it is an urgent matter.

B. Permit me to describe for you what sections of the North will be like if we do not take quick action.

C. The petition is available for your signature.

The general outline, then, reflects the many decisions you have made up to this point regarding the purpose and content of your speech, the type of audience present, the nature of the occasion itself and your own capabilities as the speaker. The question before us now is how will you make certain that your listeners will receive your message with the impact you want it to have? The wise selection of supporting material will assist the process tremendously.

The speech preparation process and the final success of the speech are aided by the development of an outline. The outline is a series of statements written in complete sentences which reveals the logical progress of the speech from the introduction, through the body of the speech to the final conclusion. These divisions of the speech, together with such aids to comprehension as transitions and internal summaries, help the listener to understand what the speaker is trying to accomplish.

Exercise

Develop an outline for a six-minute speech of information.

5. *Selecting Supporting Material*

At this stage in the development of your speech it is important for your success to give some thought to selecting the supporting material such as examples and illustrations, quotations, testimony from authorities, statistics and factual evidence. It is this supporting material which makes your basic thesis come alive. Supporting material acts as the contact point between your ideas and the experiences of the listeners. The significance of finding appropriate support material cannot be underestimated. As it is pointed out many times in this book, the communicator is successful to the extent he is able to evoke within the listener the identical image he intended. When you have an audience of one you are able to use a variety of examples in order to discover the one that speaks most clearly to the experience of your listener. When the audience is many in number, however, the attempt to relate to common experiences becomes more difficult. Therefore, you have been encouraged to learn as much as possible about the background, value systems and beliefs of your audience. The necessity to understand the audience was brought home to me most forcibly one evening when I was a guest at a men's club dinner. A local comedian provided the entertainment. He was an excellent and experienced comic. He had provided the entertainment for this men's group on many previous occasions. He was announced. The curtain opened. He appeared. He began his act with one of the dirtiest jokes I have ever heard. He met with complete silence. In the past with this group he could expect hilarious laughter and enthusiastic laughter at this type of joke. In astonishment he looked at his audience and discovered what was wrong. Someone had forgotten to tell him that it was Ladies' Night at the club! He quickly changed his routine and by the end of the act he had most of the audience enjoying themselves. If he had not been able to adapt as quickly as he did, however, the whole evening would have been a complete disaster for him and his audience. As you gain experience in choosing appropriate supporting materials you will learn to adapt to the background and values of your audience, so as to gain the maximum possible acceptance of your communication efforts.

6. Committing the Speech to Writing

It is recommended here that you commit the entire speech to writing word-for-word. Many advisors would not agree with this advice. I realize there are dangers involved in writing out the speech in this manner. One of the disadvantages usually cited is that the speaker will become too closely tied to individual words when delivering the speech, and thereby lose some degree of spontaneity. We will discuss this matter again when we talk about the delivery of speeches. It is also true that written language and oral language have different characteristics. We use more personal pronouns and shorter sentences in oral speaking. Written style emphasizes a more complex sentence structure. Our oral vocabulary is also much smaller than our written one.

With these criticisms in mind, however, I believe that the thought has not been specifically and clearly formulated until it is written down. I also feel that a better product will result when the speech is completely written out.

The length of the speech I have stressed is also an important factor to consider. In timing your speech at this point it is beneficial to read the prepared manuscript out loud at your normal speaking rate. You will most likely discover that because of time your speech needs revision.

Exercise

Give an eight- to ten-minute speech of information on a topic of your own choosing.

7. Mastering the Speech for Delivery

Opinion is divided on the best method for preparing a speech for delivery. Each speaker soon learns the procedure best suited to his own style. My advice is to take the written manuscript and read it over a number of times. With each repetition of the material, you master more of the general thoughts of the speech. This does not mean that you are memorizing the talk word-for-word. If anything is commited to memory, it is perhaps the general outline. When you have mastered the general ideas of the speech, it is then useful to get on your feet and speak out the speech in rehearsal without reference to any notes except quotations which you may wish to read word-for-word for accuracy. You will probably require two or three rehearsals to tailor the speech to the time allowed. As you practise the talk you will discover areas that you want to revise by adding or deleting. Perhaps you can find some friends who will make up an audience for you.

8. Delivering the Speech

If you have followed carefully all the steps in this process of developing a talk, you will arrive at this stage with confidence and a sense of anticipation. After all, you have prepared thoroughly for this speech occasion. You have chosen an appropriate subject. The issue has been researched accurately and you have made up your mind as to where you stand on the matter. The needs, background information and beliefs of the audience have been taken into consideration. You have chosen a specific purpose for your speech, developed a logical outline which led to a word-for-word manuscript. You have prepared the talk for delivery by means of a number of rehearsals. Because of all this effort, you can now present yourself confidently before your audience. Through this process you know that you have done all humanly possible to make the occasion a success.

You still come to the time of presentation with uncertainty and concern. These symptoms of nervousness—shaking knees, quavering voice, quickly beating heart, faint feeling, perspiring palms, drying mouth and butterflies in the stomach—all indicate

ALMOST EVERYONE FEELS A LITTLE NERVOUS...

speech fright. Your task is to control these symptoms as much as possible. It may help to know that almost everyone feels a degree of nervousness before making a public appearance. A goaltender for the Montreal Canadiens in the 1973/74 season admitted that he was sick to his stomach before every game he played. However, he had controlled this sign of nervousness by game time and it did not prevent him from playing an excellent game on goal.

As you gain experience in facing the public you will learn to minimize this distress. However, the feeling never completely leaves you. In fact, there are some experts who feel that if you are not somewhat nervous at giving an address, then you are not taking the occasion seriously enough. They also point out that when a person faces a threatening situation the human body provides additional strength through increased amounts of adrenalin in the body system. Speakers who are well prepared forget about their nervousness as soon as they get into their speech. Their desire to communicate their own thoughts to another audience erases all other concerns from their minds. Because you understand the significance of the bodily changes mentioned above, and because you have something of importance to say, your concern for your nervousness will be minimal.

Speech teachers talk of four styles of delivery: extemporaneous, memorized, read and impromptu. I recommend that you deliver most of your speeches in the extemporaneous mode. You can make use of this form of delivery when there is adequate time to prepare in the manner we have discussed in this section of the book. This mode of delivery permits direct eye contact with the audience. This is an important characteristic of successful speaking. The speaker who is able to engage an audience in this manner stands a far better chance of success over the person who spends his time staring at the floor or the ceiling or the tree outside the window. The speaker who has direct eye contact with his audience can see the reception the audience is giving his thoughts and can make adjustments where necessary. For example, when the speaker detects a number of glances which indicate a lack of understanding of a point, he is able to provide further information to clarify this misunderstanding. If it appears that the audience is not giving full attention, then the speaker must take steps to correct the situation. None of these observations are possible unless the speaker is in close eye contact with his audience. In this form of delivery the speaker should make only minimal use of notes. Too often notes become a crutch to lean upon. Eventually they become a barrier inhibiting effective communication. When you enter into direct conversation with your audience, as I am suggesting, then your voice presents a conversational tone which is also pleasing to your audience. Your voice takes on a lively tone. A pleasing variety of pace and pitch develops. As you engage in conversation in this way with your listeners, your hand and facial and body gestures develop naturally to reinforce the meaning of your words. A word of caution is in order at this point. Extemporaneous speaking requires a great deal of practice to perfect. You grow in your ability to use this form of delivery. Be prepared, then, to accept evaluation of your efforts and to strive for improvement.

In contrast to extemporaneous speaking the impromptu form of delivery takes place when the speaker is called upon to speak without any previous notice. You will be called upon to use the impromptu mode of delivery more than any other form. In school, at work, during your leisure time activities—situations requiring you to speak without formal preparation time are endless. However, the matters we have talked about in the preparation of extemporaneous speeches will help you out in the impromptu situation. The ability to quickly decide on a point of view, to select a few main points, to find interesting support material that will give impact to your information, and the skill to preface and summarize your thoughts, will assist you to communicate effectively in impromptu situations.

Of course, you could also read your manuscript word-for-word. This third form of delivery has advantages and disadvantages. In this mode of delivery your mind is freed from the task of finding the appropriate word and sentence structure because this has already been done in composing the manuscript. Since your written vocabulary is larger than your spoken vocabulary, a more interesting pattern of language may be used. The main disadvantage is the loss of direct eye contact. As a result, you may become more interested in the words themselves than in communicating meaning through them. The reader may present his manuscript without any variety of tone or pace. His whole presentation may lack vitality and interest. There are times, however, when a statement must be read word-for-word. A complex, scientific paper full of important detail must be read to the audience. A nation's statement of policy in a time of crisis with another nation must be read word-for-word so that there is no misunderstanding.

There are some speakers, finally, who prefer to deliver their information from memory. They believe that this form of delivery encompasses all the advantages of the other modes of delivery. The speaker with a memorized speech does have command of the exact wording, as long as he doesn't forget. At the same time he appears to have direct eye contact with his audience. The speaker, however, may be so concerned about the actual wording that in reality he is more in contact with the manuscript than with the audience. The memorized speech makes it more difficult for adaptation during delivery. A skilled speaker may make use of all four forms of delivery. The extemporaneous mode,

however, gives you the best opportunity to deliver your ideas in a conversational manner.

The extemporaneous approach also permits you to develop appropriate gestures to complement the content of your speech. There are two contrasting views on this matter. One group of experts argues that, since the poor use of gestures could destroy the message to be communicated, it is just as important to plan for, develop and present specific gestures as it is to choose thoughts and ideas. The other side, however, insists that the development of planned gestures leads only to a mechanical performance which inhibits communication. This second group points out that if you present your ideas in the extemporaneous fashion involving a personal, conversational approach, then the gestures will come naturally. The only thing to do to improve your use of gestures is to notice during rehearsals those gestures which detract from the message and purposely try to remove them. I recommend the second approach. In my experience I have discovered that the best approach is to help the student remove distracting gestures. I, for instance, developed two bad habits which disturbed audiences. I moved my feet as if following the four corners of a square. The points of the square appeared to be about

SOME GESTURES DETRACT FROM THE MESSAGE

one foot apart. This little shuffle became an irritating pattern that had to be removed. The other distracting gesture consisted of moving the left hand up and down with the palm up as if asking the audience to weigh the importance of the matter under discussion. These kinds of distracting gestures can be identified and removed with the help of your teacher and classmates. A viewing of your class speech on video tape will also assist you to isolate them.

During your first speaking efforts, you will not know what to do with your hands or how much to move from the spot to which you think you have become glued. But with a little experience you will "loosen up" and use your whole body, including facial expressions. It is also true that the subject itself, your compassion for it and the occasion itself will influence the kind and amount of gestures used. A microphone on a stand, for instance, limits the extent of your movement. A large audience in a huge hall requires that your hand motions be more sweeping in extent than if you are speaking to a small audience in a confined space.

Many of the things that have been said about gesturing could be repeated when considering the use of audio visual aids in speaking. Audio visual aids must complement the spoken word. The audience must be able to read the message presented. There is nothing more frustrating for a listener than not being able to decipher the printing or writing. You must control your audio visual aids. Do not let them control you. I remember attending a talk by a leading dietition. The topic was "Your Diet and Your Life Style." Before beginning, the speaker attached about twenty-five pictures on the chalk board with tape. It was an extremely hot afternoon and throughout the talk, one-by-one, the pictures fell to the floor. Not much except the speaker's frustration and disgust was communicated that afternoon.

The extemporaneous manner of delivery permits a speaker to make the most effective use of audio-visual aids. The speaker maintains eye contact naturally with the audience and does not address his remarks to the audio-visual aid. The flexibility of the extemporaneous method allows the speaker to adjust his use of the audio-visual aid based on his assessment of the audience's comprehen-sion. Your best audio-visual aid is, of course, yourself. Make certain that you dress in an appropriate manner for the occasion. This is an important factor even in a classroom speech. I have seen many an effective speech spoiled by poor or inappropriate dress and by a display of bad attitude.

Summary

There are four main styles of delivery usually mentioned: impromptu, read, memorized and extemporaneous. Extemporaneous speaking is the type recommended for classroom speaking because it offers the best opportunity to study all the variables at work. Extemporaneous speaking is used when a speaker has adequate time to prepare and research the topic. The speech is delivered with a minimum of notes, which permits good eye contact with the audience and allows the speaker to make use of feedback from the audience.

Exercise

Deliver an eight- to ten-minute persuasive speech.

9. *Evaluating the Speech*

The final task of the speaker is to evaluate the success of his efforts.

The evaluation process begins, of course, during the speech itself. The speaker who learns to overcome his concern about delivering a speech and is confident of his content and his message soon learns to observe the reaction or overt feedback from his audience. As an inexperienced speaker you will be more concerned with "getting through your material" than with how your audience is receiving it. Before long, however, you will be able to strengthen the sense of communication with your audience and actually see the signs of their reaction to your presentation. You, in turn, will be able to react to their feedback and improve your communication skills still further. For instance, in a speech on "Snakes" you may discover that you overestimated your audience's information on and interest in a subject that is very important to you. You may find it necessary to spend less time than you had planned on "The Scientific Classification of Snakes" and more time on the other aspects of your speech, such as "Snake Charming" and "Treating Snake Bites."

The remaining forms of evaluation take place when the speech is concluded. One valuable form is found in the questions and comments made by members of the audience. Try not to be defensive during this form of exchange of ideas and feelings. Do your best to be objective and respond in a helpful way to these reactions of your audience. Try to analyze the reasons why a particular question is asked. Perhaps you left out some vital information which prevented your questioner from understanding part of your presentation. Perhaps a comment offered signals that you had hit negatively at a belief held dear by a member of your audience. The question period, then, offers an opportunity to assess how good your choices were in preparing your material and how these choices related to the knowledge and commitments of your audience.

In a classroom situation the evaluation procedure is continued as the instructor and your fellow students have oral and written opportunities to offer constructive criticism. Each listener ought to be prepared, having listened attentively and creatively, to offer criticism on the strengths and weaknesses of the speech as it was presented.

Let us pause here to reflect on the topic of "Listening." The study of speech making, believe it or not, assists one to become a better listener. When you realize that the mind has the capability of dealing with far more information than the senses receive at any time, then you understand man's tendency to let his mind wander away from what a speaker is saying at a particular moment. A listener has consciously to direct his thoughts to the speaker's message in order to receive the greatest impact of the speaker's offering. Again, the same method of preparation used by a speaker may be of value to a member of an audience as he listens. The listener should consciously search for the speaker's central idea and what he intends to accomplish. The listener also needs to search for the main points and to isolate the supporting material used to develop these ideas.

The listener needs to look for, or supply himself, transitions and internal summaries and other parts of the structure of the speech. The listener needs to examine how the ideas presented match or are different from his own beliefs on the topic presented. The listener must assess the value of the speaker's use of gestures in reinforcing or detracting from the presentation of ideas.

The listener has a responsibility to prevent other barriers arising when contemplating the speaker's ideas. You may feel that the speaker's voice is bland, his ideas poorly organized, and his topic dull without any relevance to you and your situation. You may further find that the speaker has certain mannerisms which come between you and the speaker's views. You, for instance, may feel that the speaker comes with a biased point of view displaying little attempt to consider and understand other points of view. You may discover that you have to "listen through" a heavy accent or a poor usage of the English language. The situation in which you find yourself may also provide distraction. For instance, the room may be too hot, the people restless, or a door may be banging. You are able to overcome these barriers by developing your concentration and will to listen. You must constantly remind yourself that it is your responsibility to overcome all the internal and external barriers and to search for and understand to the best of your ability the meaning of the message that the speaker is presenting.

With classroom practice, and a consideration of the methods of planning and presenting ideas, and through the monitoring of the speech practices of yourself and others, I am confident that you will experience a growing competence in your efforts to communicate your thoughts and feelings to others. Good luck!

Exercise

Listen to an audio or video recording of your speech and write an evaluation of it.

SELECTED READINGS

Barnlund, Dean C.   *Interpersonal Communication: Survey and Studies.* Boston: Houghton Mifflin, 1968.

Bettinghaus, Erwin P.   *Message Preparation: The Nature of Proof.* Indianapolis: Bobbs-Merrill, 1966.

Brown, Charles T. and C. Van Riper.   *Speech and Man.* Englewood Cliffs, New Jersey: Prentice-Hall, 1966.

Bryant, D. C. and K. R. Wallace.   *Fundamentals of Public Speaking.* 5th ed. New York: Appleton-Century-Crofts, 1969.

Cathcart, Robert S.   *Post-Communication: Critical Analysis and Evaluation.* Indianapolis: Bobbs-Merrill, 1966.

Clevenger, Theodore.   *Audience Analysis.* Indianapolis: Bobbs-Merrill, 1966.

Cronkhite, Gary.   *Persuasion: Speech and Behavioral Change.* Indianapolis: Bobbs-Merrill, 1969.

Gilman, W. E., Bower Aly, and H. L. White.   *An Introduction to Speaking.* 2nd ed. New York: Macmillan Co., 1967, 1968.

Mills, Glen E.   *Message Preparation: Analysis and Structure.* Indianapolis: Bobbs-Merrill, 1966.

Minnick, Wayne C.   *The Art of Persuasion.* 2nd ed. Boston: Houghton Mifflin, 1968.

Monroe, A. H. and D. Ehninger.   *Principles and Types of Speech.* 6th ed. Glenview, Illinois: Scott, Foresman, 1967.

Smith, Alfred G.   *Communication and Culture: Readings in the Codes of Human Interaction.* Ed. Alfred G. Smith. New York: Holt, Rinehart and Winston, 1966.

Wilson, J. F. and C. Arnold.   *Public Speaking as a Liberal Art.* 2nd ed. Boston: Allyn and Bacon, 1968.

9

GROUP DISCUSSION

Ronald F. G. Campbell

In September of 1973 twenty college students gathered in their designated classroom for the first meeting of the course called "Discussion and Group Methods—Theory and Practice." Since this was the first time the course had been given, the students knew very little about its benefits for them. All they had in front of them was a course description which read as follows:

In modern business and industry most of the important decisions are made by small groups of people in consultation. The purpose of this course is to assist the individual to understand human interaction in small groups. The student will learn to develop practical discussion and group leadership abilities. This course considers techniques of group discussion. The principles of planning, conducting and participating in discussions, committee meetings and conferences will be covered. Guidelines for preparing, adapting and testing the validity of information for group discussion will also be presented. Students will participate in class group discussions on topics of their own choosing.

Student curiosity was further increased when the teacher began his first meeting with these questions: "Why have you elected to take this subject? Of what value will this course be to you? Why study group discussion?"

Some of the answers were funny. (I think!) "I needed another English course to graduate and this one fit my timetable." "I like to talk, so I thought this course would suit me." "It didn't look like there would be much writing, so I chose it." "I always lose out in discussions with my friends, so I am taking this course to help me win a few arguments."

Other responses were more appropriate: "In my opinion, in my work many decisions will be made not by individuals, but by groups. I would like to know how group decisions are made." "I was attracted by the part of the course description which promised participation in actual discussions. I feel that I need practice in getting my point across and in understanding the points of view of others." "I have taken a lot of psychology and sociology and I would like to investigate how these concepts operate in the group discussion situation."

These answers were soon followed in turn by another question: "How does a course in group discussion relate to a study of public speaking?"

I feel, first of all, that a student will benefit from such a study of group processes after taking a public speaking course as outlined in a previous section of this text. The student benefits more because a number of the skills required to be successful in a discussion situation are similar to those needed in giving a speech. The public speaker, for instance, must learn to limit the topic. The speaker is required to conduct as much research as time allows. The speaker needs to find supporting material, such as examples and illustrations which are interesting, relevant, and add impact to the acceptance of the message. The speaker is concerned with the listener in all stages of the preparation of a message. The response of the audience must be gauged by the speaker. Also, the speaker must be prepared to adapt to the demonstrated needs of the audience. And finally, the speaker must deliver the message in an interesting and clear voice, and must support the spoken word with suitable gestures. All these qualities are equally valuable to the person who takes part in a group discussion. The person who follows a public speaking course with the study of group discussion strengthens skills and knowledge previously mastered, and adds new information and techniques which will be of value in all circumstances of life.

How does one go about studying group discussion? There is, first of all, a body of knowledge to be reviewed. This research information is gleaned from psychology, anthropology, sociology, education and communication theory. Observation and controlled classroom practice help the student to apply these principles and assist the learner to view strengths and weaknesses objectively.

In the classroom I have found it advantageous to the learning process to intermingle periods of theory with opportunities for practice. In the first introductory sessions the nature of group discussion to be considered in the course is reviewed. A definition of group discussion is then presented

TOWARDS THE SOLUTION OF A SPECIFICALLY DEFINED PROBLEM

and discussed. A process of reflective thinking is introduced. Then the class, with limited understanding of the discussion process, is divided into four groups of five. Each group selects its own leader and a topic of interest to the members. Each group is given at least one week to make preparations for a discussion to be held in a fifty-minute class period. The discussion in class is recorded on audio tape. Members of the class, and the instructor, prepare a criticism of the discussion. This criticism is presented to the members of the discussion group at the next class meeting. When all the groups have completed round one of the discussion, the instructor summarizes the progress made to date and introduces new theory for class consideration. This process is repeated approximately five times in a term. As each round of discussion takes place, individual strengths and weaknesses are noted. The individual participant in this process grows in his knowledge of the group process. He also, through practice, develops skills of leadership and participation. He gains insight into his own personality and understands better the behaviour of others. I also request from each student one major paper on a specific topic which will aid his theoretical understanding of the field of group discussion. I have received papers on such topics as: "The

Causes of Breakdown in Group Discussion," "The Role of Discussion in Modern Industrial and Labour Relations," and "Styles of Leadership in Group Discussion."

Now that you understand some of the background of a course in the group process, let us begin our study with a definition of group discussion. Group discussion as understood in this text is the process by means of oral discourse, whereby a group of two or more people, through cooperative participation, under the guidance of a leader, follow a discussional pattern of reflective thinking towards the solution of a specifically defined problem. This is, of course, more easily said than done! This definition needs some explanation.

The focus of this definition is on the solution of problems. This part of the definition needs to be stressed. Group discussion is not necessary in the search for facts or evidence. This can be done better by an individual working on his own. A bull session where a group of friends sit around socially and talk about whatever comes to mind is not to be classified as a group discussion in this definition. The following situation forms a problem suitable for resolution through group discussion. John and Mary have completed one year at a community college. Both are twenty years of age. They have known each other for a number of years. They want to be married. John's parents want them to wait until they have graduated from their three-year course. Mary's parents have promised that if they do get married, they will give the same amount of support to Mary as they do now. The question is: "Should John and Mary get married now?"

The choices of problems for consideration are of course, endless. Other topics that come to mind include: "What steps, if any, should be taken to improve the city ambulance emergency service?" "Should marijuana be legalized?" "What should the role of students be in the selection of teachers?" Other matters connected with the choice of appropriate problems will be covered later. For now, keep in mind that the centre of attention is on the solution of problems.

The definition stresses, in the second place, that this is a group activity. There is a place in this process for individual initiative, but the whole spirit is based on mutual exploration and cooperative investigation of problem areas. This process is not aided by the individual who is self-centred or who is not eager to learn or know. The person who cannot accept criticism, who is not capable of assuming a questioning stance, is also out of place. The group process is inhibited by the discussant who is not able to control emotional responses.

A good discussion results when the members of the group put the good of the group first. An effective participant is a good listener and one who is willing to base judgments on realistic evidence. The good discussant is one who holds a well-developed position, but at the same time is willing to entertain arguments contrary to these beliefs and values.

It should be pointed out here that the personal qualities which contribute to good group discussion can be developed through practice and criticism. You can learn to control your personal feelings so as to assist the group in its problem solving activity. A productive discussion group made up of individuals committed to the success of the group can be an important asset to any organization.

Thirdly, according to the definition, the progress of the group is aided by the use of the process of reflective thinking. This pattern for discussion has its roots in the work

AN INDIVIDUAL WHO IS NOT EAGER TO LEARN OR KNOW

of an educational philosopher, John Dewey, who in 1910 wrote a book entitled *How We Think*. His writing led to the development of a system of steps to be followed, guiding the participants in their deliberation. In this system there are six steps: (1) definitions, (2) analysis of the problem, (3) criteria for an acceptable solution, (4) alternate solutions, (5) the preferred solution and (6) testing the best solution. Many students find it difficult to acknowledge the need for such a process within group discussion. They do not see the discipline imposed by such a logical approach. Discussion, they feel, is a spontaneous matter which would be inhibited by the straitjacket of a standardized system. The reflective thinking process, however, does assist the participant to order thinking and material to the advantage of the group. These six steps are also used in the research and planning stages of a participant's preparation. A typical outline making use of the headings of the reflective thinking process follows as an example for you to study:

Question
What steps, if any, should be taken to change the emergency ambulance system currently operating in Metropolitan Toronto?

DEFINITIONS · ANALYSIS OF THE PROBLEM · Criteria for an acceptable solution · ALTERNATIVE SOLUTIONS · THE PREFERRED SOLUTION · TESTING THE BEST SOLUTION

THE PROCESS OF REFLECTIVE THINKING

1. *Definitions*
   A. *In the question:*
      (i) *Emergency ambulance system*— this refers to the ambulances, both privately owned and government controlled, which respond to calls made through the Emergency Measures Organization.
      (ii) *Metropolitan Toronto* consists of the City of Toronto and surrounding boroughs operating together in this matter of emergency ambulance service.
   B. *Terms in discussion:*
      (i) *Private operators*—a number of ambulances are managed by private companies. They are licensed by the Province.
      (ii) *Emergency Measures Organization*—a Provincial organization established to deal with emergencies.

2. *Analysis of the Problem*
   A. *Symptoms:* Lately a number of complaints have been received concerning the length of time it has taken an emergency ambulance to reach the scene of an accident.
      (i) It is reported that it took an ambulance fifteen minutes to reach a young boy in a park who had suffered a serious head injury in a baseball game.
      (ii) Relatives of the victims of a two-car accident claimed that they waited at the scene for thirty-five minutes after the ambulance had been called.
   B. *Causes:*
      (i) The large size of the territory of Metropolitan Toronto, with insufficient men and equipment, appears to be the major cause of delays.
      (ii) An antiquated despatching system is another cause.
      (iii) There really are two systems— one provided by private companies and the other managed by a public agency. This leads to delays in the relaying of messages, differences in standards, wages and training.
      (iv) The requirement that ambulance drivers must deliver the patient to a hospital bed rather than just to the hospital emergency ward is another cause for delay.
   C. *General evaluation:* The problems in

emergency ambulance service seem to arise mainly because of a patch-work system being developed without any single agency having to demonstrate responsibility.

3. *Criteria* (to judge acceptable solutions)
   A. There must be uniform service throughout the whole of Metropolitan Toronto.
   B. An emergency ambulance should normally be on the accident scene no later than ten minutes after the report has been received.
4. *Alternate Solutions*
   A. The Province of Ontario should hire a consultant firm to prepare a study on the emergency ambulance service.
      (i) *Advantages:* All the facts will be known before any piecemeal action is taken which could further damage the emergency service.
      (ii) *Disadvantages:* Any further delay could cost lives. The morale of the employees could deteriorate during this interim period.
      No guarantee that a ten-minute limit could be achieved.
   B. The Province of Ontario should give the authority to one agency for this emergency ambulance service.
      (i) *Advantages:* Uniform service could be more easily achieved.
      (ii) *Disadvantages:* One responsible agency does not necessarily mean that adequate financial support would be given.
   C. The community fire departments should be given the responsibility for the emergency ambulance service.
      (i) *Advantages:* Fire departments seem to have the training and the capability for meeting emergencies in a short span of time.
      Fire departments have many years of experience in meeting emergencies and appear to have an adequate organization.
      A completely new organization at this stage would be appropriate.
      (ii) *Disadvantages:* Each borough has a separate fire department. Different kinds of emergency requests could cause confusion within the fire department and result in more disastrous delays.

5. *The preferred solution*
   The preferred solution seems to be a combination of A and B. If one agency were given responsibility, then some of the disparities in the service could be eliminated. The Government at the same time would have to give this agency adequate financial support to commission a long-range study and to reach the ten-minute criteria of service.

6. *Testing the best solution*
   I would recommend that a pilot operation be established in the Borough of North York. When this system met the stated criteria, then it could be expanded to the whole of Metropolitan Toronto.

The final aspect of the definition to be considered is summarized in the words "under the guidance of a leader." It is possible for a group discussion to function without a designated leader. The roles of the leader in these circumstances must be assumed by the individual participants. It is my opinion that in the beginning stages of the study and practice of group discussion, a leader is indispensible.

Up to this point we have talked about the nature of group discussion and considered in general terms how one studies it. Now let's suppose you have decided to go into the subject in greater depth. What do you need to know and how are you to put this information into practice?

As indicated earlier, the best method is to divide the class of twenty into four discussion groups of five people each. Each group selects a leader and agrees on a topic.

Summary

The study of group discussion will assist the student to investigate how decisions are made in small groups. By the discovery method the student will come to understand how the group operates, using the strengths and overcoming the weaknesses of the members. Many of the skills developed in the speech course will be of value in group dis-

GAIN UNANIMOUS ACCEPTANCE OF THE TOPIC

cussion. The use of precise language and relevant supporting materials will aid each participant in communicating ideas. Dewey's method of Reflective Thinking is adapted in this text to form a framework for the logical preparation and presentation of material.

CHOOSING SUBJECTS FOR DISCUSSION

The group will find that the task of choosing a topic is difficult. However, it is a crucial activity which has a great influence on the success or failure of the eventual discussion. The participants must do their best to gain unanimous acceptance of the topic. It is important that each member show that he is interested in the subject, and that it is relevant to life today. Under these conditions the participants will be prepared to take the discussion seriously and prepare themselves adequately. The beginning discussion group should also choose a subject that can be easily researched. Is information readily available? Are experts who will be willing to discuss the subject close at hand?

Where do you discover suitable discussion topics? Subjects may come from issues currently in the news either locally or national in scope. Editorials in the newspaper may prove a valuable source. Magazine articles also may offer the basic idea for your group.

Continuing social issues, such as poverty, euthanasia, the use of drugs, women's rights and government support for medical care are topics which can bear further illumination.

The problem chosen must be capable of having more than one solution. The final answer must not be capable of having a "yes" or "no" answer. The selected problem must be suitable for the time allowed for this discussion. This is not an important point in an informal, private discussion where everyone has the opportunity to review the problem without any time constraint. However, in public discussion on radio or television or as part of an open live community program, time is an important factor which the leader and his group must keep in mind.

If an audience is present, additional factors regarding the choice of topic must be considered. It is crucial that the audience have an acute interest in the discussion topic in order to maintain attention.

Through experience it has been shown that questions of policy are better topics for group discussion. A policy problem might be, for instance, "What changes, if any, should be made in the speed-limit laws in the Province?" Questions of fact are mostly inappropriate. An example of a question of fact is, "Is the government deficit increasing or decreasing?" Questions of value are also difficult because they depend so often not on facts and evidence but on personal opinions and beliefs. Questions such as, "What is the significance of the church in modern society?" fit into this category.

PHRASING THE PROBLEM

Once the general topic has been chosen, then it must be phrased appropriately. This, too, is a vital step. It is best in this process to state the problem in the form of a question. This helps to delimit the problem. For instance, a discussion topic "United Fund" would be of little assistance to the participants in their research, preparation and thinking. A discussion group assuming this topic would spend a great deal of time trying to gain a point of view to act as a starting point. However, if the group framed the problem as follows: "What changes should be made in the methods used by the United Fund to raise money?" the group would have a better chance to have a meaningful discussion. The question should not contain any ambiguous language which could cause difficulty in the discussion. For instance, consider this statement: "What policies should experts recommend to change the educational system in Canada?" This question would be of little value in setting the stage for a useful group discussion. Who are the experts referred to? Are they educators or economists or what? What is meant by the "educational system"? Does this refer to the Province or the local community? Perhaps it would be helpful to restate the problem as follows: 'Should changes be made in the methods of teaching mathematics in public school education?"

The question should also be phrased impartially without any possible indication of judgment of the situation or of the outcome. For example, the above question could be stated to colour the whole discussion: "What should be done to improve the inadequate teaching of mathematics in public school education?" This, of course, gives a biased slant to the whole discussion.

Summary

The subject chosen for group discussion must meet the following criteria: It must be of interest to as many participants as possible, and have the unanimous approval of all the discussants. The topic must be relevant and current. It must be capable of having more than one answer. Once the appropriate problem has been selected, it must be phrased in the form of a question. The question should not contain any ambiguous language and must be as specific as possible so as to limit the range of the discussion. Impartial terms must be used to frame the question.

THE ROLE OF THE LEADER

The leader's role starts right at the beginning of the whole group discussion process. He must be prepared to know as much as possible about the topic. Besides assisting the group to state the problem in appropriate terms, the leader helps the group establish other procedures and arrangements. He sets the date for the discussion itself. He conducts a preliminary discussion on the present views of the group on the chosen topic. He calls any planning meetings that are needed. These planning sessions are valuable as opportunities for sharing of information and ideas discovered during the individual research efforts of the participants. He helps the members to share sources of information and insights into the problem. It is the leader's responsibility to spot those members of the group who are not carrying out their research and study responsibilities. It is also during this period that the leader must discover the potential strengths and weaknesses of the discussion skills of the participants.

Having made this analysis, the leader must take steps during the discussion itself to deal with these findings. Some people are inhibited in the presence of a group and must be encouraged to contribute to the discussion. The leader must be aware of these members and try to involve them by asking them questions about the matter under discussion. Sometimes the leader can help the hesitant one by asking that person to provide a summary of what had been accomplished by the group up to that point.

It is the leader's responsibility to make certain that everyone speaks in a voice loud enough to be heard clearly by all the members of the group. If there is an audience present, the leader must encourage the mem-

EVERYONE SPEAKS IN A VOICE LOUD ENOUGH TO BE HEARD CLEARLY BY ALL

bers of the group to speak loudly enough for all to hear. When a discussion is broadcast over radio or television, it is important that the group members use their microphones correctly.

Sometimes the leader finds it necessary to limit the contributions of one or two members in favour of participation by all the discussants. The domination of one participant, no matter how well informed, may disrupt the discussion process.

The leader is responsible for guiding the group through the discussion process to a satisfactory conclusion. This task requires a great deal of experience in group methods. The leader must know as much as possible about the topic. However, this knowledge must be used judiciously. The leader's beliefs, however, must not be allowed to dominate the discussion. The leader must use this information to act as a background from which to judge contributions which are irrelevant or hinder group progress. The group leader summarizes the progress made by the participants. The leader is responsible for timing the discussion when a time limit is imposed. The leader may utilize the six steps of the reflective thinking process in outline form as follows:

1 min.	1. Statement of problem
3 min.	2. Introduction of the discussion topic
2 min.	3. Definitions
8 min.	4. Analysis of the problem
3 min.	5. Criteria by which to judge acceptable solutions
10 min.	6. Alternate solutions
7 min.	7. The preferred solution
8 min.	8. Testing the best solution
3 min.	9. Conclusion of the discussion

Finally, the leader is required to minimize unnecessary disagreements which may arise because of the clash of personalities. This does not mean that differences based on fact and logic cannot be entertained.

PARTICIPATION

It is true that the leader bears a heavy responsibility for the success of the group deliberation. The remaining participants, however, have their responsibilities. Each participant assumes the duty of developing a position on the issue by means of adequate research and the willingness to engage in a logical thinking process.

GROUP COHESIVENESS

The individual discussant also assists the group to reach its goal by active participation. Clear, thoughtful and colourful language is used to express his views. Each participant must promote group cohesiveness. This is done by minimizing irrelevant disagreements, and by helping the group to progress through the discussion process as quickly and efficiently as possible. The useful discussant helps the quiet ones in the group to speak out on the matter under discussion, and assists the leader to control those who would dominate the proceedings. Each discussion must be a learning experience for each participant. The dynamics of the group must be studied. The participant tries to understand what actually happened to the group as it struggled to solve the problem in the most reasonable manner possible. The main fault with discussion participants is that they refuse to listen closely to other discussants and weigh carefully what the other person is saying. In a discussion situation you must keep asking yourself: "What did he say?" "What is the meaning and significance of that contribution?" and 'How does it relate to my beliefs, the facts I have gathered, and the problem as I see it?"

Summary

The leader or chairman of the group bears a heavy responsibility in bringing about the success of the group in solving the chosen problem. The main task is to assist the progress of the group through the discussion process. The leader assists the individual members of the group to participate to the best of their ability. Each discussant, however, is required to make a contribution to the success of the group based upon thorough preparation.

EVALUATION

As in all forms of communication, such as public speaking and debating, the evaluation process is a significant one. I usually ask each listener to submit a written evaluation of the leader and each participant immediately at the close of the discussion. An evaluation instrument which could be helpful in this process follows:

Evaluation of Discussion

	Poor	Excellent
1. Statement of Problem Comments:		1 - 2 - 3 - 4 - 5
2. The Role of the leader		
(a) His role as chairman		1 - 2 - 3 - 4 - 5
(b) His role as participant		1 - 2 - 3 - 4 - 5
(c) Signs of preparation		1 - 2 - 3 - 4 - 5
Comments:		
3. Participants		
Name_____		1 - 2 - 3 - 4 - 5
Comments:		
Name_____		1 - 2 - 3 - 4 - 5
Comments:		
Name_____		1 - 2 - 3 - 4 - 5
Comments:		
Name_____		1 - 2 - 3 - 4 - 5
Comments:		
4. Group as a whole		1 - 2 - 3 - 4 - 5

This instrument is purposefully general in nature. This allows the critic to use his full knowledge in evaluating the discussion. When the written criticism has been completed, I usually conduct an oral class discussion on the strengths and weaknesses of the participants in the discussion. Areas for improvement are isolated and suggestions for correction are offered.

The whole discussion is recorded on audio tape. This record forms the basis for a written criticism developed by the instructor. Typical comments are reflected in the two following criticisms:

Seneca College of Applied Arts and Technology: Group Discussion

QUESTION: What steps, if any, should be taken to better safeguard air passengers and airline crew against air terrorism?
CHAIRMAN: Glenn. PARTICIPANTS: Flo, Susan, Tricia, Louis

Participation in this discussion was uneven. Some people seemed to have prepared well and others made little preparation. In general, the same criticism can be made in this discussion as has been made for most of the discussions. That is, that in-depth discussion does not take place. There was some questioning of points, but I'm not sure that this questioning contributed to the understanding of the group or contributed toward the progress of the discussion.

The definition stage provided some interesting considerations. Tricia's restatement of the question was interesting but largely ignored by the group.

The analysis stage, in my opinion, was confused as to symptoms and causes. There were many irrelevancies in the causes stage. This was not true in other aspects of the discussion. The Chairman contributed to the discussion by encouraging those who were not participating.

The criteria stage was done, in my opinion, again very poorly. Solutions were presented at this stage rather than goals, aims and objectives.

Here again, summaries would have helped in seeing what progress was being made.

The possible solutions were interesting and inventive. Some of the members of the discussion group were speaking too quietly, but the Chairman asked them to speak up. This helped the situation.

The preferred solution could have come more easily if the group had landed on the technique of a short term/long term approach to the solution of the problem. The group finally did, in essence, come to this solution. This group made good use of the division called "implementation."

The marks for this discussion were assigned as follows: *Tricia: 9.* I believe that you displayed in this discussion a good command of the topic, some thoughtful consideration of the problem, and a willingness to share this information and to discuss it with others. The only comment of real criticism would be to speak up. *Flo: 6.* I see in your participation in this discussion an improvement. You seem to be willing to share your ideas a little more than you have been in the past and to consider questions concerning your contributions. You could still participate more and do so without the use of your notes. *Glenn: 7.* The Chairman, as I have indicated, is an important person in the discussion group. You displayed a concern for those who were not participating and invited their assistance in the solution to the problem. In my opinion, you relaxed during the question period when you should still be in command of the situation, knowledgeable about the progress of the questions and concerned for those who want to enter into the discussion at that stage. The introduction was practically nonexistent and the concluding remarks did not further the progress of understanding of the problems. *Susan: 7.* Again, when you participate, you demonstrate a knowledge of the subject and clear thinking. I do believe, in this discussion, that you could have participated more. *Louis: 8.* I believe that you were well prepared and capable of discussing the whole situation. The one criticism I would have, is that you still have a tendency to question in an abrupt manner that could offend some people. Make sure that your questioning is not just for the sake of questioning, but that it contributes to the progress of the discussion."

Seneca College of Applied Arts and Technology: Group Discussion

QUESTION: What steps should all social

institutions take to prevent child abuse?
CHAIRMAN: Bill. PARTICIPANTS: Ralph, Naomi, Louise

The Chairman attempted to give a better introduction to the topic than had been given by most of the chairmen in the discussions so far. I believe that this introduction set the stage for the topic. It seems to me, however, that very often the chairmen encourage participation by members of the discussion in an artificial manner, such as: "Would someone like to open the discussion?" I believe that this encouragement for participants ought to be more subtle and sophisticated.

The discussion began well with terms to be defined. The group took a broad view of the term "social institutions." This term could have been misinterpreted if some time had not been spent on defining it. This was perhaps one of the best introductions to definition of terms. The restatement of the question amplified the topic under discussion to include mistreatment of all children in all forms. The group also stated that all rights of children ought to be considered in the discussion.

In the analysis stage, the symptoms were brought out in an interesting manner, demonstrating good personal research by most of the people present. Up to this stage I do believe that most of the people were participating well, both in the discussion itself and in assisting in the progress of the discussion in terms of the process. I do believe that also, for perhaps the first time, some in-depth discussion was taking place. The tendency has been in the past to throw out an idea without following up carefully and examining it on all sides before proceeding to the next point.

I cannot emphasize enough that internal summaries would be helpful to the progress of the discussion. I keep asking myself: "Where are we?"

The causes were reviewed carefully, although the group began to forget about their reasons for gathering and the process used to demonstrate progress.

In the criteria stage, in my opinion, the goals, objectives and solutions were mixed up. Irrelevancies began to enter into the discussion, althought this was not the reason I stopped the discussion. The reason I stopped the discussion was that I thought many of the audience had good points to offer and I wanted to take advantage of them.

On the whole, I was very pleased with this group, and I am sure that if the Chairman and the group had been allowed to continue, that they would have come forward with an excellent preferred solution.

The marks for this discussion were assigned as follows: *Bill: 8.* You as Chairman displayed a good ability to think on your feet and to present ideas without dominating the group itself. As I indicated earlier in this criticism, you could improve your contribution by helping others to start their contribution if you asked a more subtle question in line with the discussion itself. *Ralph: 8.* In this discussion, you entered into the topic more fully than you did in the last group discussion. Your contributions were well thought out and you helped the group in the business of in-depth discussion of relevant points. I believe that you could have helped more with steering the group in terms of the process itself. *Naomi: 7.* In the course you have developed in your ability to relate to others, and also to consider the contributions of others and apply your thoughts in sequential form. I still think that you need to speak up louder and to be a bit more aggressive in your presentations. *Louise: 7.* Throughout the course you have demonstrated a willingness to do excellent research and to find a considerable amount of personal opinions from experts to add to the spice of the discussion. I still think you need, at times, to listen to the real meaning behind someone else's presentation in the discussion. You don't have any problem relating to other people and expressing your opinions.

USES OF GROUP DISCUSSION

Up to this point we have been considering group discussion as a classroom exercise, revealing to the participants knowledge about human interaction, as students in small groups seek to find solutions to specific problems. This understanding and practice, however, is valuable outside the classroom as well. People find themselves daily in situa-

LET'S DISCUSS THIS, MEN!

GROUP DISCUSSION IS A VALUABLE SKILL

tions where the practice of group discussion is a valuable skill to possess.

The opportunities for the use of the techniques of group discussion may be broken down for convenience into two main areas—private and public. Private uses for discussion are found, first of all, in *study groups*. Here the analysis of the problem is of utmost significance. Definitions and explanations are also important as the participants seek to broaden their understanding of particular subject matter. Teachers often use this form of group discussion to assist students to appreciate concepts and ideas presented to them.

Conferences called (between members of an organization) to review apparent difficulties may also be classified as private group discussions. For instance, an automobile company may find that its advertising campaign is not complementary to the production efforts of its latest model. Representatives of the marketing division are asked to confer with the production division to iron out these difficulties. In this form of group discussion the emphasis is on the definition of the difficulty, its cause and the alternative solutions to the problem. Knowledgeable participants are an asset to this process.

Committee deliberation is the third main type of private discussion commonly used today. Here the definition of the committee's assignment is of prime importance. The committee operates in an informal atmosphere. One of the most inhibiting factors in the committee situation is usually the lack of adequate information. Under this condition the chairman might consider adjournment until the necessary information is obtained.

Public discussion, in contrast to private discussion, usually takes place before a large group where all members are not normally given the opportunity to participate. Public discussion is often held in an auditorium rather than in a committee room. Some public discussions may also be broadcast over radio and television. Although public discussion makes use of all the techniques of preparation of material and presentation of ideas mentioned in connection with classroom and private discussion, there are notable differences. In public discussion the participants must demonstrate carefully that progress is being made in the consideration of a topic that is of current interest. Interesting presentations in a public discussion are essential. Illustrations which make the discussion relevant for the listener are most important. Good speech and language habits are a "must" in public discussion. The introduction of the topic for public discussion must be stimulating and draw the interest of the audience members. If there are to be questions allowed from the audience, the rules permitting such participation must be clearly stated by the chairman. The *panel group* is an example of a public discussion. Here four or five members of the panel under the direction of a chairman present various points of view on a particular issue of interest to the general listening audience. Questions may be entertained by the chairman either by telephone, if the discussion is broadcast, or in person if there is a live audience present.

A *symposium-forum* is another form of public discussion. In this type of discussion three or four speeches on a specific issue are presented, usually by experts. For instance, the shortage of housing may be considered by a developer, a local government official and a private citizen, hoping to purchase his own home. The chairman in a symposium situation has a slightly different role to perform than in many other forms of discussion.

In his introduction he must explain the significance of the topic and prepare the audience for the treatment of the subject. He also introduces each participant and summarizes the discussion at the end. And it is the duty of the chairman to field the questions from the audience and direct them to the appropriate speaker.

The *colloquium* is a type of public discussion which combines the formats of the panel and the forum. The chairman and the panel begin the discussion of the issue in the usual way. If at any point a panel member feels that members of the audience could assist the deliberations by means of a question or an informed comment, then the chairman calls for audience participation.

There are many forms of private and public discussion. The most appropriate type is chosen based on the nature of the issue under discussion and the occasion at which the discussion is to take place.

Concluding Remarks

In the highly organized society in which we live more and more decisions are negotiated by people in group discussion. In the course of a day you will find yourself participating in family meetings, conferences at work, and community committees of all kinds. Discussion skills will be demonstrated daily for you on radio and television. Your knowledge of the theory of the group process,

and your experience as a discussant will help you become an effective participant in all these opportunities for problem solving.

Exercises
1. Prepare a discussion outline for the situation mentioned in the book involving the desire of John and Mary to be married.
2. Observe a group discussion on television and write a report of your experience.
3. Evaluate two aspects of the following discussion topics:
   (a) suitability of phrasing and (b) suitability for discussion:
      1. On reducing strikes in Ontario.
      2. What proportion of outstanding lawyers are graduates of Osgood Hall?
      3. How, if at all, should the organization of our armed forces be modified?
      4. Unqualified applicants should not be admitted to institutions of higher learning.
      5. What difference would the widespread use of abortion make in our views of marriage?
4. If a discussion group did not have a designated discussion leader, what actions would individuals in the group have to take to compensate for this?
5. Choose a topic and conduct a problem-solving discussion using the principles outlined in this book.

SELECTED READINGS

Gulley, Halbert E. *Discussion, Conference, and Group Process.* 2nd ed. New York: Holt, Rinehart and Winston, 1968.

Maier, Norman R. F. *Problem Solving Discussions and Conferences: Leadership Methods and Skills.* New York: McGraw-Hill, 1963.

Phillips, G. M. *Communication and the Small Group.* Indianapolis: Bobbs-Merrill, 1966.

Phillips, G. M. and E. C. Erickson. *Interpersonal Dynamics in the Small Group.* New York: Random House, 1970.

Potter, D. and M. P. Anderson. *Discussion: A Guide to Effective Practice.* 2nd ed. Belmont, California: Wadsworth Publishing Co., 1970.

Utterback, W. E. *Group Thinking and Conference Leadership.* Rev. ed. New York: Holt, Rinehart and Winston, 1964.

10

WRITTEN COMMUNICATION
Getting It Together

Vernon F. Gunckel

INTRODUCTION: Bits and Pieces

Ce que l'on conçoit bien s'énonce clairement,
Et les mots pour le dire arrivent aisément.

Whatever we conceive well we express clearly,
and words flow with ease.
L'Art Poétique Nicolas Boileau-Despréaux

Perhaps you have played the popular party game of Scrambled Words. Each person is given a list of scrambled letters and asked to unscramble them so that they form a particular word.

Listed below are the names of ten cities located in Canada. You will note that the letters are scrambled. The letters are only *bits and pieces.* Can you get these letters together in such a way that each city can be identified?
(You will find the answers at the end of this chapter)

RSTOI-SIIERVRÈ   _____ _____
DNEOMOTN   _____
HXLIFAA   _____
OLMNRÈAT   _____
CREVNAOVU   _____
TTOAWA   _____
EGRNIA   _____
RONOTOT   _____
NWPENIGI   _____
FEYEOWLLKIN   _____

How successful were you in being able to get the *bits* and *pieces,* the *letters,* together to form the names of cities?

It would certainly be no game if, every time we wanted to know something, we had to unscramble the letters. The novelty would soon wear off.

Have you ever received a note from a friend that didn't seem to make any sense?

You may have spent a considerable amount of time trying to figure out just what the writer meant. Perhaps the words were not in the right place or were incorrectly used for the expression of a particular thought?

- Now—what did she mean by that?
- He must have misunderstood me!
- This just doesn't make sense to me!
- What?

In many ways, some of the letters we receive appear to resemble our scrambled-cities game. The pieces don't seem to fit together. We have to unscramble the message. It may also be that your interpretation of what your friend thinks he has said is something very different from what *you* think he has said!

A few years ago, while teaching an English-Communication class in a community college, a friend of mine had asked his students to write a few comments about a book they had been asked to read. The book, *La Guerre, Yes Sir!* by Roch Carrier, is a succinct comment on the English-French situation in Quebec, particularly as it existed during the Second World War.

In his own way, each student had attempted to write out a description of his interpretation of the thoughts expressed in the book. Here are a few examples of some of the things the students had to say.

- Corriveau, left his community to go to war, then came back but he was dead.
- Everyone usually knows everyone in the village, and what everyone is doing. Carrier showed this at Madame Corriveau's house during the party which was held in honour of her son who died at war and who's corps was brought to her house which presently was in the living room.
- The villager's attendance at mass and all the formulas they faithfully repeat in front of Corriveau's coffin. An events is when sister Esmalda [nun] come to visit her brother in the coffin.
- If I was to write a book on French-Canada, I can't say I would go about it in any different way that Carrier did, except for some little things I would probably emphasize the community part more and I would have written authors comment, or an introduction or something, to stop the readers from guessing but other than that, I would make no changes.

Do these comments make much sense to YOU?

Are they not much like the scrambled-cities game?

If you had read the book, you might, after a period of time, be able to put the BITS and PIECES together in such a way that *you* would understand what had been written. Please don't misunderstand me. I do not want to poke fun at anyone. I have selected these examples so as to demonstrate that often what we *think* we have written is not always interpreted in the same manner. I am sure that the students who had written these comments understood what *they* had meant. But to others, the words were scrambled.

Again, let me use another example to point out rather vividly a serious problem that we have with our written communication.

A student once brought me a paper which had been poorly written. Words were misspelled. Often the words were not the ones the student had intended to convey his meaning. Sentences were incomplete. Continuity of thought was totally absent. The paper was returned to him with a very low mark. I had not failed him because I had wanted to offer some encouragement.

The next day the student, very upset, came to my office. He spoke to me very sternly. "How dare you give me a low grade! When I presented this paper to my high school English teacher last year, he gave me an A!"

Overlooking, for the moment, the fact that he had taken a paper previously written for another teacher and had passed it off on me, I was interested in how *any* teacher could have given this person the highest possible mark on what was to me a complete scramble. Being curious and concerned, I asked him for the name of the teacher for whom the paper had been written. It just so happened that during that week I had been visiting his high school in an attempt to develop a liaison between the college where I was teaching and the high schools in the community.

The next day I had a chance to visit his former teacher. After talking about things in general, I asked if he remembered my student. His reply was a very enthusiastic Yes. Pushing further, I asked him if he remembered an essay that the student had prepared for him during the previous year. With all the student papers a teacher grades in a year, I honestly didn't expect him to remember. But much to my surprise he again responded with an enthusiastic yes. He went on to describe this particular essay as "ingenious and creative." My immediate response was one of shock and disbelief. He had to be putting me on.

After a rather lengthy discussion about the nature of creative writing, he explained to me that he was aware of grammatical errors, errors in spelling and problems with the overall structure.

His belief was that the "creativeness" was more important than the identification of any errors in the mechanics of writing. My question was, "How do you know what he said?" His immediate response was, "Oh, I know him and the way in which he thinks. It all made sense to me." Having had this student in my class for only a short period of time, I acknowledged that I didn't know him and could hardly know what he had attempted to say in the paper. I am not sure I would have ever known. To top this off, the student was enrolled in the college as a business management candidate. Can you imagine what written instructions he might give to his employees?

Sentences taken from actual letters received by a governmental office in application for financial support, while they may be humorous to us, reveal what words misplaced, scrambled, can do.

- I am forwarding my marriage certificate and six children. I have seven, but one died, which was baptized on a half sheet of paper.
- I am glad to report that my husband who is missing, is dead.
- In accordance with your instructions, I have given birth to twins in the enclosed envelope.

Bits and pieces, when properly put into a form we can understand, make things intelligible to us.

ELEMENTS—STRUCTURE

Another term we might use for the Bits and Pieces is

ELEMENTS

A STRUCTURE PROVIDES A FRAMEWORK AROUND WHICH WE PLACE ELEMENTS

Bits and Pieces are *Elements*.

You and I live in a world of elements, a world of bits and pieces. We can go so far as to say that anything that exists contains *elements*. We can only understand each other when these elements are placed into some type of structure or form.

Life appears in the union of substance and form. These things are elemental. *To be without form is the void of matter, and it is the void of thought.*

Look at these *lines*. They are *elements*. These elements, much like the letters of our scrambled-cities game at the beginning of this chapter, are not in a structure that we can understand. They are only lines on paper. Can you put them together in such a way that they make sense?

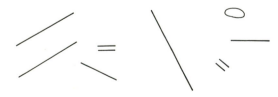

Look at these *words*. They are also *elements*.

THAT OF THE IMPRESS YOU IT WELL IS WRITTEN WILL HOPED IMPORTANCE THIS CHAPTER COMMUNICATION UPON

The *words,* while recognizable to us, are not placed in a form or STRUCTURE that we can comprehend.

A *Structure* provides a framework around which we can build by using *Elements*.

Can you get the words, the *elements*, together in such a way that they will provide you with a *structure* which will make sense to you?

How did you do?

Did you get it all together?

After some period of time you may be able to put these *elements* together in such a manner that they will make sense to you. The lines, letters, and words are only the *elements* and not the thought itself. They are understood only when placed in a *structure* or form that is familiar to you.

If you place the lines, as shown in our first illustration, into a familiar structure, we will see a stick figure of a man.

If you place the *words* into a familiar *structure,* you will see that I have a message for you.

IT IS HOPED THAT THIS CHAPTER WILL IMPRESS UPON YOU THE IMPORTANCE OF WELL WRITTEN COMMUNICATION.

Everything is composed of *elements*. When put into a *structure* that you and I can understand, these elements take on a familiar form.

Can you think of any instances when what may appear to be structure may also be an element? How can something be both an element and a structure at one and the same time?

Let's look at an example.

Leaves and branches are the *elements* that make up the *structure* that we call a tree. The tree is the structure and the leaves and branches the elements. However, if we place the tree in a forest, it then becomes an element in the structure that is the forest. We can also go in the other direction. The *leaves* are *structure* and the *veins* and *chemicals* which make up the composition of each leaf are *elements*.

Let us return to the scrambled sentence in our illustration. The *letters*, or elements, formed *words*. The *words* are known to us; therefore we can say that they are in a structure because they are familiar to us. But if these words are scrambled, they cannot be readily understood as a complete thought until they have been placed into a *structure*.

After we have unscrambled the words and placed them into a message that makes sense, is it possible that the message which makes up a sentence can, like the tree, be an element as well?

If you say yes, you are correct!

When the sentence is placed in a *paragraph*, it is only one of several sentences. Standing by itself, without other sentences, it might not have the full impact or understanding that we desire. It is at this point that the sentence becomes the *Element* and the paragraph the *Structure*.

In the same way, the paragraph becomes an *element* when placed in position with other paragraphs to form a larger piece of communication.

Does this all sound very complicated to you?

Just think what our communication would be like if we didn't understand how these *elements* and *structures* can affect what we want to say.

Have you ever stopped to think that everything that is written in the English language is based on only **26** ELEMENTS?

We call these elements, in *Structure*, the *Alphabet*. The great writing of Shakespeare, Dante, Tennyson, Milton, and Dryden is based on an alphabet of only 26 letters!

If you are a musician, have you ever realized that all of the music written in the Western world has been based on only **8** notes taken from that *structure* that we call the Major Musical Scale?

Think about this!

The great symphonies of Beethoven, Mozart, and Tchaikovsky; the organ and choral works of J. S. Bach; the rock of Guess Who, King Biscuit Boy, or the songs of Anne Murray or Stompin' Tom Connors—all are developed around the eight *elements* that make up what we know as the Major Musical Scale. Whether the music is classical, country and Western, jazz, or rock, it makes no difference. When we say that we don't like a type of music, we are actually saying that we don't like the configuration in which the notes have been placed.

Our Thoughts are given meaning for others when we use elements in structure in order to communicate.

Expressing a thought means giving it a form that is recognizable to another person. Shakespeare has described it as the poetic process, but it is what actually takes place in every person who thinks, speaks or writes.

And, as imagination bodies forth
The forms of things unknown, the poet's
* pen*
Turns them to shapes, and gives to airy
* nothing*
A local habitation and a name.
*   A Midsummer Night's Dream,*
*   Act V, Scene 1*

An unformed thought, a thought not yet turned to shape, is only a vague impression, sensed but not grasped, an airy nothing, until given a local habitation and a name. The local habitation is its embodiment in some image associated with remembered sense experience. That image must have a name, a word, a sound that stands for it. By this process, it is given recognizable form. We create words from our thoughts so that we may identify our thoughts to others. If our elements are placed into a structure others can understand, we have begun the process of communication.

Getting It Together:
1 Anything that exists contains *elements*.
2 A *structure* provides a framework around which to build.
3 When given a place in a structure YOU and I can understand, *elements* take on a familiar form.
4 Our thoughts are given meaning to others in that we use *elements* in *structure* in order to communicate.

WELL WRITTEN COMMUNICATION COMMUNICATES

Grammar: A Key to Understanding
How many times have you communicated in writing during the last 24 hours?

How many times have others communicated with you in writing in the same time period?

Perhaps you read a book or received a letter from a friend.

It may be that you have just completed an essay for class or sent a note to a friend.

Maybe you have filled in an application for a job or have written a driver's licence examination.

THE WRITTEN WORD REMAINS VITAL

While most of our personal interactions are based on face-to-face encounters, much of our communication is in written form. Letters to friends or business associates, legal documents, newspapers, books, magazines, interdepartmental memorandums, essays, business reports, are only a few of the examples of written communication.

Even though the telephone, radio and television have provided us with an extension of ourselves in the form of amazing technological tools for communicating, the written word remains vital in our society.

As a student, you will be asked to write that essay which will be due for class next Monday morning.

As an employer, you might be asked to draw up a set of written directives for your employees.

As a job seeker, you will write a letter of application and will compile a résumé of your qualifications and experience.

Individuals still read the great books, protect themselves or their possessions with legal documents, retain jobs through written negotiated contracts, keep historical records, write letters, and attempt to express inner feelings in written form.

How important our writing becomes when seen in this light!

How does one prevent being misunderstood when speaking or writing?

How does one know if what one has to say in written form is understood by most?

Some years ago, a rather large industrial corporation was facing a walkout of its employees because of a memorandum issued by their employer. The employer was an intelligent and personable individual, but he lacked one important skill. He could not communicate well in writing. He had not learned how to place elements (words) into a structure which would be clearly understood by most. His memorandum to his employees was to communicate to them that they would be required to work shorter hours with an increase in pay.

This doesn't sound like something to make a man walk off his job, does it? The memorandum, however, was phrased in such a way that the employees understood it quite differently. They interpreted the memorandum to say that some jobs would be cut, leaving some individuals unemployed, and that because of increased costs at the plant, there would be no cost-of-living increase for the year.

The employer could not understand what the problem was until he had called in a communication expert, the shop foreman, a labour negotiator, and representatives of the employees. All this simply because the employer could not communicate clearly. The memorandum had made sense to him, but he forgot or failed to realize that others might interpret the message differently.

In the past few years I have met many businessmen, teachers, and other people in all walks of our society who have returned to school during the evening hours in order to learn how to communicate better in writing. In some instances, promotions in a company had been withheld until the person could demonstrate that he could communicate well in writing. I have seen various companies pay the tuition for many of their employees so that they might take advantage of learning the skill they should have possessed years before. These individuals had come to realize just how important written communication was in their day-to-day interactions. They wanted to learn how to prevent being misunderstood in their written communication and how to communicate more effectively.

The key to better writing is contained in that discipline which we call

GRAMMAR

For various reasons, your reaction to this word may be something less than positive. The very word seems to cause many students to express their feelings in a nonverbal way by rolling back their eyes. If you are one of those rare individuals who may *not* react in this manner, then hats off to you! For those of you who think negatively, I hope that when the discipline of grammar is fully understood, you will come to see how vital it is in our written communication.

The Purpose of Grammar is

to provide that structure within which to place the elements of our language;

to provide a foundation from which we communicate with one another in an effective manner; and

to preserve our language.

Whenever I have raised the issue of the importance of grammar with my students, some will point out to me various writers who seem consistently to break the rules of the discipline. I will quickly point out that *good* writers may deviate from the rules of grammar because they do so with a full knowledge of what they are doing. It is done for a specific purpose such as developing a stylistic device and *not* because they are unaware of the grammatical structure.

What if everyone wrote without using any guidelines in order to insure that his messages were being received as they had been intended? Imagine the chaos that would ensue! All of our communication would be much like the scrambled-cities game. If everyone spoke or wrote without any kind of common language structure, we would have to unscramble everything that was said. And worse, if there were no common structure, we would have no way of knowing what was spoken or written.

Never give the excuse that many writers do not follow the rules of grammar in order to defend your own inability to use your language well.

Near the beginning of this chapter I mentioned an incident regarding an essay that a student had given me which had been written earlier for another teacher. In talking with his high school instructor, I was told that the rules of grammar were unimportant. It was the student's "ingeniousness and creativeness" that was important.

I cannot understand how one can separate the creative idea from the structure of language and still communicate. If one's creative thought cannot be placed in a structure that is recognizable, then how am I, or any person for that matter, going to know just how creative and ingenious that writer or speaker is?

The unfortunate thing is that this is not an isolated experience. I have met many individuals who subscribe to the idea that grammar is unimportant. Students have enrolled in a creative writing class thinking that good writing is independent of grammar.

The aim of this chapter is not to make you a grammarian but to impress upon you the importance of knowing the basic skills of the discipline.

Test Yourself
1. Can you write a sentence that can be understood by others?
2. Do you ever have people tell you they cannot understand what you have written?
3. Can you organize your thoughts on paper in such a way that another person can follow your line of thinking?

Sentences, not words, are the essence of speech, just as equations and functions, and not bare numbers, are the real meat of mathematics . . . .
As we shall see, the patterns of sentence structure that guide words are more important than the words.

Benjamin Lee Whorf

There is no short cut to good writing. Without the basic skills necessary, you will encounter great difficulty in trying to put your thoughts into words. The first step to clear writing is to know these basic skills. At the end of this chapter, I have suggested resources that will help you in reviewing your knowledge of these skills.

Grammar is the guide to clear writing.
It is a key to understanding.
It is the foundation in which we share a commonness in the structure of language.

WRITING AND SPEAKING: Understanding the Differences

I hold that a word is something more than the noise it makes; it is also the way it looks on the page.

T. S. Eliot

Have you ever listened to a TV or radio news commentator who has just given some vital information but you seem to have missed it because you were not paying close attention? You wished he might repeat what he had said. It went by so quickly.

Perhaps you have had a speaker at your school who had some important things to say but you missed many of the points because he was so absorbed in his written text. He simply forgot that you were out there. After a few frustrating pages, you simply tuned out.

What was the problem in both these examples?

While grammar is a basic skill in our endeavours to communicate with one another, there are other factors which are equally important. One of these is the recognition that *there is a difference in a written and spoken style in communication.* On the surface, this may appear obvious; however, we do not always pay full attention to these differences.

On the other hand, it may be that you have heard a speaker that you thought was interesting. You could remember the major points he had discussed.

You have just read a book and thoroughly enjoyed it. You got so much out of it.

The latter two examples demonstrate that the communicators took into account the dif-

DEAR SNUFFY, PLEASE BE MINE. YOURS SINCERELY, MUGGSY

THERE IS A DIFFERENCE IN A WRITTEN AND SPOKEN STYLE

ferences in spoken and written style in communication. This was not the case in our first two examples.

I have found that many radio and TV newsmen have difficulty in communicating on the air if their backgrounds lie in the area of print journalism. Like the commentator in our first example, such individuals have been trained to write for the *eye* rather than the *ear*. If we are reading a newspaper or magazine, we can go back and reread what we didn't understand. When something is spoken, we cannot do the same unless the speaker is in our presence and we have some opportunity to ask him to repeat what he has said. The commentator was writing for the *eye* and this is where the difficulty may have begun.

In the second example, the speaker did not allow for feedback. If he had looked up from his prepared speech and noted that his audience was asleep, he would have had immediate feedback as to his inability to communicate verbally. Again, this is an example in which someone had prepared something for the *eye* and not for the *ear*. In both examples, the material may have been excellent but it was used in the wrong situation.

Written communication is intended primarily for the eye. Spoken communication is primarily intended for the ear.

To a large degree, an understanding of these differences will determine your effectiveness in communicating with others.

Verbal and Written Styles in Communication:
RECOGNIZING THE DIFFERENCES

Written	*Spoken*
Intended for the *Eye*	Intended for the *Ear*
No means for *direct feedback*	*Allows* for *direct feedback*
May be absorbed by the reader at his *leisure*	Must be understood *at the moment* of delivery
A *reader* may proceed *at his own rate of speed*	The *listener* proceeds *at the pace the speaker has set*

A *reader* can *think* upon what has been written and turn to outside sources for *consultation*	A *listener cannot reflect* for fear of losing the remainder of the words spoken
Written material must *ultimately* be understood by the reader. One can *think* upon or look up words, concepts, or phrases not understood.	Must be *instantly* understood to the listener

Summary

Before we apply what we have learned to the actual writing process, let us summarize the main points we have discussed.

1. Our communication may appear to be scrambled BITS and PIECES if our ideas are not understood by others.

2. Anything that exists contains ELEMENTS. We can only understand each other in that these *elements* are placed into some type of form recognizable to us.

3. A STRUCTURE provides a framework around which we place *elements*.

4. Words, phrases, and sentences are *elements* when placed in the *structure* of our written or spoken communication.

5. A purpose of GRAMMAR is to provide *structure* within which to place the *elements* of our language.

6. *Grammar* is the guide to clear writing. It is a key to understanding.

7. An understanding of the differences in WRITTEN and SPOKEN styles of communication will determine, in large measure, your effectiveness in communicating with others.

APPLICATION

The Writing Process

PREPARING TO WRITE

With your understanding of the differences between the written and spoken styles in communication, the basic skills of grammar at your fingertips, and a feel for the importance of placing elements in structure, you are ready to begin the *process of writing.*

If your intention is to communicate *something* clearly to *someone* by writing about it, you will find The Writing Process diagram of benefit to you. Use it as a guide as you prepare to write. However, this is only one ap-

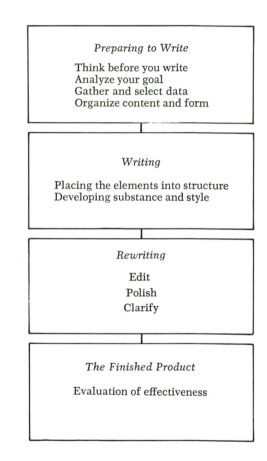

Preparing to Write

Think before you write
Analyze your goal
Gather and select data
Organize content and form

Writing

Placing the elements into structure
Developing substance and style

Rewriting

Edit
Polish
Clarify

The Finished Product

Evaluation of effectiveness

proach to the process of writing. *There is no one correct method.* Through experimentation and analysis, you will be able to determine what approach works best for you. Each individual approaches his writing differently and develops his own style.

While the elements in the Writing Process diagram may, in some measure, be applied to most types of writing, it is primarily intended for use in the preparation of essays and research papers.

An essay is any short written composition

EACH INDIVIDUAL DEVELOPS HIS OWN STYLE

dealing with a single subject, usually from a personal point of view.

A research paper, sometimes referred to as a term paper or information paper, is a systematic study and investigation in some specific area of interest. It is undertaken to establish facts by gathering data in order to increase one's knowledge on a given subject.

An *essay* is a short composition.

A *research paper* is more lengthy. The length is determined by the amount of information needed to complete an investigation.

An *essay* is written primarily as an expression of the author's personal views, or opinion.

A *research paper*, unlike the essay, is *not* an expression of the author's personal views. It is the examination of data in order to gain information or increased knowledge on a given subject.

An *essay*, because it is primarily an expression of one's opinion, does not necessarily require extensive factual data. That is not to say that the essay cannot contain such data in order to reinforce one's own viewpoint. When properly used, facts can add argumentative value to your essay.

A *research paper* consists of an unbiased account of a topic documented with pertinent and valid information in support of whatever statements one makes. The paper will, when completed, consist of evidence drawn from numerous sources and presented in a logical manner, a summary of one's research, and conclusions drawn upon the evidence.

With these definitions in mind, let us proceed with an approach to The Writing Process.

Think Before You Write!

. . . there are three kinds of authors. First those who write without thinking. They write from a full memory, from reminiscences; it may be, even straight out of other people's books. This class is the most numerous. Then come those who do their thinking whilst they are writing . . . there is no lack of them. Last of all come those authors who think before they write. They are rare.

Arthur Schopenhauer

The first impulse many students have when receiving an assignment for a written composition is simply to sit down and just begin writing. While this may have some benefit in getting your ideas down on paper so that you may see them, such work must *never* be considered as the final product. Papers which are written in this manner reflect the fact that the writer has given no thought to any particular organization or direction. No consideration has been made as to the purpose of the assignment or the goal to be attained. As a result, the paper becomes nothing more than a loose disjointed series of ramblings—a scramble. *If you don't know where you are going with your subject, you cannot expect your readers to know.*

Before you begin to write, *Stop* and *Think*.

What is the purpose of my writing? Do I understand the assignment? If my subject has not been chosen for me, how do I go about finding one? What is the nature of my paper? Is it a research paper written from factual data? Is it an opinion paper, an essay, expressing what I believe? To whom am I writing? What do I want to know about the topic? How shall I go about developing my idea? What results do I want?

These and other questions provide a preliminary analysis by which you will determine the approach you will take to your writing. To prevent an ineffective piece of written communication, you must *think before you write*.

Analyze Your Goal

It follows that the next step in your preparation should be an analysis of your goal. What you write is written to *someone* for some *reason*. When you write, you must at all times keep in mind who is to receive the communication. Just because YOU may understand what you have written, it may not be so with your receiver.

If you are asked to select a topic, do so with your receiver in mind. Consider that another human being will read your paper.

At what level do I write? In other words, what is the experience of my receiver? Does the paper go beyond the receiver's present range of knowledge?

Only through a thorough preliminary analysis can a writer determine which ideas will be relevant and important to his subject and his purpose. In fact, superficial and rambling remarks are likely to occur when the writer, even if he has a purpose, proceeds without having thought of a procedure for achieving it.

Gather and Select Data

Thinking means shuffling, relating, selecting the contents of one's mind so as to assimilate novelty, digest it, and create order.
                                    Jacques Barzun

Writing a paper is not an easy task. It is hard work. There are no short cuts. A step-by-step procedure in going about gathering and selecting data will be of great importance as you prepare to write.

1. Begin where you are.

Many times I have had students ask me, "Where do I begin?" Students will panic, running off in all directions, not knowing where they are going. How surprised they are when I say, *Begin with yourself!*

Too often we underestimate ourselves as a rich reservoir of knowledge gained through our own experience. You may be amazed at just how much you actually know about a given subject. If you have selected the subject yourself, you must have chosen it because it interests you. If it interests you, then the chances are that you already have *some* knowledge about it. When the subject has been chosen for you, you can still start with yourself.

The first step in gathering and selecting data for your paper is to sit down in a quiet spot and take an inventory of your knowledge of the subject. Take out a sheet of paper. Divide the paper vertically into two equal parts. At the top left hand side, place the heading—"What I know about this subject." At the top right hand side of the paper place the heading—"Information I have found."

Begin with the left hand column of what you know about the subject. It may be a great amount of material or it may be little. At any rate, through this procedure, you will have some idea as to exactly where you are in relation to the subject. Often you will find that what you know about a subject may serve as an excellent self-starter in finding your additional information. One word of caution, however, never confuse what you know about a subject with what you *think* you know. Always be certain to check your information, especially quotations and specific data. Take nothing for granted. You will want your paper to be accurate.

When you have fully reflected on what *you* know about the subject, you are ready to begin searching for additional information.

2. Find information for your subject.

Using the same sheet of paper, move to the right hand column with the heading—*Information I have found.* Rather than write out all of your notes here, use this part of the paper as a resource finder for easy identification of your material. This will be helpful when you finally sit down and organize the material you have collected.

List the *source* and a *brief statement* in your own words as to the nature of the material.

Example:
Source: Pearson, Lester B. *Mike: The*

Memoirs of the Rt. Hon. Lester B. Pearson, Vol. I. Toronto: University of Toronto Press, 1972, p. 171.

Statement: Pearson comments on Chamberlain's presentation to the British House of Commons on May 7 regarding the interpretation of recent developments with Germany.

While the library is the first place you may look for information, don't overlook other valuable resources. Books are not the only place where you will find data. Other than yourself, another source of information is people. *Interviews* with individuals who may have knowledge and some understanding of your subject may prove to be a real asset.

For example, if you are writing a paper on "Preventive Dentistry," there is probably no better place to begin than with your family dentist. Beyond what he may know, he can direct you to other sources of information. If you live in a city where there is a School of Dentistry, all the better. Use individuals as resources to supplement the material you find in books and other printed materials.

3. Take notes on what you find.

Let us first turn our attention to books as a source of information. Most people do not know how to take notes. As a result, they become frustrated when they spend a great amount of time in simply becoming a human duplicating machine. They copy down everything! This is *not* note-taking.

When reading for information:
A. *Don't* copy entire pages of books on note cards or on sheets of paper.
B. *Don't* read information you already know.
C. *Don't* read material that is obviously not directed toward your subject.
but
A. *Do* learn to skim material.
B. *Do* take down only information which actually pertains to your subject.
C. *Do* set up a system by which you can easily identify your information when you have completed your inquiry.

Many people have the idea that taking notes means to copy verbatim, word for word, large amounts of material from books. *Notes* are bits of information and not duplications of pages taken from books. Lift out *only* those items which *directly relate* to your subject. It may not even be necessary to copy entire sentences unless you are making use of a quotation or other specific data.

Don't waste a lot of your valuable time reading something you already know. Learn to skim the material, focusing on those important items that catch your attention. Be selective. By learning to skim material for important information, you will be able to bypass those items that you may already have or that do not relate directly to your subject.

Be certain that when you take notes you identify the source. This information will be valuable to you when you are preparing your Bibliography at the end of the paper. Transfer the source information you have to the half sheet of paper marked *Information I have found.* When you select and organize your data, you can lift out references as they apply to specific subject areas. Your identification should include:

Author's name
Title of Reference
Facts of Publication:
   edition
   volume number
   place of publication
   date of publication
   page number(s) from which the information has been taken

When you are interviewing individuals, take along a note pad so that you can jot down important information. Some students will take along a tape recorder from which they will assimilate their notes at a later time. In either situation, it might be a good idea if you ask the person to be interviewed if he minds being recorded or having you take notes as he talks. If you are taking notes and time permits, you may wish to read back some of your interpretations of what you believe he has said. It may be necessary to check for accuracy especially if you are dealing with some very complicated materials.

DON'T DUMP EVERYTHING INTO YOUR PAPER

4. Select material to be included in your paper.

Don't feel that you must include everything you have found on a given subject. Don't try to impress your reader by dumping everything you have collected into your paper. Some people have the idea that just because they have the information they have to use it whether it applies or not.

Select only that material which directly relates to your subject.

Don't be a bit surprised if you find that *most* of what you have won't be included. The formula to use when deciding if the material is relevant to the subject is, *When in doubt, leave it out.* Use the half-sheet of paper headed—"Information I have found" as a screen for sifting out material you do not need.

With your material selected, you may now move on to the next step in preparation for the *process of writing.*

Organize Content and Form

If you were setting out on a journey from Vancouver, British Columbia, to Saskatoon, Saskatchewan, the chances are you would turn to a road atlas. If you do not consult an atlas, you may well find yourself in Red Deer, Alberta, Prince George British Columbia, or in a location other than the one you wanted.

If you want to travel from one point to another, you don't just get in a car and begin driving without knowing how to get to the place where you are going. Many people use this approach when it comes to writing a paper. No thought is given as to where they are going or how they are going to accomplish their goal. What is the destination?

We also have a road map for writing. We call it an *Outline.* It is probably the most important tool you will use in your preparation to write.

OUTLINE STRUCTURE

Subject: (the General Topic)

Thesis: (State in a *single* declarative sentence.)

INTRODUCTION: *Body of the Paper*

I. Main Point (Indicate each main point with a Roman numeral.)

A main point is your central "talking" point.

A main point should be stated in a single sentence. A main point must be distinct from the other main points but *all* points must *directly* relate to the Thesis.

A. Sub-point (A sub-point provides support for the main point under which it is placed. It must directly relate to that point.)

1. Examples (Examples should *directly* relate to the sub-point under which it is placed.)

II. Second Main Point.
  A.
  B.
    1.
    2.
  C.

III. Third Main Point
  A.
    1.
  B.

CONCLUSION:

Caution: Avoid *too many* Main Points.

☐ An outline is useful in that it arranges the materials into an orderly fashion. It is an organized storehouse of ideas.

☐ An outline enumerates important ideas to be developed in the paper.

☐ An outline will give you a perspective as you examine the main lines of thought.

☐ An outline enables you to check the adequacy of the forms of support in relation to your subject.

☐ An outline will show you the relationships among the parts to the whole, the subject.

There are several types of outlines. Some individuals prefer simply to list topics while others may use words or phrases. I recommend a complete sentence outline.

A sentence outline makes the writer really think about his subject. Each point is written as a single sentence.

Let me take you step by step in the process of outline development.

1. State the subject title at the top of your paper.

2. Write a *thesis sentence*.

What is it you specifically want to say about the subject? You should be able to state this in a *single* declarative sentence. A simple sentence is one that does not contain a clause. It is not a compound sentence. A simple sentence consisting of a subject and verb provides a good clue as to whether or not your subject is limited. For example, if your subject is about the Canadian Indian, you can see that the topic is far too general. What is it you want to say about the Canadian Indian? When what you want to say is stated specifically, you have your *Thesis Sentence*. The Thesis Sentence is important in that it is from this that you will develop your main lines of thought in the outline.

3. Develop your main points.

What are the main things you want to say about your thesis? List them.

Do they all *directly* relate to your thesis? If not, then they do not belong. Keep only those points which *directly* relate and are part of the Thesis Statement. This method will prevent you from including material that is not necessary.

Your outline will assist you in selecting pertinent material from your notes. You may find that you will need to do additional research on your topic.

If you are talking about the Canadian Indians of the Pacific Region, then obviously any material on the Ojibways would be out of place, for they are located in what is called the St. Lawrence Basin, south of the Laurentian Plateau.

Do your main points overlap? If so, eliminate those that do.

State each main thought in a single sentence just as you have done with your Thesis Sentence. This technique will help you stay on track.

With the main points in front of you, you now need to concern yourself with *an order of arrangement*. How best can you arrange your thoughts so as to communicate effectively? There are many patterns of arrangement which can be used. The most common, however, are the *Topical Order*, the *Space Order*, and the *Time Order*.

A *Topical Order* of Arrangement enables you to place each main point into a topical sequence. For example, in talking about the Indians of the Pacific Region, each main point may be a specific tribe.

A *Space Order* of Arrangement places points into a logical sequence moving in a specific direction, from north to south, east to west, up to down, down to up, from left to right. This method enables the reader to follow systematically your line of thought. For example, if you were talking about the major Indian tribes of the North American West, you might begin with the tribes of the Southwestern United States. From here you would move up to the Pacific Coast tribes and then on to the Northwest tribes.

A *Time Order* of Arrangement places your information into a chronological order. This may be divided into past, present, and future or any other segment of time. For example, if you are writing a paper on the major Indian treaties in Canada, you may divide the order into those treaties made with the Province of Canada, or pre-Confederation, and those made after Confederation. The selection of an order of arrangement provides a consistent point of view. Your reader can follow you step by step. You have placed your elements into a structure he can identify.

4. Develop your sub-points.

A sub-point is *directly* related to the main point under which it is placed. If it does not directly relate, then it should not be included in that particular position. You may follow the same approach to the sub-point as you did with the development of your main points. However, this time you are relating the sub-point to the main point rather than directly to the Thesis Statement. If your sub-points are well prepared, then they will directly relate to the main point which directly relates to the Thesis.

You may also select an order of arrangement for your sub-points. Your main points may be in a *Space Order* but your sub-points may be organized in a *Topical Order*. For example:

		Major Indian Tribes of the North American West
Space Order	I.	Southwest American
Topical Order		Indians
		A. Apache
		B. Navajo, etc.
Space Order	II.	Pacific Coast Indians
Topical Order		A.
		B
Space Order	III.	Northwestern Indians
Topical Order		A.
		B.

One word of caution. Once a pattern has been established for a level in your outline, don't change it. If you have selected a Topical Order for your main points, *all* of the main points *must* be organized in this fashion. If your sub-points are arranged in a Space Order, then *all* of the sub-points in your outline must be of the same order. Changing an order at one of these points could cause problems. Rather than having your elements carefully placed in a clear structure you would have a scramble of the elements.

5. List specific examples.

Examples may be placed in your outline using Arabic numbers, *e.g.,* 1, 2, 3, *etc.* At this level of your outline, you do not need to write a sentence. A word or phrase will do. Examples must directly relate to that which is immediately above it.

6. Write the Introduction and Conclusion.

The outline is the body of your paper. With the outline completed, you are now ready to write the Introduction and Conclusion to your paper. Saving the writing of the Introduction until last will provide you with a more effective approach. You cannot introduce something you have not met. With the total perspective of the outline in front of you, the Introduction and Conclusion will do the job required. The outline provides you with a vantage point from which to write.

Your outline is now completed and you are ready to write your paper.

WRITING

Placing the Elements into Structure

Using the outline you have prepared, you are now ready to put the pieces together in the form of your written paper. The Main Points of the outline become the major sections of your paper with the Sub-Points making up the paragraphs and sentences of each section.

The first writing is to be considered a draft copy. It is *not* the finished product. You may find that you will add and subtract material as you go along with your writing. However, it is not wise to deviate too far from the prepared outline. If your outline has been carefully and thoughtfully developed, the pieces should fit together well as you write. Use the outline as your guide.

Developing Substance and Style

> *Le Style c'est l'homme même.*
> *The Style is the man himself.*
> Leclerc de Buffon
> *Discours sur le Style*

> *Style is the dress of thoughts.*
> Lord Chesterfield

While grammar will provide you with the structure in which to place language, it will not give you imagination or insight. A style of writing is not something dictated. It is nurtured. The style belongs to the individual. The chapters in this text will serve as a good example. Written by five authors, there are, you will note, definite differences in style. While each of us may share a common goal in communicating with you, we do not share a common style. Each author has gone about his writing in his own way. Like the clothes fashioned by a Pucci, a Pierre Cardin, or a Christian Dior, a particular style of writing belongs to its creator.

When listening to a piece of music, you may be able to identify the composer by his style. He uses the same musical scale other composers use but places the notes in an order reflecting his own interpretation of music.

The film style of Donald Shebib is readily seen in such creations as *Going Down the Road* and *Between Friends*.

A style belongs to its creator. So it is with writing. The great poets and novelists can be identified by their style of writing. A writing style is something which is developed through experimentation, analysis, and reflection. It is a part of you. Your paper will reflect the style that is you.

The *substance* of the material you have included in your paper must be identified. This is done by placing a footnote at the bottom of the page, or with a collection of footnotes at the conclusion of your paper.

Individual instructors may differ on how these footnotes are to be placed in your paper. They must be included at some point; otherwise, you are practising plagiarism, taking credit for something which is not original to you.

Upon completion of your draft copy of the paper, you are now ready to begin the process of rewriting and composing the finished product.

REWRITING

The major part of your writing has been completed with the development of your rought draft. You are now ready to put on the finishing touches. The rewriting of your paper is not to be taken lightly. It is important. The finished product should be *accurate, easy to read,* and *complete* in every way.

I have provided you with a checklist which will help you to identify those areas which may need to be rewritten. This list is by no means complete. You may add to it. It does, however, contain the major points to check.

Edit, Polish, and Clarify
1. Take out any material which does not belong.

2. Rewrite areas in which there are obvious distortions and distractions.
3. Check for accuracy of statements and sources.
4. Note any inconsistency in style.
5. Omit needless words.
6. Correct spelling and punctuation errors.
7. Watch for any grammatical errors and problems with language structure.
8. Identify all resource materials by the use of footnotes and a bibliography.
9. Compare the organization of your material with your outline.
10. Clarify any difficult terms or concepts.
11. Prepare smooth transitions between major sections.

THE FINISHED PRODUCT

With your rewriting completed, you may now write your paper in its final form. Your paper should reflect your best quality of work. It should be *neatly* typed or written in ink. Many instructors ask their students to type the paper. If typed, be certain it is not smudged, messy, or marked through with erasures. If written by hand, use ink and by all means *write legibly!* You don't want your reader to stop reading your paper after the first page because of poor handwriting. You should have great pride and satisfaction in your finished product.

The finished product, your research paper, should contain the following:

A title page
An outline
The written paper complete
with footnotes
A bibliography

You are now ready to present your paper for reading and evaluation.

There are two sources of evaluation—yourself and your reader. The information contained in the paper and the process of writing the paper should give *you* increased knowledge. You should know more about your subject than you did when you began your research. Through your writing efforts, you have had an opportunity to learn new techniques and skills. If you have accomplished all this, then the paper has been effective for *you*.

Another indication of your effectiveness will be noted by the grade if it is to be handed in to an instructor as a completed assignment. Beyond that, how do you know if you have accomplished what you had set out to do?

The evaluation of your effectiveness in communicating an idea by the process of writing will be seen in the response of your reader. An accurate description and analysis of your paper will indicate to you whether or not you have reached the goal. Through evaluation, you will learn other methods by which you may develop your writing skills.

CORRESPONDENCE

You have just finished your morning coffee while reading the newspaper. You are glancing through the business section when your attention is drawn to a job advertisement. It looks good to you. The advertisement asks that you apply in writing *and that you* submit a résumé *of your experience and qualifications.*

Asking a person to apply for a job in writing and with a résumé of his experience and qualifications is a common practice among employers.

How does one go about applying in writing for a job?

What is a résumé?

The purpose of this section of the chapter is to assist you in preparing (1) a letter of job application, (2) a résumé, and (3) a letter of job acceptance should the position advertised be offered to you.

The steps involved in the Writing Process Diagram can be practised, in large measure, by the letter writer. While you are not preparing a lengthy research paper, you are going to practice many of the same skills.

1. You must *think before you write*.
2. You must *analyze your goal*.
3. You must be able to *gather and select data*.
4. You must be able to *organize content and form*.
5. You must present your material in a *logical manner*.
6. You must demonstrate an ability to *write well* which involves a knowledge of basic *grammar* skills, *punctuation, and spelling*.
7. You must have the ability to *express yourself well in writing*.

YOU MUST SELL YOURSELF

LETTER OF APPLICATION

What Is The Purpose of a Job Application Letter?

The prime purpose of the job application letter is to get an interview. You will inform your reader of your qualifications and will indicate your interest in the position advertised. You will want your reader to be interested enough in you that he will invite you to meet with him. *You* will need to determine exactly what you have to offer this particular employer and why *you* are the best person for the job. If you think this sounds like an exercise in salesmanship, you are right! *You must sell yourself.*

What Information Should a Job Application Letter Contain?

There is more importance attached to a letter of application than you might realize. The letter tells a great deal about You. Keep in mind that the reader has never met you. This letter is his first introduction to you. First impressions tell much about an applicant. Remember that you want that interview.

A messy or poorly constructed letter will

Letter *of* *Application*

104 Saturn Way
Toronto, Ontario
M3B 4K8
May 23, 1975

Mr. J. T. Hill
Director of Personnel
E. W. Fawcett Corporation
30 W. James St.
Toronto, Ontario
M1B 2S4

Dear Mr. Hill:

    In response to your recent advertisement in the
GLOBE AND MAIL for an assistant sales manager, I submit my name for consideration for this position. Included with this letter is a résumé listing my qualifications. I believe that my qualifications and experience will interest you.

    For the past five years, I have been working as
a salesman for the L. Sturgis Company, Ltd., in Toronto.
I have enjoyed my work and feel that I have made a contribution to the company. However, because the company
is small, advancement is limited. I believe your
company can offer me more of an opportunity for personal development.

    If you have any questions, I would be pleased
to answer them in a personal interview at your convenience.

    Thank you for your consideration.

              Sincerely,

              Robert M Doss

              Robert M. Doss

Enclosed: Résumé

Letter of Application

621 Pine Ridge Road
Toronto, Ontario
L3T 4K8
May 23, 1975

Mr. J. T. Hill
Director of Personnel
E. W. Fawcett Corporation
30 W. James St.
Toronto, Ontario
M1B 2S4

Dear Mr. Hill:

In response to your recent advertisement in the GLOBE AND MAIL for a management trainee, I wish to submit my name for consideration for this position. Included with this letter is a résumé listing my qualifications.

This spring I will graduate from the business management program at Seneca College of Applied Arts and Technology. I believe that this program has prepared me for the business world. For your information, I have also included a listing of the courses I have taken while at Seneca.

For the past three summers, I have worked in my father's hardware store helping him maintain his business records and serving as a salesman. I feel that I have gained a considerable amount of experience.

If you would like to consider my application, I will be most pleased to come to your office for an interview.

Thank you for your consideration.

Sincerely,

Marvin Sims

Marvin I. Sims

Enclosed: Résumé

quickly find its way into the wastepaper basket.

Any consideration for a position may end as soon as the reader notices that you can't spell.

Your letter has coffee stains on it.

You have folded the letter incorrectly.

Do these things sound trite to you? Any one or a combination of these things may cause you to lose out. Don't be fooled. They are major considerations that many employers take into account when receiving a letter of application.

How should the letter look and what must it contain?

1. Write your letter on *plain*, good quality, bond paper, 8½ x 11. *Do not* use personal or company letterhead stationery. A typewritten letter is always best.
2. Be neat.
   There should be no erasures, coffee stains, or other distracting marks on either the letter or résumé.
3. A well written letter is *most important*.
   Watch closely for grammatical errors, spelling mistakes, and errors in punctuation.
4. Be to the point.
   Don't try to be cute. Write in a business-like manner.
5. The letter should contain only that information which will inform your reader as to just why you qualify for the job.
6. Include a résumé with the application.

RÉSUMÉ

What is the Purpose of a Résumé?

A résumé, sometimes referred to as a personal data sheet, should be included with your letter of application. The purpose of the résumé is to inform the reader of your qualifications and experience.

The résumé should be written *before* the job application letter. While it is true that the employer will probably read the letter first, you may use some of the contents of the résumé in the letter.

What Should a Résumé Contain?

A résumé must be accurate and complete. Appearance is very important.

Make the résumé appealing but honest.

Do *not* print or duplicate a résumé. It should always be a typewritten original.

A good résumé usually is divided into six major parts.

1. *Personal Data*
   This includes such important data as name, birth date, marital status, address, and telephone. Some individuals include height, weight, and condition of health. These last three factors would be determined by the nature of the job for which you are applying. If these items are important for the particular position you are seeking, then by all means include the information.

2. *Education*
   List your educational background in chronological order with the most recent first.

   This section should contain the name of the school, its location, and the length of time you attended. Also, list your status on leaving. For example, if you graduated with a diploma, so indicate. If you received a degree, indicate the type of degree and when it was received. If you are a university graduate, give your major area of study.

3. *Work Experience*
   List *ALL* jobs in chronological order with the present or most recent one at the top of your list. *Do not* leave out any major jobs. If you have a time gap in your work experience, the reader will wonder why you have left something out. This could be serious. He may think that you have something to hide and will want to know why. *Be honest!* Exclude nothing.

4. *Extracurricular Activities*
   Don't shy away from informing your reader of your extracurricular activities at school or in your spare time. This is a very important part of the résumé for some employers. Many believe that an individual who has maintained a good grade average in school and has been active in extracurricular activities shows initiative and industry.

   An individual who is employed all day, but who takes time to work in civic organizations

Résumé

Personal Data

Name:	Robert M. Doss
Date of Birth:	June 28, 1949
Marital Status:	Married
Height:	5' 8"
Weight:	160
Health:	Excellent
Address:	104 Saturn Way Toronto, Ontario M3B 4K8
Telephone:	(416) 661-4321

Education

University of Toronto   1967 to 1971   Graduated with
  College of Business   B. A. degree
  Toronto, Ontario
  Major: Business Administration

York Mills High School   1962 to 1967   Graduated Grade 13
  Toronto, Ontario   with honours

Work Experience

1971-1974   Salesman   L. Sturgis Company, Ltd.
                           Toronto, Ontario
                           Duties: selling and servicing
                                     accounts for duplicating
                                     equipment

1969-1971   Cashier   T. A. Gibson Company
                           Toronto, Ontario
                           Duties: worked part-time receiving
                                     money from customers for
                                     goods and services received.

Extracurricular Activities

University: Member of the Business Management Club
             Business Manager of the student newspaper
             Member of the University of Toronto Band
             Recipient of Edna Williams Scholarship
High School: Sr. Class Vice President
              Debate Club
              York Mills Drum Corps

Other Related Information

Hobbies and Interests: music
                          model railroading
                          hockey

References

Mr. Kenneth Jones, President   Mr. Philip Garson, Manager
L. Sturgis Company   Bank of Ontario
1615 MacDonald St.   432 Jamestown St.
Toronto, Ontario   Toronto, Ontario
M5B 3L6   M5B 2M5

Reverend Mr. Robert Fell
Christ the King United Church of Canada
3010 Westmont Avenue
Willowdale, Ontario
M8Q 6M2

EXTRACURRICULAR ACTIVITIES

demonstrates vitality. This part of your résumé also gives the reader some insight into your personality, your leadership ability, and the way in which you work with others.

5. Other Relevant Information

This part of the résumé is directly related to the position you are seeking. You may wish to include a listing of your courses of study while in school or any other data which may reinforce your application.

6. References

You may list three to five references.

You might include a personal or character reference, a professional reference, and a credit reference.

The purpose of the character reference is to establish your integrity.

The professional reference may be one of your fellow employees or your supervisor. It should be someone who knows how you work.

A credit reference indicates to the reader that your creditors will not be after you while on the job.

LETTER OF ACCEPTANCE

What is the Purpose of a Letter of Acceptance?

The purpose of the letter of acceptance is to notify your employer officially that you have accepted the conditions of employment as they have been presented to you. In some instances, a letter of acceptance might serve as a legal contract of employment.

What Should a Letter of Acceptance Contain?

You should:

1. thank your employer for giving you an opportunity to be a part of his company:
2. indicate the terms of employment you have accepted, including salary, and
3. note the date you will begin work as agreed upon by you and your employer.

In most instances, references usually are not requested until after an interview. However, you should include them in the résumé. There are times when a name familiar to the reader may help you to get that job.

Letter _of_ _Acceptance_

104 Saturn Way
Toronto, Ontario
M3B 4K8
June 17, 1975

Mr. J. T. Hill
Director of Personnel
E. W. Fawcett Corporation
30 W. James St.
Toronto, Ontario
M1B 2S4

Dear Mr. Hill:

     Thank you for your letter of June 16, 1975, offering
me the position of Assistant Sales Manager of the E. W.
Fawcett Corporation. According to the terms set forth in
your letter, I will report to work on July 2, 1975, and
my starting annual salary will be $13,900.

     I appreciate this opportunity to serve your company.
I hope that I will be able to make a valuable contribution
to the sales program.

                    Sincerely,

                    Robert M Doss

                    Robert M. Doss

Answers to the Scramble Cities Game

TROIS-RIVIÈRES	OTTAWA
EDMONTON	REGINA
HALIFAX	TORONTO
MONTRÉAL	WINNIPEG
VANCOUVER	YELLOWKNIFE

SELECTED READINGS

Blumenthal, Joseph. *English 2600:* A Programmed Course in Grammar and Usage. Third edition. New York: Harcourt, Brace and World, Inc., 1969.

Blumenthal, Joseph. *English 3200:* A Programmed Course in Grammar and Usage. Second edition. New York: Harcourt Brace Javanovich, Inc., 1972.

Casty, Alan. *Building Writing Skills.* New York: Harcourt Brace Javanovich, Inc., 1971.

Murphy, Herta A. and Charles E. Peck. *Effective Business Communications.* Toronto: McGraw-Hill Book Company, 1972.

Perrin, Porter. *Writer's Guide and Index to English.* Chicago: Scott, Foresman and Company, 1959.

Shurter, Robert L., J. Peter Williamson, and Wayne G. Broehl. *Business Research and Report Writing.* Toronto: McGraw-Hill Book Company, 1965.

Strunk, William Jr. and E. B. White. *The Elements of Style.* New York: The Macmillan Company, 1962.

GLOSSARY

Actualizor   A person who operates from a position of self-worth rather than deficiency. Actualizors do not compete with others for need satisfaction. Instead, they try to establish a trusting relationship with others within which mutual need satisfaction is possible.

Adaptors   Behaviours performed impulsively to reduce or step up stimulation, and thus to adjust stimuli levels within a person. Examples are drumming fingers, scratching, picking or rubbing oneself, crossing legs, forward and backward leaning, covering mouth with hand, covering eyes with hand, and biting lips.

Affect   To alter a relationship between our own organism and the environment in which we find ourselves.

Affects   Displays of emotion in the human face and body. There are probably seven pure or "primary" facial emotions: anger, fear, disgust, sadness, surprise, happiness and interest. "Mixed emotions"—several hundred of them—are created by combining various elements of the pure emotions. Fear, for example, may be shown in the eyes, with sorrow shown in the mouth, resulting in the expression of "guilt."

Ambiguity   State of being capable of more than one interpretation.

Audience analysis   The review of the characteristics of an audience in terms of age, socioeconomic level, knowledge of subject, education and accepted authorities.

Central Idea   The main theme of a speech, expressed in a single sentence.

Channel   The pathway linking media and receivers, along which information "flows." The primary channel in face-to-face communication is air, through which flow visual, auditory and chemical messages. Some theorists define channels in terms of the different senses, viz. visual channel, auditory channel, olfactory channel (smell and taste), and tactile (touch) channel.

Code   A set of rules which directs both the organization of stimuli (sounds, body movements, graphics, etc.) into informational stimuli—or "messages"—and the interpretation of them in a meaningful way by a receiver. Thus, the rules of spelling, grammar, syntax, etc. comprise part of the language code. Different kinds of rules underlie nonverbal codes such as smoke signalling, painting, music, emblems, facial expressions, touch, etc.

Communication   The interaction of people, animals or inanimate objects, during which information generated by one or more of the interactants is processed by at least one of the other interactants, resulting in the production of meaning in the mind of the processor. (See *Interpersonal communication*.)

Confrontation   The act of testing one's perception of another person's behaviour, usually *with* the other person.

Connotative meaning   Our personal thoughts, feelings and experiences about the thing, event or concept that a word refers to. The connotative meaning represents our own private meanings that are additional to the primary meaning embodied in the "denotative" meaning of the word.

Context   Information which is in the environment of a message and which has some relevance to that message's interpretation. Context may include information from the cultural setting, the social and physical circumstances, and any verbal and nonverbal information generated by some sender prior or subsequent to a particular message. What a person shows on his face, for example, may help you to interpret his words. You determine the precise meaning of the word "run" in the following sentences by interpreting it in the light of the other words: "I ran into my friend the other day," versus "I ran into my friend's car the other day."

Creative meaning   Meaning which is invented, given, or assigned by an individual or group of individuals. *Personal creative meaning*, sometimes referred to as "connotative" meaning, is most closely related to personal experience. *Shared creative meaning*, or "denotative" meaning, denotes or refers to something we basically share in common.

Denotative meaning A brief, objective dictionary explanation of the primary meanings of a word in a variety of contexts. Synonyms and pictures are frequently used in a dictionary to indicate more precisely the denotative meaning.

Determinants In communication, those factors which determine our effectiveness. Among the more common communication determinants is the recognition that one cannot *not* communicate, that each person is unique, that fields of experience vary, that feedback plays an important role in our communicative efforts.

Discursive The mode of "discourse" which involves the naming of concepts and the articulation of their relationships, statement-making, questioning, etc. Discursive communication tends to be continuous, sequential and "logically" organized. Ordinary language is the most common code used for discursive purposes, though mathematics can be employed discursively as well, e.g. $1 + 1 = 2$. (See *Nondiscursive*.)

Dyadic communication A dialogue between two people who are important to each other in an intimate, face-to-face interaction.

Ego state An individual's experience or conception of himself. The dynamic unity which the person senses within himself.

Elements Bits and pieces. Anything that exists contains elements. In communicating with others, these elements can be understood only when placed in a structure or framework which is familiar to us.

Emblem Any behaviour which is used as a substitute for words. Examples are the hitch-hiking sign, peace sign, sign of the cross, sports officials' signs, nonspontaneous deliberate facial expressions, and various obscene gestures. Emblems are employed when verbalization is uncustomary, difficult, impossible or less effective.

Empathy A characteristic of a person which enables him to experience what others are experiencing, and thus to appreciate the attitudes and emotions of another.

Empathic listening Listening to *understand* rather than to evaluate. Empathic listening involves listening *with* rather than *to* another person. It involves seeing the person you are listening to as he sees himself; moving away from the centre of your world and experiencing the centre of his world. Empathic listening means trying to understand what the message means *to the speaker*.

Essay Any short written composition dealing with a single subject, usually from a personal point of view. An essay, because it is primarily an expression of one's opinion, does not necessarily require extensive factual data. That is not to say that the essay cannot contain such data in order to reinforce one's own viewpoint. When properly used, facts can add argumentative value to an essay.

Entertainment speech A speech in which the subject is treated from a humorous point of view.

Extemporaneous speaking The presentation of ideas in a situation where adequate preparation time is available, rehearsal has taken place and the speech is delivered with a minimum of notes, allowing for direct eye contact with the audience.

External feedback Verbal or nonverbal information which is generated by a source beyond a person and which informs him how his appearance or behaviour is being perceived. A person may nod his head while you are speaking; he may say "Right!"; he may lean toward you and smile. These are all examples of *positive* external feedback. On the other hand, if he failed to nod his head, frowned, leaned away from you, and broke eye contact, then he would be sending you *negative* external feedback.

Extralanguage All human-generated non-speech sounds, such as gasps, snores, sneezes, whistles, foot-stamping, paper-shuffling, etc.

Feedback The response the receiver sends back to the sender to tell him how he is doing at communicating. Feedback gives us the opportunity to correct our efforts if we do not succeed on the first attempt at communicating. (See *Internal and External feedback*.)

Field of experience   The sum total of each person's experiences. A person's field of experience includes his basic communication skills, level of knowledge, attitudes, social background and cultural heritage. The sender can send messages and the receiver can interpret messages only in terms of the experience each has had.

Five basic elements of speech making   Audience, subject matter, speaker, occasion and desired result.

General outline   A series of sentences forming a skeleton of a speech and indicating the relationship of the ideas.

General purpose   The purpose is the reason for giving a speech. There are five: to inform, persuade, entertain, enquire or reinforce.

Group Discussion   The process, by means of oral discourse, whereby a group of two or more people, through cooperative participation under the guidance of a leader, follow a discussional pattern of reflective thinking towards the solution of a specifically defined problem.

Illustrators   Any behaviour which provides the receiver with nonverbal "commentary" on some verbal behaviour occurring simultaneously or immediately before or after. Most illustration is done with the hands and face ("talking with the hands" is perhaps the more common activity), though the trunk and limbs are sometimes used.

Impromptu speaking   The presentation of ideas without any prior notice or time for preparation.

Inference   A conclusion or deduction based on facts, information or indications.

Informative speech   A speech in which a point of view is explained.

Information   When a set of stimuli of whatever kind—graphics, colours, sounds, smells, movements, etc.—are manipulated according to certain rules (see *Code*), they become *coded stimuli*, or simply "information." But throughout the chapter on nonverbal communication, the term information has been used *loosely* to refer to *any* stimuli that can be processed meaningfully by a receiver, whether or not these stimuli are deliberately coded or manipulated by a sender. The spontaneous scratching of an arm, for example, is not deliberately coded—it is just an act— yet this behaviour can be *decoded* meaningfully by a receiver. Thus, information may be defined as coded or decodable stimuli. Knowledge of the correct code enables receivers to interpret, to assign meaning, to the raw stimuli.

Innate   That which is present in the individual at birth, or his genetic inheritance.

Internal feedback   Information generated within a person, which informs him about his own behaviour. When we hear ourselves speaking, or see or feel our bodies moving, we are receiving internal feedback. If we received no internal feedback, we literally wouldn't know what we were doing, and thus wouldn't be able to function at all.

Interaction   A process during which two or more people relate to one another by communicating.

Internal frame of reference   Our subjective world. Our interpretation of the world around us is confined by our limited field of experience. Our internal frame of reference leads us to *see* what we *want* to see and *only* what our experience will allow us to see.

Internal summary   The part of a speech which indicates the speaker's progress and the intention to move to a new aspect of the speech.

Interpersonal   The dynamic relationship between two or more people.

Interpersonal communication   A complex process of human interaction, in which information is conveyed from person to person verbally and nonverbally through closely shared language, experience and perception in such a way as to achieve the transfer of a close approximation of intended meaning.

Introjecting Absorbing into oneself environmental influences and personal characteristics of other persons.

Manipulator A person who tries to satisfy his basic needs by manipulating people. He doesn't care about the needs of others or about the relationship between himself and others. He lacks sensitivity.

Manuscript speech The presentation of ideas in complete written form and delivered word for word.

Masks A screen of words, actions or even silence that keeps a part of the real you from public view. We frequently want to keep part of ourselves "private" because we are afraid of how people might react.

Meaning (word) The symbolizing, signifying or representing of all experiences, both public (denotative) and private (connotative), that could attach themselves to a word.

Medium A device for displaying messages, such as a radio, a TV, a canvas, a book, a face, a body.

Message The information the sender, or source, sends to his receiver. The message may be verbal or nonverbal. A message is any signal capable of being interpreted meaningfully.

Metacommunication The process of sending and receiving verbal and nonverbal indicators that inform the receiver how a sender's message should be interpreted. Verbal indicators would include voice inflection, loudness, pitch, rate, etc. Nonverbal indicators would include facial expressions and gestures.

Model (Communication) A representation, facsimile, or analogue of the communication process, designed for purposes of description and/or prediction, and often rendered in a graphic form.

Motivation An incentive or an inducement for behaving in a certain manner. We usually act the way we do for a reason, and that rea-

son has to do with a personal reward of some sort.

Noise Anything which interferes with the reception of messages. Communication difficulties, or noise, can occur in one of five categories, viz. *difficulties* that exist primarily within and about the sender; that exist within the receiver; which occur within both the sender and receiver either jointly or separately; external to the sender and/or receiver; and related to all areas of the communication situation.

Norm A representative or standard value or pattern for a group.

Nondiscursive Communication that does *not* follow the organizational pattern of discourse, but tends to be discontinuous, nonsequential and nonrational (but not irrational), and which functions not to make statements, but to present information in an "all-at-once" manner. A facial expression is nondiscursive communication. So are hand illustrators, body movements, paintings, graphic symbols, instrumental music. (See *Discursive*.)

Nonverbal communication The process of establishing relationships between senders and receivers, based on information mediated by body or body-related variables, and by paralinguistic and extralinguistic variables.

Order of arrangement Arrangement of thoughts and ideas into a topical or logical sequence. In preparing an outline, the more common orders of arrangement may include the Topic Order, the Space Order, and/or the Time Order.

Originality The development of a fresh, personal approach to material.

Paralanguage All aspects of speech beyond the words themselves, such as tone, volume, stuttering, pausing, etc. Roughly speaking, paralanguage is *how* you say things, rather than *what* you say.

Paranoid Mental disorganization characterized by persistent delusions and hallucinations.

Perception A process of selecting, organizing and interpreting the information we receive from our five senses (vision, touch, taste, smell and hearing).

Persuasive speech A speech in which the speaker tries to convince the audience to accept a point of view or to change a course of action.

Process An action signifying that something is in motion, ongoing, ever-changing and never static. Communication must be thought of as a process. Like a circle, communication has no beginning and no end. Something has taken place before the communication event and something will continue after the event.

Psyche One's mental energy.

Public speaking "The purposeful exchange of information and feeling."

Receiver The destination for the message. A receiver is the one who receives the signal, the message, which has been sent by the sender or source. A receiver may be an individual listening, watching, or reading. Receivers can also be a group of people, such as observers at a hockey game.

Reflective thinking A series of logical steps to be followed in the discussion process.

Regulators Any behaviour (head nods, smiles, words, etc.) which functions to influence the process of sending and receiving information. Regulators influence turn-taking, listening behaviour, topic selection, rate of sending, volume and tone, and a host of other variables. Regulators serve as "traffic signs" to guide the entire process of initiating, maintaining and terminating interactions.

Relevance The important connections between objects or people.

Research paper A systematic study and investigation in some area of interest. It is undertaken to establish facts by gathering data in order to increase one's knowledge of a given subject. It is sometimes also referred to as a "term," or "information paper."

Role A classification of a set of functions and expectations as to how those functions will be carried out. For example, the roles of teacher, doctor and waitress have unique functions, characteristics and expectations of how their functions will be performed.

Role living The functions and expectations of the role consume the real you. You begin to present more and more of the role and less and less of yourself. You see and judge yourself in terms of your performance in the role rather than your performance as a unique human being.

Role playing You are *playing* a part and the foundation of the part is the real you. You realize that a role has a set of functions and expectations as to how the functions must be carried out, but you also realize that the real you must be *visible* in the role as well. There are times when the real you will be *more* or *less* visible than at others, but in each situation the real you is visible in the role.

Schizoid A personality type tending towards dissociation of the emotional from the intellectual life.

Self The *real* you. The self is the sum total of your experiences with yourself and with others. It represents the completely objective picture of you—your personality, character, feelings, belief and attitudes as they really are.

Self-concept The picture you have of yourself. It is the sum total of the beliefs you have about the kind of person you are. You develop the self-concept according to (1) your observations and interpretations of your own behaviour (2) your observations and interpretations of other people's behaviour towards you.

Self-disclosure The revelation of information about yourself that would be considered of a "personal" nature, i.e. hopes, fears, needs. This kind of personal information is normally revealed only in a climate of trust and when the person revealing the information wants to develop a closer relationship with the other party.

Sender   The transmitter of information. The sender may be an individual speaking, writing, drawing, gesturing; or a communication organization such as a newspaper, magazine, printing house, radio or television station, etc. (See *Source*.)

Sensitivity   Is the ability to be at the centre of your world and the other person's world at the same time. Sensitivity is the ability to understand accurately what another person is thinking and feeling and to interact with him with his best interests in mind.

Social culture   The knowledge, institutions, and expectations of a society learned by members of that social community.

Source   The originator, or coder of communication messages. In face-to-face communication, the sender and source are the same person (See *Sender*.)

Speech of enquiry   A speech which examines various points of view on a particular topic.

Speech of reinforcement   A speech which builds on beliefs already held.

Structure   A framework around which we can place elements. Elements take on meaning for us when placed in a structure which is familiar to us.

Sub-culture   A smaller group within a society with common language, religion or social beliefs; e.g. any ethnic group in a larger society.

Subject sentence   A sentence which incorporates the general purpose and the desired end result.

Supporting material   The examples, illustrations, quotations, etc. which provide relevant contact between the subject matter and the experience of the listener.

Thesis sentence   A single declarative sentence from which the main points in an outline are developed.

Transactional analysis   A system of examining interaction within oneself or between people, based on the concept of ego states.

Transactions   A unit of exchange of verbal and nonverbal behaviour between people.

WIGO stands for *what is going on* around us. It represents the sum total of the information that is available to us through the five senses at any particular moment in time.

WIMTU stands for *what it means to us*. The "it" is the WIS—the information selected from the world around us. Once we select information from the world around us, we organize the information and interpret it in relation to our own experience. We have now decided what that information means to us.

WIS stands for *what is selected* for interpretation, from what is going on around us at any particular moment in time. We tend to select information according to our interests, needs or desires.

APPENDIX
Human
Communication Exercises

Donald L. MacRae
Robert M. Soucie

INTRODUCTION

We hope that the following exercises will provide you with opportunities to apply and broaden your understanding of the human communication principles discussed in this book. Each exercise has been carefully chosen to encourage involvement and participation, and to foster in your group the development of a warm, open atmosphere.

The exercises can be used for many different purposes, and in a wide variety of contexts. For this reason, we have chosen not to set precise objectives for each of them, but have simply arranged them in broad categories that may suggest ways in which they can be used successfully. Taken together, the exercises have been designed to:

1. develop sensitivity to emotions, needs and past experiences—both yours and others';
2. increase awareness of your own communication behaviour and the behaviour of others, and to deepen your appreciation of the effects this behaviour has on human relationships;
3. heighten your sense of responsibility for your communication behaviour.

Because some of these exercises may prove somewhat stressful or unsettling for certain persons, the teacher or group leader ought to use them cautiously. *We recommend that he give the participants the choice of opting out of a particular exercise after he has explained the format, or at any time during the exercise.*

GETTING TO KNOW EACH OTHER

1. *Old What's-His-Name*
Take whatever time is necessary for each person to walk around the room and learn (1) every person's full name and (2) at least one piece of information about him. When everyone has completed the assignment, test everyone in the room. This exercise might be repeated at intervals during the course.

2. *I'm From—*
Each member of the group is asked to name the city from which he comes and explain to the group at least five interesting features of it (e.g. types of industry, historical sites, etc.).

3. *Mingling*
Members of the group walk around the room mingling with each other for about 3 to 5 minutes but say nothing. At the end of the 5 minutes each person chooses another person to sit and talk with for approximately 10 minutes. These twosomes should learn enough about each other to introduce each other to another person. The twosomes then mingle around the room for about 5 minutes, saying nothing, and then decide on another couple that they would like to talk with. Each person in the original twosome introduces his partner to the newly formed foursome.

4. *Uniqueness*
Each member of the group spends a few minutes studying the other members of the group in order to decide on one word that best depicts a unique personal characteristic that sets him apart from other members of the group (e.g. slimmest, oldest, longest hair etc.). Each member then explain the word he chose and the reasons for choosing it.

5. *Who I Am or What I Am*

Each member of the group is asked to write 10 statements on a sheet of paper that indicate "who I am" or "what I am." Members of the group are then instructed to circulate in the room with the statement sheets attached to their person or held in front of them. They are not allowed to speak. When two people meet, they should established eye contact and study each other's statements for approximately 2 or 3 minutes. After everyone has met everyone else at least once, they should find the one or two members that they would be particularly interested in talking with, form a small group and ask questions of each other based on the information on the statement sheets.

6. *First Impressions*
Small groups of 4 to 6 people. Each person in the group prepares a one- to two-minute introduction of himself that will be presented orally to the group. After each oral introduction has been given, the other members of the group write their "first impressions" of that person on a standard-size sheet of paper without identifying themselves.

These first impressions are handed to the group chairman who reads them aloud. The person about whom these first impressions were written then reacts to the "impressions" in terms of their accuracy, points he was surprised to hear, and his feelings about the impressions. This exercise is then repeated for each member of the group.

7. *Experience Sharing*

Small groups of 3 or 4 people. Each member of the group will share with the group an experience that he feels comfortable in talking about that occurred between the ages of 1 and 5 years. After each member of the group has recounted an experience from the 1 to 5 age bracket, then have each member of the group share an experience from the 5 to 10, 10 to 20 and 20 to 30 age brackets.

8. *Charades*

This exercise is effective in large or small groups. Each person in this group "acts out" something suggested by one of the following subjects:

1. an animal
2. how to make something
3. name of a movie
4. name of a book
5. a quotation
6. a current expression
7. name of a play
8. name of a famous person

The other members of the group must guess what the member is acting out.

9. *The Mystery Object*

Each member of the group brings an object to the next meeting. The object should be one that is not easily recognized by touch (e.g. a kazoo). The group members are then blindfolded and each person, in turn, passes his object around the group. Each group member feels the object and explains what he thinks it is.

10. *Brain Games*

Small groups of 4 to 6 people.

a) Using six wooden matches, construct four equilateral triangles. Each side of each triangle must be the full length of the match.

b) Connect all nine dots shown below by drawing four straight lines without retracing any of the lines.

moving your pencil from the paper and without retracing any of the lines.

c) Place six coins in two rows as shown below. Change the pattern to two rows of four coins by moving only one coin.

d) In the diagram below, the first three mugs are full and the last three mugs are empty. Change the arrangement by touching only *one* of the mugs so that no full mug is next to an empty one.

e) How many squares can you count in the diagram below?

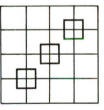

f) By adding one line, change the number below to six.

IX

11. *Group Poem*

Small groups of 4 to 6 people. The group first decides on the subject for their poem (e.g. love, understanding, honesty, freedom, etc.) and any requirements for the format of the poem. One person in the group begins by contributing the first line. The next person contributes the second line, and so on, until the poem is completed. The poems should be recorded by a member of the group as they are being written and later read to the larger group for discussion.

12. *Clowning*

One large group formed in the shape of a circle. One member of the group is appointed to go to the centre of the circle and *clown*— i.e. perform a silly trick, tell a joke, sing a song, do a dance, etc. After the "first act," the "performer" appoints the next person who will go to the centre of the circle and clown.

13. *The Gibberish Demonstration*

(Gibberish is unintelligible speech, meaningless sounds or ungrammatical talk.)

Each participant, either in front of the large group or in small groups of 4 to 6 people, is asked to pantomime the demonstration of something and to narrate the pantomime with gibberish. For example, the participant might demonstrate how to thread a needle, play a guitar or swing a golf club while at the same time explaining what he is doing in "gibberish."

14. *Tension Releasers*

1) Members of the group lie in a circle on the floor with each person resting his head on the body of someone else. The first person says "Ha!" The second person says "Ha! Ha!" Each person adds one "Ha!" to what the person before him said until the last person in the group has made his contribution—if you make it that far.

2) Members of the group become instruments in an orchestra. Each person uses only his voice and body to create the sound. A leader is appointed to direct the orchestra of nose-players, face-slappers and buttocks-beaters through a musical selection chosen by the group.

3) Members of the group "create" a machine. The first member of the group goes to the centre of the room and begins repeating a body movement and perhaps adding a sound or sounds. The next member of the group stands behind the first member as he continues his movement and sounds, and repeats a different body movement, adding a sound if he chooses. And, so it goes until all members of the group are participating in the operation of their machine.

15. *Impromptu Debates*

Ask members of the group to suggest a number of controversial topics for debate, e.g. (1) abortion on demand (2) legalized marijuana (3) trial marriages, etc. Members of the group then decide which topic they would like to debate. Divide the group evenly into *affirmative* (those members who support the proposition) and *negative* (those who oppose the proposition). The first speaker from the affirmative side begins and speaks in support of the proposition for approximately one minute. Then the first speaker from the negative side speaks for one minute against the proposition. This process continues, alternating between the affirmative and negative sides, until everyone has spoken. At this point, divide the group into smaller groups of 4 to 6 people and let these groups continue the discussion of the debate question.

16. *The Word Is*

The group (or small groups) create a new word for the "English" language and assign it a meaning. For example, the groups decide to create the word *virpo* and assign it the meaning of "a superior performance." The word *virpo* now replaces the word "super" as in "super group" in your vocabulary. Each member of the group should use the word frequently in conversation with people outside the group over a period of several weeks or several months. At the end of a predetermined time (e.g. 6 weeks) the group gets together again to discuss: (1) the degree of acceptance the word has received in other people's vocabulary, (2) where and under what circumstances you saw or heard the new word used and, (3) ways that other people used the word.

GETTING TO KNOW EACH OTHER BETTER!

1. *Personal Coat of Arms*

Large or small groups. Each person draws a personal coat of arms on a sheet of paper (small groups) or acetate sheets (for a large group showing, on overhead projector). Each coat of arms should represent or depict personal characteristics, attributes, interests, etc. of the author. Mottos might also be a part of your coat of arms. After the pictures are completed each person will display his coat of arms and explain the significance of its parts to the group.

2. *Birth Order Groups*
Divide the large group up into smaller groups by having all of those people who were the eldest in their family in one group, youngest in their family in another, and people who had older and younger brothers and sisters in another group. These groups then discuss the various frustrations, responsibilities, and feelings that they experienced as they grew up that related to their birth order in the family.

3. *The Astrology Grouping*
Divide the large group up into smaller groups according to the sign they were born under, i.e. Scorpio, Virgo, Capricorn, etc. Provide each group with a personality portrait of the sign they were born under and ask each member of the group to compare his personality with the personality portrait and share his comparison with the group.

4. *Show and Tell*
Each participant should bring to the group (approximately 4 to 6 people) a number of snapshots (or 8mm film etc.) that depict the periods in his life from 1 to 5 years, 5 to 10 years, etc. Pictures might show happy times, sad times, candid movements, etc. Each participant is then asked to show the pictures chronologically to the group and explain the significance of each.

5. *The Centre of Attention*
Each member of the group, in turn, stands out in front of the other members of the group as if in a public speaking situation for approximately 1 to 2 minutes. Members of the group focus their complete attention on the person at the front while he establishes eye contact with each member of the group. After each group member has been "the centre of attention," form small groups of 4 to 6 people and discuss your individual experiences, e.g. thoughts, feelings, fears, etc. when you were the centre of attention.

6. *The Centre of Positive Attention*
Large groups should be broken into groups of 5 or 6 people. Each group should sit in a circle with as much separation between the groups as possible. Each person in the group, in turn, moves his chair slightly outside the circle and becomes the "centre of positive attention." The other members of the group, in turn, explain positive points about the person, e.g. personality traits, looks, attitudes, etc. The person outside the circle then returns his chair to the circle and responds to the positive feedback he received, e.g. how he felt, comments that came as a surprise, etc.

7. *The Centre of Negative Attention*
Same as previous exercise except that negative feedback is given in place of the positive.

8. *Musical Sharing*
Two or three members of the group bring in a variety of recorded musical selections. After a selection chosen by the group has been played, smaller groups are formed and each person in the small groups discusses his reaction to the musical selection, e.g. messages, thoughts, images, feelings, etc.

9. *Sentence Completion*
Small groups of 4 to 6 people. Each member is asked to complete sentence "A" from the following sentences. Then each member is asked to complete sentence "B" and so on. You might want to change groups after every five or so sentences, or you might find that the groups will not want to change.

A. When I think of Canada, I . . . .
B. In the future, I see myself . . . .
C. When I feel rejected by another person I . . . .
D. I need/don't need people because . . . .
E. When I feel I am being manipulated I . . . .
F. I can express my feelings best when . . . .
G. I am happiest when . . . .
H. I am the grouchiest when . . . .
I. I hate . . . .
J. My most positive personality trait is . . . .
K. My weakest personality trait is . . . .
L. Premarital sex is . . . .
M. I fear . . . .
N. The time I like best is . . . .
O. The one thing I would find difficult to discuss in this group is . . . .

P. When I think of my parents, I think of . . . .
Q. If I could have one question answered, it would be . . . .
R. Sometimes I am reserved when . . . .
S. Sex is . . . .
T. I can only trust another person if . . . .
U. The last time I felt under pressure was . . . .
V. Right now I am feeling . . . .
W. When I reach 65 . . . .
X. The only thing that stands out in my mind from yesterday is . . . .
Y. I only give that little bit extra when . . . .
Z. The one time in my life when I felt like a big Zero was when . . . .

10. *Colour Me*

Small groups of 4 to 6 people. Each person in the group chooses a colour that he feels best fits the personality of each of the other members of the group, and also a colour that best reflects his own personality. Beginning with one member of the group, each other member explains the colour he chose for him and his reasons for choosing that colour. When everyone in the group has explained their colour for that person and their reasons for choosing it, that person then explains the colour he chose for himself and his reasons for choosing it. He may also at that time respond to the colour comments made by the other members of the group. This exercise is then repeated with each of the members of the group. Instead of choosing colours you might choose animals, cars, etc.

11. *If I Could Be*

Small groups of 4 to 6 people. Each person in the group decides on a well-known personality that he would like to be. Each person in the group, in turn, names the person he would like to be and the reasons for his choice. You might also want to have each person in the group choose another person *in the group* that he would want to be and explain the reasons for his choice.

12. *The Snoffalopagus*

This exercise can be done in large groups or in small groups. Each member of the group writes 5 to 8 characteristics that best describe himself. Beside each of the characteristics listed, each person should write the name of an animal that could be identified with that characteristic, i.e. strong—bull, gentle—lamb, etc. Each person then draws an imaginary animal, combining parts from each of the animals listed beside his own personal characteristics, and attaches a name to this newly created beast. When everyone is finished, members of the group show their creations to the group and explain the significance of the various parts of their animal. If this exercise is done with large groups, the pictures can be drawn on acetate for showing on an overhead projector.

13. *The Fantasy Farm*

Large groups or small groups. Group members either sit in a circle with their eyes closed or lie on the floor with their eyes closed. Someone is asked to begin a fantasy involving the entire group. Other group members may contribute to the story or they may choose to remain silent. You might want to put a time limit on this exercise, e.g. 10 to 20 minutes. Following the exercise, group members might want to discuss (1) fantasy content (2) roles played by members of the group (3) feelings experienced (4) tensions created (5) group cohesiveness.

14. *Nicknames*

Small groups of 4 to 6 people. This exercise is most effective after the group has been together as a group on at least two (or more) occasions. The group will discuss nicknames for each member of the group in turn. Starting with person "1," members of the group will suggest nicknames and explain their reasons for the suggestions. The person who is receiving the nicknames may veto any name. Once a nickname has been agreed upon, the name should be recorded along with the reasons given for suggesting that name. After each member of the group has a nickname, the recorded nicknames and the reasons for their choice may be read to the large group.

15. *Our Group Presents—*

Small groups of 4 to 6 people. Each group is asked to write a 4- or 5-minute skit on a topic of their own choosing. The topic could relate to the material being covered in class or to personal experiences, etc. Once the scripts have been written, the groups will be asked to perform their skits for the other groups and to be prepared to discuss the messages they were trying to act out.

16. *Summary and Inferences*

Groups of 3 people. Person "A," person "B" and person "C." Person A begins by talking for 2 to 4 minutes about his life, from childhood to the present. Person B then takes 2 minutes to summarize what he heard person A say. Person C then takes 2 minutes to explain what he inferred from what person A said (the conclusions he drew about person A from what person A said). Person A may then respond to persons B and C.

17. *Experiencing Dyadic Communication*

A day or two prior to using this exercise, the teacher or session leader should ask each member of the group to write 3 to 5 intimate questions on a sheet of paper and submit them anonymously to the leader for collating and reproduction. Questions might range from "Will you explain an experience from your past that you are ashamed of?" to "How do you feel about crying in front of people?"

Group members pair off, preferably with a person that they do not know well. The pairs are given copies of the reproduced "intimate" questions. The pairs should have approximately one hour to complete this exercise. Each person will alternate asking his partner a question from the list.

RULES
1. You must be prepared to answer any question that you ask your partner.
2. You may refuse to answer any questions posed by your partner.
3. Your communication with your partner must be held in strict confidence.

After the exercise has been completed, 2, 3 or 4 pairs get together and discuss their experience.

18. *My Epitaph*

For the next session, each group member is asked to prepare three cardboard cutouts of tombstones. On one tombstone, write your epitaph as it might have appeared had you died 10 or 15 years ago. On the second write your epitaph as it might appear should you die today, and on the third write your epitaph as it might appear should you die 10 or 15 years from today. Form groups of 4 to 6 people, and each member of the group, in turn, explains his tombstones.

19. *Good Times, Bad Times*

Each person lists at least five objects that are associated in his mind with the good times he's had, then five objects associated with bad times. The group breaks into triads and discusses the lists. Every ten minutes or so participants switch to another triad and continue their discussions.

20. *Three Good Reasons*

Each person thinks about two things he is unwilling to reveal to any member of the group. Then he writes down at least three reasons why he is unwilling to reveal them, without giving any hint as to what these things are. The group leader collects the lists (no names on them), and reads them aloud. The group then discusses the process of self-disclosure, using the collected material as a jumping-off point.

21. Each person designs two crests—one to represent himself as he currently sees himself, and one to represent the way he would like to be. The crests are signed and posted in the classroom.

22. *Satisfaction Graph*

Each person draws "X" and "Y" axes on a piece of paper, labelling the vertical axis "Satisfaction," and the horizontal axis "Time." He divides the vertical axis into 20 separate sections, and enters each year since his birth along the horizontal axis, e.g. 1949, 1950, etc. Then he plots his "satisfaction" year by year. After explaining to the group why he drew the graph the way he did, he returns it to the leader, who posts it in the classroom.

23. *Pass It On*

Arrange the group into a circle. One member whispers two or three sentences to a person next to him and tells him to "pass it on." After several rounds in which different persons initiate the message, discuss what happened, then focus on such issues as one-way versus two-way communication, the influence of the listener on a message, memory factors, etc.

24. A Is for Aardvark

Members of the group are given an 8 x 10 sheet of acetate and a black grease pencil. They are asked to listen carefully to the following description of an animal, and then draw it. They are to give their animals a name, and to sign their creation. The pictures are shown on an overhead projector and a discussion follows of the perceptual issues involved in such a task. (See Chapters 3 and 4 of this book.)

A massively-built, short-legged quadruped with long ears, rounded snout, long extensile tongue, thick pointed tail, and large powerful claws. The body is stout, with an arched back.

25. You and Others Crossword Puzzle

Working in groups of three, construct a crossword puzzle using the terms in the Glossary of this book. Puzzles can be duplicated and used as classroom quizzes.

26. Things That Bother Me

Small groups of 4 to 6 people. Members of the groups are given 10 minutes to write a list of five things that bother them. These "things" could range from their own behaviour, to the behaviour of others, to situations they find themselves in, etc. After the lists are prepared, each member of the group, in turn, reads his list and explains his reasons for writing each "thing" on the list. The members of the group then discuss ways of dealing with these bothersome things. Then, move on to the next member of the group and repeat the same process.

27. Things I Wanted to Say

Group members imagine leaving the group for the last time, getting onto the bus or into their cars, looking back and remembering a number of things that they wanted to say to the group, or individual members of the group. Group members then begin to talk about these "things they wanted to say."

NONVERBAL COMMUNICATION

1. Voice/Appearance Matching

Take Polaroid photographs of 5 males and 5 females who are unknown to the group. Be sure these persons are about the same age, that they are posed in the same way with respect to posture, positioning of arms, background, etc., and finally, that they all have "neutral" facial expressions. Select a brief (6- to 8-sentence) passage of your choice and record these 10 persons on audiotape as they read the passage. Be sure to give them practice reading it beforehand, and that the passage is easy to read. Also ensure that none of them has an accent that is readily identifiable. Number the photos randomly and put them on a bulletin board for all to see. Then play the recorded voices to the group, repeating once, and ask members to try and match the photos with the voices. After determining how well the group did, elicit reasons for their choices, then go on to discuss the relationships between physical appearance and vocal characteristics. (See *Beyond Words* and *Nonverbal Communication in Human Interaction* in the Selected Readings section of Chapter 5 for background and theory.)

2. Rubabble

Write emotion-names (pity, anger, fear, happiness, etc.) on slips of paper and put them in a container. List these emotions on the blackboard. Each member of the group draws a slip and, one by one, stands up and attempts to convey this emotion to the rest vocally, but without using language. He is allowed to use only the word "rubabble" in his message. His slip of paper is returned to the container after his turn is over. The other members will try to identify the emotion, but should keep their eyes closed during the "performances" so as to eliminate any visual clues that may influence their judgements.

3. Can You Guess the Emotion?

Make up separate slips of paper for each of the following emotions: anger, happiness, fear, surprise, sadness, disgust and interest, and list them on the blackboard. Type up a card reading "Nonverbal vocal cues of various kinds may reveal the emotional state of the speaker." Members pick an emotion slip from a container, then attempt to read the above sentence in such a way as to convey the chosen emotion. The slips are returned to the container after each "performance." Group members close their eyes while listening and trying to guess the emotion conveyed.

4. *How's That Again?*

Try learning, from scratch, how to smoke a cigarette simply by following someone's verbal instructions. Select one of the group and, without looking at him, follow his instructions on how to smoke, beginning with removing the cigarette and match from their packages, through the lighting and smoking processes. This exercise will prove highly entertaining if you simply follow the instructions blindly! For example, when you are handed the cigarette package and are told to "open it," or to "take out a cigarette," try ripping the package open! When you are instructed to "put the cigarette in your mouth," put it in sideways, or filter-end last, or under your tongue! Use your imagination when asked to "strike the match", "light it", etc. This exercise will graphically demonstrate the point that sometimes it is far easier to communicate by *showing* nonverbally, than by *telling* verbally. This exercise will also work with other complex processes like tying shoelaces, drawing an abstract figure, etc. (Note to instructor: you may want to use a person not a member of your group, who hasn't read this textbook.)

5. *Space and Territory*

Ask members to perform one or more of the following experiments and report their results to the group.

1. Ride an elevator and wait until you and another person are the only occupants. Position yourself as close to this person as you can without actually touching him. Carefully observe his nonverbal reactions—face, eyes, body posture and tension, body orientation, etc.

2. Visit a restaurant and sit at the counter beside someone. Slowly, and as inconspicuously as possible, spread out your dishes, utensils, personal objects, etc. in his direction, taking over *his* space as completely as possible. All the while, watch for his nonverbal reactions to your "invasion."

3. Ride a public transit vehicle that has many double seats with no one in them. Sit down right beside someone occupying such a double seat. Watch the nonverbal reactions.

4. Enter a line-up out of turn, and carefully observe the reactions you get.

5. Walk between people who are conversing, without excusing yourself, ducking, etc.

Pick a situation where you could have easily walked around them. What kind of reaction do you get?

6. Find an empty seat in a bar with a drink nearby. Move the drink to another table and wait till the owner returns. Note his reactions.

7. As you talk to someone, slowly move toward him. Get as close as you can, and observe his nonverbal behaviour closely on the way in.

8. Sit in someone's favourite chair and note the reactions.

NOTE: You will obviously have to use prudence in doing some of these space and territory exercises. Also, when watching for reactions, be particularly sensitive to another person freezing or omitting behaviours you would normally expect to find. Just because he doesn't move, or give you a dirty look or whatever, it doesn't necessarily follow that he had *no* reaction; often the absence of normally occurring behaviour is itself significant.

6. *Emblems We All Know*

Break the group into fours, and appoint a secretary for each. Allow 20 minutes for them to draw up as complete a list of emblems as they can. Each should be numbered, and well-known to the typical Canadian (if there is such a person!). The secretaries will then read their group's lists, acting out each emblem in turn. Two-thirds of the entire group must recognize the emblem and agree with its meaning; otherwise, it will be struck from the list. One person in the group will draw up an emblem master-list from the various small-group lists, and this will be duplicated and distributed to all. During the course of the semester, members will be encouraged to add to the list whenever they can.

7. *Foreign Emblem Day*

Give group members a week to collect emblems, in any way they can (including reading) that are not used in our culture. Spend a session demonstrating them to the group. Follow with a discussion on the coding elements of emblems that are similar across cultures, e.g. the open and closed fist, touching the head or heart, movements away from the body versus towards the body, presenting the palm versus presenting the back of the hand, etc.

8. *Silent Videos*

Select a TV program or movie involving two or more persons interacting with each other, and show it to the group without a sound. Each member makes notes of all the adaptors he sees, and will be prepared to discuss them in a group session immediately following. Game and talk shows on TV are particularly good sources of adaptors. When selecting a film, try to choose one that records people interacting spontaneously, rather than following a script. (See Chapter 6 of this book, and Ekman's *Semiotica* article in Chapter 5's Selected Readings list for background on adaptors.)

9. *Eye, Eye, Eye!*

Ride an elevator or bus and look at people right in the eye for as long as you can. Discuss the reactions you get with your group. Did they vary from person to person? What influences do setting, personality, mood, age, and sex have on the reactions? Try *not* looking as someone at all when he is speaking to you. What happens to the interaction?

10. *Don't Dim Your Lights*

As you walk past a person you don't know, continue to look at him carefully. Don't drop your gaze (or "dim your lights," as Goffman puts it). In your group, discuss the reactions you got.

11. *Squint Your Eyes*

Narrow, or "squint" your eyes the next time you converse with a friend. Then ask him how he felt when you did this. Report the results to your group.

12. *Let's Face It*

After studying how emotions are coded by the face (see Ekman 1973, Harrison, and Knapp in the Chapter 5 Selected Readings list), each member of the group cuts out 10 pictures of faces from magazines and newspapers. Avoid collecting more than one smiling face each, and faces that are larger than 3 x 3. Do not include faces that involve such behaviours as winking, lip-biting, coughing, shouting, talking, etc. Spread all the pictures on the floor and, as a group, sort them into separate piles according to the emotion, or emotions, displayed in the face. You will most likely have some "neutral" expressions, and also a number of faces which you can't agree

about. Staple all the similar faces on separate sheets of bristleboard, maintaining space between each face. Include the "can't agree" faces on one board. Label each sheet with the appropriate emotion names(s), and put them on the wall or bulletin board for the duration of the course (they tend to be quite decorative!). As you learn more about facial expressions, you may find that you want to switch faces to other categories, or to relabel certain ones. Do so.

13. *Three-Stage Decoding*

Assemble a variety of "emotion faces" clipped from magazines or newspapers, each one at least 3 x 5. Divide the group into threes and distribute the faces among them. A leader in each group covers a face with a piece of cardboard, and then uncovers it in 3 stages, stopping just below the brows and just below the eyes, before removing the cover completely. At each stage, members record on paper their best guesses as to the emotions they see. Discuss the results in the light of Ekman's work in Knapp (see Chapter 5 Selected Readings list).

14. *I Don't See What You Mean*

With the rest of the group observing, two members sit back-to-back in the centre of the class, and begin a five-minute conversation with each other on some topic of mutual interest to them. They are not to turn around during their conversation. Another pair does the same thing, and then another. A group discussion follows, in which the 6 persons explain how the lack of normal visual feedback affected them. The group leader focuses the discussion on the importance of non-verbal behaviours for regulating the process of interaction.

15. *Just What Is Going On Here?*

Half the group leave the room. The remaining members are told that shortly they will be interacting with the group outside the room. They are instructed to maintain occasional eye contact, but to completely withhold *all* other vocal, verbal and non-verbal feedback during their interactions. The group outside is recalled, and everyone is told that the returning members are to sit down in pairs with the others and spend five minutes telling them about their past history and their plans for the future. Afterwards, the "speakers" are encouraged to explain their reactions to the situations they found themselves in, and the "listeners" report on the nonverbal behaviours of the "speakers." A general discussion follows on the nature and importance of verbal, vocal, and especially nonverbal, feedback in the regulation of interactions.

16. *Are You Clothes-minded?*

Gather 12 large, full-length pictures of clothed figures, cut the heads off, and paste them on separate bristleboard sheets. Ensure that you have a very diverse sampling of clothes — neat/sloppy, expensive/inexpensive, bold/conservative, etc. Do not use any pictures that involve unusual body types or body postures, or unusual arm/leg behaviours. Number the pictures and show them, one by one, to the group (use an opaque projector for large groups). Have each person rate them separately on the scales at the end of Chapter 6 of this book. Mark the scales using the number of the stimuli pictures, e.g.

Nervous *17 68 114 2 35 10 129* Relaxed. Explore the similarities and differences in the group perceptions. Attempt to discover the reasons certain judgments were made. In the time remaining, discuss how clothes affect our perceptions of another's mood, character, personality, status, role, class, culture, etc. As a variation, one half of the group can see the pictures with the heads in place, and are instructed to rate the *entire* picture. The other half proceeds as above. Compare the groups' judgments and focus the discussion on the ways in which facial and clothes cues combine with each other to foster impressions.

17. *Silence Please!*

As members of the group enter the room, they are told they must remain silent for the entire session, and relate to each other only through nonverbal behaviours—gesturing, pantomiming, charades, facial expressions, dancing, etc., This is an excellent exercise for the first meeting of the group.

SELECTED READINGS

Boocock, Sarane and E. O. Schild. *Simulation Games in Learning.* Beverly Hills, Cal.: Sage Publications, Inc., 1968.

Boyd, Neva. *Handbook of Games.* Chicago: H. T. Fitzsimmons Co., 1945.

Gunther, B. *Sense Relaxation: Below Your Mind.* New York: Collier Books, 1968.

Gunther, B. *What to Do Until the Messiah Comes.* New York: Collier Books, 1971.

James, M., and D. Jongeward. *Born to Win: Transactional Analysis with Gestalt Experiments.* Reading, Mass.: Addison-Wesley, 1971.

Johnson, David W. *Reaching Out.* Englewood Cliffs, New Jersey: Prentice-Hall, Inc., 1972.

Krupar, Karen R. *Communication Games.* New York: The Free Press, 1973.

Lewis, H., and H. Streitfield. *Growth Games.* New York: Bantam, 1971.

Luce, R. D. and R. Raiffa. *Games And Decisions.* New York: John Wiley & Sons, 1957.

Maier, N. R. F., A. R. Solem, and A. A. Maier. *Supervisory and Executive Development: A Manual for Role Playing.* New York: Wiley, 1967.

Malamud, D. I., and S. Machover. *Toward Self-Understanding: Group Techniques in Self-Confrontation.* Springfield, Ill.: Thomas, 1965.

NTL Institute for Applied Behavioural Science. *Twenty Exercises for Trainers.* Washington, D.C., 1972.

Nylen, D., J. R. Mitchell, and A. Stour (eds.). *Handbook of Staff Development and Human Relations Training: Materials Developed for Use in Africa* (rev. ed.). Washington, D.C.: Ntl Institute for Applied Behavioral Science, 1967.

Otto, H. A. *Group Methods to Actualize Human Potential: A Handbook* (2nd ed.). Beverly Hills: Holistic Press, 1970.

Pfeiffer, J. W., and R. Heslin.   *Instrumentation in Human Relations Training: A Guide to 75 Instruments with Wide Application to the Behavioral Sciences.* San Diego: University Associates, 1973.

Pfeiffer, J. W., and J. E. Jones.   *A Handbook of Structured Experiences for Human Relations Training*, Volumes I (rev.), II (rev.), III (rev.) and IV. San Diego: University Associates, 1974, 1974, 1974 and 1973.

Pfeiffer, J. W., and J. E. Jones.   *The 1972, 1973 and 1974 Annual Handbooks for Group Facilitators.* San Diego: University Associates, 1972, 1973, 1974.

Satir, V.   *Conjoint Family Therapy: A Guide to Theory and Technique.* Palo Alto, Ca.: Science and Behavior Books, 1967.

Schmuck, R. A., P. J. Runkel, et al.   *Handbook of Organization Development in Schools.* Palo Alto, Ca.: National Press Books, 1972.

Schutz, W. C.   *Joy: Expanding Human Awareness.* New York: Grove Press, 1967.

Spolin, Viola.   *Improvisation for the Theater.* Evanston, Illinois: Northwestern University Press, 1972.

Stevens, John O.   *Awareness: Exploring, Experimenting, Experiencing.* New York: Bantam Books, Inc., 1973.

About the Authors and the Illustrator

Donald L. MacRae was born and raised in Sarnia, Ontario. Following a career as a television announcer, writer and producer, Mr. MacRae became a teacher of Speech and Interpersonal Communication at Seneca College. He has served as President of the Canadian Speech Association and has acted as a communication consultant to business and industry. He is the author of several articles on the speech-communication process and has appeared on the Channel 19 "Integrity in Communication" television series.

Ronald F. G. Campbell is currently Dean of the Finch/Sheppard Campus of Seneca College. His past career has included service in the Presbyterian ministry, and at Cornell University (Professor of Communication), and the University of Guelph (Director of Continuing Education). He has also acted as Superintendent of University, College and Adult Education for the Ontario Educational Communications Authority.

Vernon F. Gunckel is Chairman of Creative and Communication Arts at Seneca College. He has been Assistant Professor of Communication at California State University, San José, and Coordinator of the Department of Language and Communications at Canadore College for Applied Arts and Technology in North Bay, Ontario. Mr. Gunckel is an ordained minister of the United Methodist Church.

Carl J. Hartleib has been psychology instructor and counsellor at Seneca College since 1968. He has had considerable experience as a T-Group leader and as a psychological consultant to business. In addition, Mr. Hartleib has taught psychology at the Toronto Police College and has been instrumental in developing a program for Youth Bureau officers. He is also involved in the development of psychological workshops for personal growth and interpersonal communication.

Robert M. Soucie has served as a member of the executive of the Canadian Speech Association. He has written several articles on nonverbal communication and has appeared on Channel 19's "Integrity in Communication" series. Besides teaching nonverbal communication for several years, he has given many workshops in this area to professional, educational and business groups.

Isaac Bickerstaff is a *nom de plume*, first used by the great Irish satirist Jonathan Swift in 1708 as a means of dodging lawsuits, jail terms, summary executions, duels and other such unpleasantries. For much the same reason, the name is now employed by Don Evans, a Canadian cartoonist and writer.

ISBN 0·07·082256·5